CHRISTY CAMPBELL

Weapons of War

Peter Bedrick Books
New York

First American edition published in 1983 by
Peter Bedrick Books
125 East 23 Street
New York, N.Y. 10010

355.8
C187w

Originally published as War Facts Now by Fontana
Paperbacks. Published by agreement with Fontana
Paperbacks, London

ISBN 0-911745-13-0
LC 83-71621

Manufactured in the United States of America
Distributed in the USA by Harper & Row
and in Canada by Book Center, Montreal

84-6277

'The more constructive East-West relationship which the Allies seek requires tangible signs that the Soviet Union is prepared to abandon the disturbing build-up of its military strength, to desist from resorting to force and intimidation and to cease creating or exploiting situations of crisis and instability in the Third World.'

Soviet Military Power,
published by the US Department of Defence,
1981

'Peace from a "position of strength" is what the men in Washington would like to have. These days they are not concerned about the equality and equal security of the sides, and are bent on developing new, increasingly more destructive weapons of mass annihilation, on securing military superiority over the Soviet Union, and establishing hegemony and direct domination over other countries and nations.'

Whence the Threat to Peace,
published by the USSR Ministry of Defence,
1982

Contents

Part Two: **Total War**

Acknowledgments

The author would particularly like to thank Mark Hewish, Antony Preston, David Isby and Brendan Gallagher for their help and advice.

Note on Abbreviations

Scratch the subject of defence and acronyms, abbreviations and buzzwords fly out. Of necessity many of these abbreviations are used in the book as the language of military technology is one of the most cumbersome in the world. A much fuller glossary is given at the end of the book and the language of electronic warfare is examined on pages 108-10. Meanwhile some key abbreviations are given below.

CBW Chemical biological warfare
ECM Electronic countermeasures
ER Enhanced radiation
ICBM Intercontinental ballistic missile
KT Kilotron
MIRV Multiple independently targeted
 re-entry vehicle
MT Megaton
NBC Nuclear, biological, chemical
PGM Precision guided munition
RV Re-entry vehicle
SAC Strategic Air Command
SALT Strategic Arms Limitation Talks
SLBM Submarine-launched ballistic missile
SSBN Ballistic missile submarine
 nuclear-powered
TNF Theatre nuclear forces
WP Warsaw Pact

Introduction

There are 178 sovereign governments in the world today. All of them regard safeguarding the security of their people against threats from without or from within as their first duty. To this end they raise armed forces and undertake the development and manufacture of weapons or import them. Armed force is the monopoly of the state and only the state can make its use legitimate. When that monopoly is threatened from within by terrorist action or paramilitary political organization, the state takes action to defeat the threat by using its own monopoly of force.

Armed force exists to threaten physical violence to the human body and the things that support life, whether with a club, a plastic bullet or a nuclear warhead, to impose will or prevent the imposition of will. When coercion does not work and a defence is offered, a state of war exists – cattle raids, peasants' revolts, barons' revolts, wars of dynastic succession, wars of empire, wars of liberation, wars of revolution, wars of pique, wars of pride, punitive expeditions, wars of religion, wars of ideology, wars of race, wars of commerce, wars for loot, wars for sugar, wars for slaves, wars for gold, wars for oil, civil wars and world wars, wars for combinations of these reasons and wars for none of these reasons at all.

The fighting for the Falklands showed how diplomacy breaks down and wars begin. In its early stages, an eminent British military historian compared the war in the South Atlantic to a seventeenth-century colonial contest for some remote spice or sugar island. In fact colonial wars have almost always been fought for a perceived practical pay-off in terms of raw materials, markets or bases for further strategic advantage. There are no such dividends in the Falklands for either side to offset the cost in lives and sunken warships – in spite of long-term promises of oil. The invasion was launched because of internal Argentinian politics. A defence and counter-offensive was made by Great Britain and the war began because diplomacy could not enforce the imposition of a political principle – that an aggressor should be denied the fruits of his aggression. As a war of high principle, fought with very few civilians in the way, it became almost a gladiatorial spectacle with the relative merits of weapons systems being the major concern and politics pushed to one side. The same cannot be true for the war in the Lebanon.

Modern wars begin for political reasons and the tensions which underwrite the amassing of great armaments are political tensions. So far a state of disarmed peace holds more terrors for the world than does a state of preparedness for war – however primitive. When wars end, with surrender or victory, the passions that caused them and the terrors unleashed in their waging do not disappear, the spiritual and economic mobilization required for their conduct cannot be dismantled as easily as a battleship in a breaker's yard. Both the First and Second World Wars lasted for years and reached into the deepest recesses of a nation's will to wage war – indeed, this was the fundamental target under attack and the fundamental asset to be defended whether in the front line or in a factory.

Guerrilla insurgencies aside, modern war is different. High technology superpowers can destroy each other within a matter of hours. As a US general said about a war in Europe, 'What you see is what you get – it's all over on Day One.'

Thus the nature of modern weapons means that the modulations of previous 'total wars' are inadmissible. The United States had virtually no army in 1917 and 1941 and a scant arms industry – it had to find the time to build both. The German army actually began to demobilize after the fall of France in 1940 while Britain was becoming a siege-socialist state.

Preparation for nuclear war excludes the luxury of time. The piling up of massive armaments is a background hum of peace, not an adrenalin-surging cry for vengeance. For the Soviet Union it is relatively straightforward. The armed forces are the saviour of the nation and the vanguard of Marxism-Leninism. A deeply ordered society finds little difficulty in pumping an ever bigger proportion of its brain and spending power into bigger and bigger armaments – the capitalist imperialists are doing just the same.

Capitalist-imperialist democrats, however, have their problems. Democratic freedoms are subjugated in preparing for total war as they once were in its waging – it is not a negotiable social contract. Weapons programmes (such as the British Chevaline project to improve the Royal Navy's Polaris missiles) are sanctioned in secret. Dissidents and trade unionists who might betray the siege in times of crisis must be monitored and arrangements made for their neutralization. Plans are laid for 'surviving' a nuclear conflict which protect a government machine but abandon the urban populations. A secret, self-serving bureaucracy grows up to administer the process.

The government of a nuclear-armed state and indeed one which represents a nuclear target such as West Germany does not worry about whether or not it can persuade its citizens to fight a nuclear war – it has to persuade them to *prepare* for one. For a nuclear power this does not necessarily mean gathering together, arming and training large quantities of fighting men. It means spending very large sums of money on capital-intensive nuclear-weapons systems. The Spitfire is far more important than the pilot.

The secret British Chevaline project would have been impossible in the United States. A similar project would have to be subjected to public scrutiny at every step of the way. This is because the initial military proposal must be approved by the appropriate service and the Department of Defence (DoD), and then the project must by law be put out to commercial tender. (There are some exceptions such as Project Stealth where secrecy is an inherent component of the project.) Congress reviews each line item in the Research and Development budget and then the procurement budget. All this is done in open session with full press briefings – details can be kept secret but the existence of a weapons development programme cannot. The DoD presents an annual arms control impact statement to Congress assessing the political implications of new weapons system developments.

While the state of the world makes soldiers as essential as farmers and doctors, it raises weapon science and military technology to be as or more important than medical, food and energy science or any other kind of life-enabling endeavour. This is truer of the twentieth century than of any other – an immense investment of talent and treasure in weapon development and growth in their destructive power to the point reached midway through the century with the perfection of the hydrogen bomb and invulnerable means of its delivery over oceans and continents – the point at which the possibility of waging war as a rational instrument of policy broke down.

This book, with its mass of data, chronologies, tables, comparisons and maps and its brief analyses of strategic and tactical problems, is about the contemporary world, the state of things as they are now and how they are likely to be in the near future. This introduction, however, is rooted in the recent past and stresses the importance of the dialogue between the dynamics of war and weapon research itself and war and weapon research as a controllable political tool for democracies and dictatorships alike.

Military planners are charged by their political masters with having the right weapons and the right strategy to deter the potential foe or win the potential battle and not much political philosophy. But one such military planner, Marshal V. D Sokolovsky, ex-Chief of the Soviet General Staff, wrote in the 1960s:

> In determining the essence of war, Marxism-Leninism uses as its point of departure the position that war is not an aim in itself, but only a tool of politics. The acceptance of war as a tool of politics also determines the interrelation of military strategy and politics, which is based on the principle of the full dependence of the former on the latter. These scientific Marxist concepts are and were opposed by the representatives of the bourgeois metaphysical approach to war, who deny the class nature of war. They are inclined to see the causes of war in the "psychological make-up of man", in the overpopulation of the earth and in racist geopolitics.

In fact the doctrine that war should be an instrument of policy, derived somewhat crudely from the writings of the German military philosopher Karl von Clausewitz, was older than Marx, is certainly not the monopoly of Marxists, and was developed to a very sophisticated level in the nineteenth century. By 1914 European governments could regard their great armies and arms-building programmes, plus the complex and intricate plans for their use, as legitimate or indeed the only means of resolving great conflicts of national interests. Britain possessed a great and modern navy to contain German expansionism, to project power across a world empire, and to choke an aggressor to death through economic blockade. Germany built a high-seas fleet to challenge this containment and seek all the imperial trappings of world power. French, Russian, German and Austrian General Staffs had intricate plans to mobilize and move mass armies by strict timetable, crossing Europe by railway if necessary, overwhelming the enemy in a short series of decisive battles. This war could be scientifically planned and made more intelligent with the use of the new technologies of telecommunications and aerial reconnaissance. Each side believed they could win this steam-powered war within weeks.

It did not work out that way. Automatic weapons and quick-firing artillery, already technically mature by 1900, blunted the power of the offensive and put the armies of Europe into trenches. The war escaped from the bounds of political policy. It brought down the political structure of the old Europe and put, for the time being, into the hands of the victors the new devices of dynamic war, the tank, the aircraft and the submarine that had sought and brought the decisions of 1917-18.

Politically the war developed a whole momentum of its own – the manpower needs of the war swept millions into the fighting, and civilian populations, including women, were mobilized to an unprecedented extent to supply its industrial needs. Propaganda campaigns were mounted in the relatively new mass-literacy media and urban civilian populations were subjected to starvation by blockade and aerial and artillery bombardment.

The brief flickering faith of the 1920s in the outlawing of war as an instrument of policy expired with the economic turmoil of the time, the rise of the dictators and the failure of the League of Nations to impose covenants without swords. The military planners of Nazi Germany had seized on the tank, the aircraft and submarine and forged them into weapons which could and did sweep aside any opposition to German policy, first by threat and then in battle itself. All this was linked to the second great weapons revolution of the century. The weapon technology of 1936-9, fast hard-hitting tanks capable of independent operation, ocean-going submarines, 300 mph+ all-metal aircraft and massive mobile firepower for attacking infantry, opened up a window that had been closed since 1918 – the chance not of fighting a war of attrition, but of waging a lightning war of decision with armed force as the lancet for the pursuit of policy. All the new technical devices (with the exception of the operational atomic bomb) with which the Second World War would be fought, including radar and jet engines, were developed in this period.

Just as in 1914-18, however, the outcome of the war in Europe and the Pacific after the containment of Germany and Japan's lightning victories was ultimately decided by a massive war of attrition, with strategic bombing and U-boat warfare replacing economic blockades and trenches, but fought at its highest technological point by physicists, not chemists and metallurgists as previously. German military strength was eroded on the Eastern Front where the Russian Army learned how to counter the techniques of Blitzkreig just in time, and turned massive forces of armour and tactical air power vengefully back on the invaders.

The strategic bombing of Germany by the RAF and USAAF wore down Germany's industrial base and the area bombing policy was aimed at destroying the will of the German people to go on fighting although this was as unsuccessful as the Blitz on Britain had been in 1940-1. The Second World War was total war on a scale the First World War did not reach. It began with air raid shelters and gas masks not brass bands and soldiers bedecked with flowers marching to the railway station. It was the war of mass deportation, slave labour, area bombing, genocide, kamikaze, V2 rockets, firestorms, U-boat wolfpacks – the war of Rotterdam, Hamburg, Oradour-sur-Glane, Dresden, Auschwitz and Hiroshima.

The destruction of Hiroshima and Nagasaki by atomic weapons seemed to change everything. The war was over, democracy had survived, the ideology of National Socialism was destroyed and its absolute evils exposed, and the ruthless military power of Japan was broken. Yet the world was altered in a way that it had not been in 1918-19 when the costs of general war between industrial nations seemed to put it beyond the bounds of rational policy.

The military power of the United States had entered Europe decisively and this time would stay. The Soviet Union had projected its power to the Elbe. For a while the United States was able to use its monopoly of the bomb and the capacity for strategic nuclear warfare as a rational instrument of policy, just as a fast carrier force might be used – first by attacking Japan and then sheltering the old European battleground under a nuclear umbrella. If the Soviet ground forces should move further west, the US could destroy Russian cities with atom bombs without retaliation. On 31 January 1950 President Truman announced his decision to build a thermonuclear weapon two hundred times as powerful as the Hiroshima bomb – within two years a test device was exploded at Eniwetok Atoll and by 1955 this enormous destructive power had been contained in an operational bomb.

Simultaneously the so-called 'Teapot' committee set up to explore the possibilities of the intercontinental ballistic missile concluded that this programme should be given top priority. The Pandora's box of German missile technology was being opened at White Sands and Redstone and the multi-stage intercontinental ballistic missile (ICBM) was soon to become a reality. This nuclear 'defence' became a cornerstone of the North Atlantic Treaty Organization and for a while the United States seemed tempted to use nuclear weapons in Korea and Indo-China. During the Dulles era in the early 1950s, nuclear capacity became almost the exclusive military basis of US foreign policy.

However morally repugnant the idea of limited war may have been to the Western allies, the so-called 'bisection debate' began in US military circles very soon after the explosion of Russia's bomb – deterrence became, in most eyes, separated from and even opposed to defence. It was argued that the awesome destructiveness of nuclear weapons had split the conduct of war in two. The armoured divisions, aircraft carrier and ground attack aircraft that had fought the battles of 1945 had been instruments of total war but, compared with the destructiveness of the nuclear arsenal, their offensive capacity was strictly localized. The justification for limited war was still that of Clausewitz – military power should at all times be subordinate to national policy. A thermonuclear exchange and the mutual self-destruction of the superpowers represented the complete breakdown of rational policy, and this view formed the basis of Pentagon orthodoxy in the late 1950s. The object of the nuclear arsenals was not defence but pure deterrence. Nevertheless, 'conventional forces', whether armoured divisions or cruisers, remained the instruments for securing the policy objectives of the nuclear powers. Before the United States was sucked into the jungles of South-east Asia the role of her conventional forces was clear. The enormous manpower on the ground in Germany, the squadrons of fighter aircraft and tactical aircraft, the vast US military aid to the NATO allies, the British Army of the Rhine, the rearmed German *Bundeswehr*, the trans-Atlantic supply line and the naval power to protect it – all this constituted a conventional 'tripwire' which the equally conventional forces of the Warsaw Pact would have to pull before the Third World War arrived.

However, there are serious flaws in this doctrine, made graver by the fact that the very existence of these forces is intended to confer real options which may be exercised in a crisis. The 'tripwire' approach is based on a strategy which is flexible yet backed up by the most powerful deterrent necessary. In the face of provocation, the response is calculated to force the aggressor to consider the consequences of scaling each rung of the 'escalation ladder'. In the 1960s the United States was able to exploit the central Russian strategic nuclear deficiencies and leave a whole range of tactical front-line capabilities on land and sea relatively weak. Today the enormous Soviet investment in both strategic and conventional forces, including naval power and particularly attack submarines, has thrown this equation off balance.

As far as the conventional warfare aspects are concerned, the Warsaw Pact armies have always enjoyed the advantages of position, scale and homogeneity of equipment, and are fast catching up the West in the technical sophistication of their weapons. Since the late 1950s the only way to counter this threat has been the widespread deployment of tactical nuclear weapons for use on the European battlefield. By 1960 there were large numbers of Honest John artillery rockets in Germany, each armed with a warhead bigger than the Hiroshima bomb. With the Soviet Union beginning to challenge the United States' strategic strike power, the Pentagon looked to the use of tactical weapons alone, without the use of strategic weapons. However, the projected use of tactical weapons caused a serious split within NATO. The Europeans saw escalation itself as a deterrent, knowing that if cities rather than troop concentrations become the target of tactical weapons, Central Europe would be reduced to an irradiated desert.

By the late 1960s once again policy and technology were marching together. The underlying military and nuclear superiority enjoyed by the United States throughout the period of the Cold War, the Cuba crisis and beyond was being matched by the Soviet Union.

Soviet conventional ground and naval forces have been growing at 5 per cent a year for over a decade, but a far more important shift has taken place in the strategic balance. In the early 1960s, in spite of vociferous political and cultural attacks in some Western countries, the nuclear deterrent was accepted and seemed to be working well. By the time of the Cuba crisis, however, ICBM-delivered thermonuclear weapons were becoming so numerous, their guidance systems so accurate and reconnaissance so sophisticated, that they were capable of destroying enemy nuclear forces, and especially bomber bases, in one thunderous pre-emptive strike. The United States, with its strategic superiority, had the capability to knock out the Soviet deterrent before the bombers had left their bases.

Theoretically this 'counterforce option' gave the Russians a greatly increased incentive to use strategic weapons in any conflict right from the start – but as the climb-down at Cuba proved, Russian adventuring in fact could be contained if not completely deterred.

Towards the end of the 1960s, however, the Soviet Union was fast closing the gap. In 1961 the United States had sixty-three ICBMs and some hundred submarine-launched Polaris Als, and the Russians some fifty ICBMs. Ten years later the figures were as follows: United States – 1054 ICBM, 656 SLBM; Soviet Union – 1510 ICBM, 440 SLBM. With mutually assured destruction as the alternative, US foreign policy would have to find a new direction faced with an adversary of equivalent power.

The first bilateral Strategic Arms Limitation Talks (SALT) began in 1969. In May 1972 the Brezhnev-Nixon Moscow summit yielded three major documents: the Treaty on Anti-ballistic Missile Systems; the Interim Agreement and Protocol on Strategic Offensive Missiles; and Basic Principles of Relations between the United States of America and the Union of Soviet Socialist Republics. The Anti-ballistic Missile Treaty was a major breakthrough. It was agreed by treaty that the Soviet Union and the United States could deploy two ABM systems each, one to guard the national capital and another to guard a retaliatory strike missile base.

SALT 1 was an interim agreement to last for five years. It placed head-count limits on offensive intercontinental ballistic missiles of both sides and ballistic missile submarines. SALT 1 put ceilings on numbers, did not enforce actual reductions and did not cover nuclear bombers, tactical nuclear forces based in Europe or constrict technological improvements to the strategic systems it sought to limit.

With SALT 1 in force, the military planners of the Soviet Union could already regard their strategic forces as more than effective and resources could now be devoted to continued build-up of conventional forces in Europe, the deployment of sophisticated theatre nuclear weapons such as the SS-20 intermediate-range ballistic missile and the *Backfire* bomber, and the continued buildup of the Soviet Navy and through it the projection of Soviet military power into the Third World.

The European NATO allies felt desperately exposed. Britain's independent deterrent was wearing out and the secret Chevaline front-end improvement programme could only extend its life in the short term. The West Germans felt the SS-20s breathing down their necks and wanted to restore the credibility of the 'coupling' of European defence to the Unites States' core arsenal. In October 1977 Chancellor Schmidt made a private but highly influential speech in London which accelerated the political process of NATO theatre nuclear weapon modernization.

Soviet power projection did the same thing to the United States as they found the results of living with SALT-style parity increasingly unpalatable. Not only had they been successfully challenged at the strategic level but on a general-force level as well.

In 1945 the Soviet Navy was little more than a coast defence force. By 1967 its Commander in Chief, Admiral Gorshkov, could report, 'The Soviet Navy has been converted in the full sense of the word into an offensive type of long range armed force which could exert a decisive influence on the course of an armed struggle in theatres of military operations of vast extent, and which is also capable of supporting state interests at sea in peacetime.' By 1980, after an immense construction programme, it was well equipped to do just that, and the Soviet Navy rivalled the US Navy in surface warships (with the exception of strike aircraft carriers) and had great superiority in submarines with more than 250 first-line boats in service and a building programme of one a month.

Seapower and long-range strategic transport airpower is for the projection of policy beyond national borders. The Soviets used this capability in the wake of the collapse of the last great European empire in Africa – when the Portuguese withdrew from Angola in 1976 the Soviets poured in military equipment, East German military advisers and a 10,000-strong Cuban expeditionary force to defeat the US backed forces, and in 1977-8 Soviet transport aircraft and helicopters intervened decisively in the Ethiopian-Somali war in the Horn of Africa. Détente, meanwhile, was already dying. The concept of 'linkage' – a package of grain sales, trade deals, technology interchange and liberalization within the USSR on such issues as Jewish emigration crossed too many political or economic interests within the United States to be effectively linked to the vital issue of arms control. The new Presidency of Jimmy Carter in 1976 seemed to give SALT 2 a fresh chance but the political consensus within the United States itself was crumbling fast. Fear of Soviet missile numbers, fear of losing the cherished technological advantage, the failures in Africa, the lost promise of peace in the Middle East at Camp David, the energy crisis, humiliation in Iran, the hostage crisis, the Soviet invasion of Afghanistan and the threat of an invasion of Poland, all conspired to bury détente and usher in the Republican

Presidency of Ronald Reagan with General Haig as Secretary of State and Caspar Weinberger as Secretary of Defence.

In 1970 at the height of the Vietnam War the United States spent $77 billion on defence. By 1985, President Reagan says, he wants a defence budget of $376 billion. Inflation bridges a large part of this huge gap but in 1982 in real dollar terms US defence spending outstrips the peak Vietnam era figure – why?

The political reasons have been covered. Internal economic reasons are another. The military reasons are these. First is a new determination to match the Soviet Union's central conventional military capacity in Europe. This means new tanks, new ground attack and tactical aircraft and new-generation air superiority fighters. It also means a continued imperative with European political connivance for the modernization of theatre nuclear weapons with new systems such as the Tomahawk cruise missile and Pershing II missiles.

In 1974 it was announced that the United States was increasing research and development of a new kind of weapon, the neutron bomb, which went some way to solving the problem of Soviet conventional superiority in Europe.

Neutron weapons deliver high radiation combined with comparatively low blast and flash damage. The radiation attacks organic matter within a controllable radius, leaving equipment and structures more or less intact. The Pentagon wanted 8-in and 155-mm neutron artillery shells and one-kiloton (1 KT) warheads for Lance missiles. However, a pattern of neutron shell air-bursts over a Soviet tank formation rolling westwards would not stop it in its tracks. It would be some hours before the irradiated crew began to die, by which time strategic weapons may well have been used. It has been argued that operational neutron weapons will seriously lower the nuclear threshold, removing those crisis options from the battlefield that the very existence of conventional weapons is designed to give by the blurring of the dividing line between conventional and nuclear weapons. To this argument the then NATO Commander-in-Chief, General Alexander Haig, gave the answer at the beginning of 1978, 'that he did not believe that in any way neutron weapons lessen the essential control associated with the anguishing decision to employ nuclear weapons in any instance.'

The second reason for new United States military spending is a determination to match Soviet power and intervention ability on a global scale. Faced with its chain of bases and satellites, often taken over directly from the retreating colonial power, US and Western navies have had little choice other than to adopt a defensive posture, concentrating resources for example on anti-submarine warfare to combat the threat of the Soviet submarine fleet. But above all the fact that one third of the United States' oil comes from the Persian Gulf, over 60 per cent of Western Europe's and 70 per cent of Japan's oil comes from the same source makes an effective military long arm a US military priority.

In his last State of the Union speech, with the American hostages still held in Iran, Russian troops in Afghanistan and all the firepower of the US strategic arsenal and navy strike carriers unable to get either troops or hostages out, President Carter declared the readiness of the United States to apply force if necessary to ensure the supply of oil. President Reagan went so far as to suggest stationing American troops in the Gulf or at least within operational reach. Extension of overseas bases, new warships, tactical transports and helicopters therefore are an important part of forward US military planning for the new 'Rapid Deployment Force'.

The third military reason is the approaching obsolescence of the American strategic triad itself, land-based intercontinental missiles, B-52 strategic bombers and Poseidon missile equipped submarines. The B-1B carrying cruise missiles, the MX missile and the Trident missile submarines are the new prongs of the triad with projected operational lives stretching well into the next century.

In May 1981, addressing West Point cadets on his commitment to higher military spending, President Reagan told them, 'I am happy to tell you that the people of America have recovered from what can only be a temporary aberration.' Referring to the demise of SALT 2 he said 'any controversy now would be over which weapons the United States should produce and not whether it should forsake weaponry for treaties and agreements.'

In the 1980s weapons have become policy, and no longer the means by which policy may be carried out. This book henceforth is designed to show the reader the implications of this change, what those weapons are, what they are intended to do, what they cost, and what the plans are for their use.

Part One
Limited War

1 • The Battle for Europe

The continent of Europe expressed geographically stretches from the western tip of Portugal to the Ural Mountains 800 km east of Moscow – 10 million square kilometres and 600 million people.

In March 1948 a coalition of countries in Western Europe which had been liberated from German occupation by Anglo-US-Canadian military power signed in Brussels a fifty-year military treaty of mutual assistance. Meanwhile, the United States, Canada and the Brussels nations – Britain, France, the Netherlands, Belgium and Luxembourg – began negotiations for the larger North Atlantic Security Treaty which was signed on 4 April 1949 with Portugal, Iceland, Denmark, Norway and Italy joining this new North Atlantic Treaty Organization. Greece and Turkey joined NATO in 1951 and West Germany in 1954.

In May 1955 the Soviet Union and a coalition of those eastern European countries liberated in 1944-5 by Soviet forces – Poland, Czechoslovakia, Hungary, Romania, Bulgaria, East Germany and Albania – signed the Warsaw Pact mutual defence treaty as a nominal answer to the re-arming of West Germany within NATO. European countries not tied to military pacts are Austria, Sweden, Switzerland, Ireland and Yugoslavia (which broke with the Soviet Union in 1949). Finland, although neutral, signed a ten-year treaty of non-aggression with the USSR in 1948. Spain signed a defence agreement with the US in September 1953 and joined NATO as a full member in June 1982. France withdrew from NATO military command in March 1966 and Albania broke with the Warsaw Pact in September 1968. Greece withdrew from NATO military command in 1974 and rejoined in 1981.

Europe is where the conflicting security interests of the superpowers converge head on. US-Soviet military rivalry physically collides in NATO's centre section along the border of the two Germanies. If deterrence fails here, NATO can forget its flanks.

The accords of the NATO pact do not demand an automatic declaration of war in the case of an attack on one of its members although the will of the United States to respond is the bedrock of NATO's credibility. The Warsaw Pact is constituted in a similar way, defining itself as a purely defensive coalition with the 'gains of socialism', 'revolutionary achievements' and the 'cause of peace' as the objects – to be defended by pre-emptive means, if necessary. Clause 4 of its constitution declares 'that each signatory shall immediately either individually or in agreement with other parties come to the assistance of the state or states attacked with all such means as it deems necessary, including armed force.' A marshal of the Soviet Union has always been the Warsaw C-in-C just as an American general and admiral have always been NATO's land and sea supreme commanders – SACEUR and SACLANT respectively.

There is a fundamental difference between the two coalitions. The Soviet Union provides a far greater proportion of Warsaw Pact combat power and standardized equipment than does the United States for NATO (the US provides 10 per cent of NATO's ground forces, 20 per cent of its seapower and 25 per cent of its tactical airpower); and the military assets of the Warsaw Pact are concentrated geographically around and closely integrated with the dominant military power. The resources of NATO are widely dispersed with the dominant military power separated by the Atlantic ocean. The burden of NATO's conventional military planning on land and sea is how to contain a Warsaw Pact thrust for long enough to allow the United States reserve forces to be mobilized and safely delivered in time to hold the line in Europe. From 1943 onwards the Soviet Union emerged as the dominant power on the continent of Europe and has continued to expand militarily, opposed by American power which is based not on geography but on political commitment. Such a power base is vulnerable to severance at both ends, by moves for European independence and for American isolationism. This is the so-called 'de-coupling' issue, the term used by NATO to embrace moves and circumstances which might break the Western Europe-US link.

The symbolic counter to de-coupling is the basing of US ground forces on the ground in Europe itself, as much as a hostage to American public opinion and political willpower as an effective military deployment.

The development of the Soviet ability to hit the United States with intercontinental ballistic missiles raised the stakes not only for Americans but for Europeans sheltering under the US nuclear umbrella.

In this new environment of nuclear parity rather than US strategic superiority, in 1967 NATO had to adopt a flexible response policy in parallel with the strategic doctrine of the US, offering a defence at the level of violence of the attack and escalating in proportion. The most important 'rung' of the escalation ladder (other than to start it in the first place) is to use nuclear weapons and since the NATO Nuclear Planning Group agreed on guidelines in the late 1960s it has been the Alliance's policy to respond to an overwhelming conventional attack by using battlefield nuclear weapons.

Going Nuclear

The mechanism for the first employment by NATO of battlefield nuclear weapons is very complex. In theory, the governments of all the fifteen states of the Alliance should be consulted; in practice it would have to be different.

Say Soviet tanks and motor rifle divisions are punching across central Germany and an embattled US Army Divisional HQ cannot hold the line without firing its enhanced radiation Lance missiles. The request goes to Corps, to CENTAG HQ, to AFCENT, to SHAPE and SACEUR and thence to the US National Command Authority where the US President would take the decision, probably in consultation with the German Chancellor. The time all this would take is twenty-four hours and the tactical moment long since passed.

There is a nuclear planning staff at SHAPE (Supreme Headquarters Allied Powers Europe) which bases its planning on the NATO document MC 14/3 of 1967 – the so-called 'Athens guidelines', the Nuclear Planning Group guidelines of 1969, the preliminary strike role guidelines of 1972, and the bi-annual Ministerial guidelines.

The fundamental NATO document MC 14/3 differentiates between three kinds of nuclear response: direct retaliation, deliberate escalation and general nuclear response.

The release of theatre nuclear weapons is authorized by the US National Command Authority. This means that the US President would always decide about the use of theatre nuclear weapons, although Britain has some say. A group of British liaison officers constantly monitor US operational plans involving British nuclear weapons and Britain has a general right of veto.

The nuclear weapons of NATO allies are released for use, with certain exceptions, only after consultations by the North Atlantic Council. Generally the same also applies to the American tactical nuclear weapons which would be released for operational use by the American president through CIN-CEUR.

SHAPE also prepares its own target list, the operations plan of SACEUR. At its disposal are aircraft, Pershing I missiles and submarine-launched Poseidon missiles which would be used in component operations as soon as a political decision had been made for their release. Part of these missiles and aircraft are in constant readiness (quick reaction alert, or QRA) for operational use immediately after an attack. These intermediate-range strike forces are supplemented by the battlefield systems – Lance missiles, Atomic Demolition Munitions and Nike Hercules nuclear air-defence missiles and nuclear-capable howitzers.

The preparation of graduated operational options has only just begun, and the operational use of these systems is as yet by no means clear. This vagueness is considered by some politicians not as a drawback but an advantage. As far as operational planning is concerned, the SACEUR and the American system are linked in several ways. Some of the Single Integrated Operational Plan (SIOP) forces are assigned to NATO, and special 'limited nuclear options' with intercontinental weapons are intended for strikes on Soviet medium-range weapons.

Published Soviet doctrine envisages a war in Europe's Central Sector brought about by NATO adventurism. A massive land

and air offensive rolls back this aggression and penetrates deep into enemy territory destroying the opposing forces in the process. If the enemy should resort at the eleventh hour to a nuclear tactical defence, either localized or theatre-wide, then any restraints on the use of theatre nuclear weapons are removed, becoming the main and legitimate means of destroying the enemy in battle, while hesitant half-measures would throw away the advantages of initiative. This implies pre-emptive attacks on counterforce targets, not just a single salvo but a sustained barrage until all targetable objectives are destroyed. The Soviets would employ their long arm, the SS-20s based in western Russia, which could blanket NATO's rear springboard for long-range theatre forces, the United Kingdom, which is dense with counterforce targets. In this gameplan, deterrence has signally failed for Britain and West Germany but the United States is still intact. Would the US use their core strategic arsenal to save what's left of Europe?

If hostilities on European soil should represent total war to those Europeans unfortunate enough to get in the way, this may still represent limited war to the United States. Ironically, further basing of US nuclear power physically in Europe can serve to rattle further European nerves as this might represent a US commitment to fight in Europe rather than sacrifice its own cities in a full strategic exchange.

In October 1981 President Reagan made a casual remark to a group of newspaper editors which set adrenalin pulsing across the Atlantic. The President mentioned that he 'could see where you could have an exchange of tactical weapons against troops in the field without bringing either one of the major powers to pushing the button.' The West German press in particular leapt at the remark, splashing the story that the US was planning for a nuclear war confined only to Europe while the Soviet leadership was able to reap the rewards of a major propaganda coup against a background of large-scale anti-nuclear demonstrations, claiming that the US 'would like to put the whole risk of a thermonuclear catastrophe on Western Europe while remaining on the sidelines'. The result was a statement issued by President Reagan which attempted to clarify what US and NATO policy in Europe actually was; it is repeated here in full to put in context the assessment of capabilities that follows.

American policy towards deterring conflict in Europe has not changed for over twenty years. Our strategy remains as it has been, one of flexible response: maintaining an assured military capability to deter the use of force – conventional or nuclear – by the Warsaw Pact at the lowest possible level.

As all Presidents have acknowledged, any use of nuclear weapons would have the most profound consequences. In a nuclear war all mankind would lose. Indeed, the awful and incalculable risk associated with any use of nuclear weapons themselves serves to deter their use. The suggestion that the United States could even consider fighting a nuclear war at Europe's expense is an outright deception.

The essence of the United States nuclear strategy is that no aggressor should believe that the use of nuclear weapons in Europe could reasonably be limited to Europe. Indeed, it is the joint European-American commitment to share the burden of our common defence which assures the peace.

Thus we regard any military threat to Europe as a threat to the United States itself.

Three hundred and seventy-five thousand United States servicemen provide the living guarantee of this unshakable United States commitment to the peace and security of Europe.

The Warsaw Pact

The army that beat the Wehrmacht in 1945 still had over a million horses providing an essential part of its logistic train. By the mid-1970s it had become the most formidable, fast-moving, hard-hitting and technically competent striking force the world had ever seen. In the 1960s the Soviet Army began a large-scale modernization programme of its conventional and theatre nuclear land and air forces to transform a balanced defensive-offensive army into one geared to fast-paced offensive operations on minimal mobilization times. This programme has included deployment of new-generation T-64 and T-72 tanks in Soviet front-line forces based in Germany, Hungary and western Russia. Towed artillery has been progressively replaced by self-propelled weapons. Infantry mobility and firepower has been enhanced by the deployment of BMP infantry combat vehicles, airborne assault vehicles and tactical transport aircraft and helicopters. Tactical nuclear and chemical warfare capability has been transformed with the upgrading of nuclear-capable artillery, and introduction of the more accurate SS-21 and SS-X-23 tactical missiles with advanced warheads replacing the twenty-year-old FROGs, Scuds and Scaleboards and the formidable SS-20 mobile intermediate-range missile with a MIRV warhead which from bases in Western Russia can command a huge arc of targets in the whole of western Europe.

'Frontal Aviation' organized into tactical air armies, is the largest component of the Soviet Air Force and the introduction during the 1970s of modern combat aircraft such as the Sukhoi Su-17 *Fitter C*, the MiG-23 *Flogger B*, the MiG-25 *Foxbat*, Su-24 *Fencer*, and Mi-24 *Hind* combat helicopter has turned Soviet tactical airpower from a basically defensive force into a formidable nuclear-capable offensive instrument.

This unprecedented flexibility, mobility, firepower and mass has been achieved for a reason. These capabilities deliver to Soviet military planners and their political clients a subtle and wide range of options in Europe. Soviet strategic power can inflict damage on the continental United States as a prelude to a war on the continent, its armies could overrun western Europe very quickly from bases in East Germany and Czechoslovakia, its theatre nuclear weapons could support conventional operations in the crucial Central Sector (see page 41) by long-range strikes into NATO rear areas including Britain. NATO forces cannot really cope with chemical combat, as has been proven in exercises, and has no promising prospects of being able to do so. Frontal Aviation can challenge NATO for air superiority over western Europe, initial efforts could be rapidly reinforced and re-supplied, and the Atlantic umbilical could be effectively cut by Soviet sea power.

Soviet Combat Doctrine

The foundation of Soviet combat doctrine is 'Combined Arms Warfare' employing varied weapons and bringing them together in the most effective manner to the maximum advantage. At the 'Front' level, which is the largest field formation in wartime, there is a combined-arms commander who can control co-ordinated ground, air, missile, air defence and, if necessary, naval formations to carry out missions and reach objectives delineated by the General Staff. A Front could be composed of three to five combined arms armies, one or two tank armies, airborne, aviation, missile, engineer, signal, intelligence, train, reconnaissance and special forces.

The tank and combined-arms armies include three to five tank and motor rifle divisions and are administrative units capable of independent operations. The component tank divisions are formed around three tank regiments, one motor rifle regiment, one artillery regiment, one air defence regiment and other support formations. Three airborne rifle regiments form the airborne divisions with ancillary backup. The motor rifle divisions have a similar square structure with three motor rifle regiments, one tank regiment, one artillery regiment and one air defence regiment, plus many combat and service support units.

As many as five Fronts may combine in a Theatre of Military Operations whose commander will be a three-star General directly responsible to the General Staff. This body functions to control the operations of the five services (the Strategic Rocket Forces, Ground Forces, Air Defence, Air Forces and Navy) while individual service chiefs are reponsible for the training and support of troops and the development of weapons and tactics.

The modern combat capabilities outlined above and their lucid combined-arms organization for maximum effect all facilitate the tenets of Soviet military planning for the successful capture of a relatively intact western Europe. This doctrine emphasizes the objective, surprise, mass, the earliest possible destruction of defensive ability, rapid occupation and the expedient isolation of the United States. Victory is the goal, regardless of who started the war and why.

The use of nuclear or chemical weapons is part of this process of clearing a path for armour and airmobile forces and disarming NATO's nuclear means of response if necessary. The Soviet Army has the delivery systems, the training and equipment for operating on a nuclear/chemical battlefield and a range of chemical agents to draw on. Non-persistent agents, for example, could be used to clear poorly prepared defensive forces at a river-crossing or air landing zone without damaging the terrain or preventing the advancing Soviet forces with their effective Nuclear-Biological-Chemical (NBC) protection from seizing the position. More persistent agents could interdict supply routes or airfields (see pages 100-3).

Assembly and staging for assaults take place in optimum conditions for secrecy such as night or bad weather to avoid detection and are aided by deception plans. The assault is preceded by a massive firepower pounding followed by attacks on narrow fronts piling up attrition-proof numbers against the defence. Around two thirds of total strength is in the first echelon with a second and sometimes a third behind. When the crust is broken through, armour fans out on multiple axes, driving for deep objectives, crossing rivers seized by helicopter and airborne forces and bypassing bottlenecks. Sustained rates of advance under conventional conditions should average 30 km per day against a determined defence. This puncture technique would be repeated on a broad front by multiple tank army probes denying the defenders the chance to concentrate their efforts and allowing the attackers' reserves to be switched into the line of least resistance. Soviet doctrine deems defence to be a temporary expedient to be employed locally while on the offensive in other sectors, or during consolidation after attack, to gain time, cover a withdrawal or repel an attack by a superior enemy force.

The NATO Response

As we have seen, NATO was adopting the policy of flexible response with a strong conventional layer just as the Soviet armed forces were embarking on their massive modernization programme. The doctrine of massive retaliation which had sufficed in the 1950s was reappraised and, faced with expanding Soviet power, a predominantly conventional defence was judged too expensive, a predominantly nuclear defence too unstable. Thus flexible response was formally adopted in December 1967 and it remains the foundation of NATO strategy for a limited war in its Central Sector today. It strives to deny the Soviets any hope of success unless they attack with such weight that compelling US interests would be compromised, making the risk of rapid escalation excessive. It predicates a strong forward defence plus the versatility to cope with aggression at the appropriate level on the conflict scale and escalate under control if necessary. In defence, NATO looks to the new lethality of modern weapons and modern mobility as a substitute for abundance. The US Army's field manual FM-100-5 states: 'Swiftly massed field artillery, totally mobile tank and mechanized infantry battalions, airmobile and armour weapons, assault helicopters, close air support aircraft and, in some circumstances, tactical employment of nuclear weapons offer us the means to concentrate overhelming combat power and to decisively alter force ratios when and where we choose'.

It is not, of course, as simple as that. A doctrinal debate is taking place in the US and among NATO armed forces which attempts to resolve some of the contradictions that defence against massive Soviet conventional power throws up. The old style of 'firepower attrition' simply does not work against huge numbers, and great enthusiasm has been expressed by US Army planners for the Israeli style of self-sustaining brigade units. Mobility always exists to put effective firepower in place but the advocates of 'manoeuvre warfare' argue that a smaller army can throw the ponderous juggernaut off balance with judo-like application of force as the *Bundeswehr* intends to do. Sceptics would say that the US and NATO armies in defence have no choice since the opportunities to manoeuvre will only be open to the side making the decisions, the attacker not the defender.

Defence brings further dilemmas. If the use of battlefield nuclear weapons is expected from the outset, then the defenders must disperse to reduce vulnerability. Conventional forces attacking on a narrow front could quickly crack this diluted crust, but if NATO strength were concentrated forward to repel attacks on a broad front, they could be utterly destroyed if caught by a sudden resort to battlefield nuclear weapons. The US doctrine in the case of the expected breakthrough is to go into a precisely choreographed rolling defence that depends on 'reinforcing laterally with on-line withdrawals to prepared secondary positions' (they currently exist only on maps). All of this represents a very complex piece of command and control under the best possible conditions. In wartime, when every electronic countermeasure weapon will be aimed at dismembering command systems anyway, the successful execution of such a military manoeuvre becomes highly problematical.

A recent German Army staff study has come up with a different solution. Geography determines five natural entry routes into West Germany, and as the number of enemy tanks and fighting vehicles in the spearhead units is known, the number of targets to be destroyed can be calculated: it is about 3000. The new lethality of conventional munitions provides enough stopping-power to cope: mines rapidly dispersed from tube launchers and fuel air explosives delivered by rocket (see pages 78-81). The tank itself is toppled from its pedestal with an emphasis on light armoured vehicles equipped with missiles on elevating launch platforms, effectively achieving double the range of the attacking tanks' guns. The defenders employ a leapfrog technique in this rolling barrier defence strategy so as to present the attacker with a fresh and fully supplied defending force still possessing superior firepower.

Air forces would now be released from the responsibility of close air support or missions into the enemy rear to concentration on air defence because the superior defensive firepower would be enough to destroy enemy armour in the killing zones and heavy artillery rockets with 200 km range could cover the West German frontier from as few as five launch sites.

NATO Central Sector

The NATO Central Sector, the heart of the Federal German Republic, is the most productive and populous part of Europe, dense with cities, factories and human beings. It is also the most critical place on which the collective military power of the Warsaw Pact forces is brought to bear. Accidents of history have built in disadvantages for the putative defenders. The North German Plain, a key axis of approach, is defended by the British Army of the Rhine aided by rear-based Dutch and Belgian brigades. The German *Bundeswehr* is split in three, the United States with its great military power in the South being responsible for the most easily defended terrain. The three French divisions based in Germany are not integrated within NATO; indeed, the withdrawal of France in 1968 cut the Al'_ance's east-west lines of communication leaving the supply lines running parallel to the front from the North Sea ports to Bremerhaven, Rotterdam and Antwerp with very little room for manoeuvre. If strong Warsaw Pact mobile armoured elements cracked through the crust, NATO's main line of resistance would be enveloped unless friendly forces regrouped behind the Rhine, the first major defensible feature to the rear. French planning has no intention of 'fencing with the enemy all the way to the Pyrenées' and its Pluton tactical nuclear missiles are targeted on Soviet lines of approach in Germany.

NATO's conventional manpower is actually smaller today than in the days of massive retaliation when it was supposed to act as a 'tripwire' for the United States. The strength of the West German armed forces, however, has greatly increased in manpower and armour, doubled defence budgets from 1970 to 1978 funding these efforts. Half of the ground forces in NATO's Central Sector are German, half of the land-based air defence, a third of the combat aircraft, and all the ships and a large proportion of the naval airpower in the Baltic.

Soviet forces alone match NATO forces with twenty-four Category 1 (75 per cent readiness) divisions in East Germany and Czechoslovakia facing twenty-four NATO divisions in West Germany. This forward-based Soviet power could be rapidly reinforced by road within forty-eight hours by forces in European Russia which could also replace the two Soviet divisions in Poland and four more in Hungary. A further eight armies composed of twenty divisions and three airborne divisions with 6800 tanks are maintained in the Baltic, Byelorussian and Carpathian Military Districts.

NATO reserves, in contrast, are simply earmarked to bring existing formations up to strength; nearly all of NATO's uncommitted combat strength is in the United States. The moving of these vast numbers of men and material from the US depends on pre-positioning stocks and munitions in Europe and the capabilities of America's strategic air- and sealift. The capacity of ports and airfields to handle this transfer of resources is adequate, provided they can function undamaged, but all would be prime targets for missile attacks or mining. NATO's SACLANT command must further contain attacks on the sea lanes across the Atlantic and to the Middle East if the Alliance is going to stay in one piece or even sustain a defensive battle in Germany which may, for the moment, be holding the line.

The Warsaw Pact forces too have their problems. Since December 1981 when there was a virtual military coup, the people of Poland, right in the middle of the line of communication, have been held within the grip of orthodox Soviet communism only by the imposition of martial law. Warsaw is a vital hub of rail and road communications. The prospect of a truculent trade union presence is as unwelcome to the Kremlin as the shutdown of the British Polaris base at Faslane, Scotland, by Civil Service Union maintenance workers in 1981 was to NATO, although the respective authorities' reactions were very different.* Czechoslovakia was kept in line only by full-scale invasion in August 1968 with five Soviet divisions remaining as a permanent garrison, while Rumania has attempted to pursue an independent line of its own. Whatever the cracks in the Alliance, there is no doubting the unbreakable dominance of the Soviet armed forces but even here there are deficiencies. Category I divisions are rarely up to full readiness and in the Group of Soviet Forces Germany, 25 per cent of the enlisted personnel are recruits who are rotated every six months into the divisions, teenagers who have in some cases not even completed their basic training. Few of the Soviet Frontal Aviation's fighter and ground attack squadrons match the Western counterpart's capabilities or standards and there are doubts about the combat efficiency of Soviet tanks. Given the very size of this offensive bludgeon, some analysts who doubt the fashionable 'short sharp shock', week-long war hypothesis nurture doubts about how it could be adequately fuelled and controlled once set rolling.

* The Faslane workers were put under Naval regulations

SOVIET FORCES and NATO MILITARY SECTORS
in Central Europe

W. German

Dutch

W. German   3rd
                 (4

British

NETHERLANDS

Belgian

Northag
Centag   8th Guards A
                      (1 tk div, 3 M

W. German

Bonn

Weir

BELGIUM

United States

Frankfurt

United

Wurzburg

LUX

FRANCE   WEST GERMANY

(French)

NATO total in Europe
84 Divs (inc 3 airborne/airmobile)
13 Divs (inc 2 USMC) in US plus Canadian Brigade

Stuttgart

On Central + Northern region
39 Divs are forward deployed and
3 from US via rapid airborne reinforcement

NATO Central and Northern Region. Airpower in Place
1,340 Fighter/Strike
445 Interceptor
200 Recce

Baltic Sea

Rostock

2nd Guards Tank Army
(1 tk div, 2 MR divs)

Soviet Forces Germany

th Air Army
5 combat aircraft)

BERLIN

div)

20th Guards Army
(3 MR div)

deburg

Cottbus

AST GERMANY

E. German divs

1st Guards Tank Army
(3 tk div, 1 MR div)

Dresden

HQ Army Boleslav
(1 tk div, 1 MR div)

PRAGUE

Milovce

Pilsen

HQ Army Olomouc
(1 tk div, 2 MR div)

Central Group of Forces
(100 tactical aircraft)

German

AUSTRIA

POLAND

15 Polish divs

CZECHOSLOVAKIA

10 Czech divs

Warsaw Pact total in Europe

173 Divs (inc 9 airborne/airmobile)
and 15 Divs in Central Soviet Union

On Central + Northern Region
104 Divs,
50+ of which could launch operations
soon after mobilisation

**Central and Northern Region.
Airpower in Place**

1,580 Fighter/Strike
2,595 Interceptor
  415 Recce

NATO North Flank

Norway forbids the presence of permanently stationed foreign troops or nuclear weapons upon its soil. Most of Norway's armed forces, however, are earmarked for AFNORTH (Allied Forces Northern Europe), the NATO command whose HQ is at Kolsaas near Oslo and British and Dutch Marines regularly exercise in rapid reinforcement of the area and warfare in Arctic conditions. A Norwegian infantry battalion acts as a tripwire along the 120-mile frontier with the Soviet Union in the far north – an area of great strategic significance. A Soviet sonar line stretches from the North Cape to Spitzbergen and a US equivalent extends out to Jan Mayen from the North Cape.

Considerable Soviet military power is piled up against NATO's North Flank – two motor rifle divisions and a naval infantry regiment in the Kola peninsula and seven more motor rifle and an airborne division in the Leningrad military district. They are there first to protect the Northern Fleet, the core of the Soviet Union's strategic seaborne deterrent, but they could also move to take over Northern Norway very rapidly in a 'limited war' either as a token counter to a US move elsewhere (in the Middle East, for example) or to seize a springboard for the projection of naval and air power over the Atlantic.

NATO South Flank

Greek and Turkish enmity has caused the most serious division within NATO since its inception. Greece left the Alliance in 1974 over the Cyprus dispute and rejoined with strings attached in 1981. In the same year Turkey with its very large army was held together by a military takeover suppressing all political activity. Greece and Turkey defend an area distinct from the Centre Sector and avenues of approach further west are blocked by Italy although Libyan attitudes are causing alarm. NATO outnumbers its rivals at sea and could bottle up the Soviet Black Sea fleet if necessary. The Soviet Mediterranean squadron depends on replenishing at sea. The US 6th Fleet, however, was cut in half in 1980 when the *Nimitz* set sail for the Arabian Sea in response to the increasing tension in the Middle East. Soviet submarines in the relatively shallow Mediterranean can exploit sea-water temperature differences and dense merchant traffic to avoid detection or shadow the Sixth Fleet so closely as to allow minimal reaction times in the case of attack by cruise missiles.

NATO's Fears

In the early 1970s NATO defence planning was based on the assumption that there would be considerable warning of an attack. This was replaced in 1975/6 by an alarmist fear that the Warsaw Pact could overwhelm NATO conventional forces with just twenty-nine divisions, punching through the forward defence without a detectable mobilization period, the main body of the enemy coming into action a few hours after leaving their assembly areas and crossing the Rhine within forty-eight hours. Pact capabilities were therefore closely studied in 1976 and as a result the monitoring system, which keeps watch electronically or by satellite reconnaissance on over 700 key 'indicators' of Pact activities, was stepped up.

A 'bolt from the blue' or surprise attack employing theatre nuclear weapons at once was judged unlikely although possible. Two days would be the minimum mobilization period for an attack on the West, the minimum time to convert Category II Divisions to Category I and get 85 per cent of available airpower combat ready. Eight to fourteen days would be the optimum, after which advantages would diminish due to NATO's counterbuildup. Nevertheless this analysis did little to satisfy those who, faced with Soviet military superiority in Europe, real or imaginary, were demanding bold initiatives to redress the balance.

Initiatives to bolster NATO's deterrent and defensive abilities were presented in a proposal by the US Secretary of Defence and delivered in London by President Carter to NATO ministers in May 1977. The assembled politicians agreed to generate annual defence budget increases in real terms of around 3 per cent across five years from 1979 to pay for these efforts. Quick-fix improvements were essentially complete by mid-1979, especially in war reserve ammunition and anti-tank weapons. Stocks of air-to-air, ground-to-ground and anti-tank missiles were increased; but anxieties were still expressed that the physical separation of the US Army in Europe from ammo dumps west of the Rhine and in Britain was still too great and, further, that these sites were very vulnerable to air, commando and gas attack.

The Soviet superiority in armour was another prime concern: simply providing more anti-tank missiles to infantry was not regarded as a sufficient answer. Heavy TOW anti-tank missiles mounted on helicopters and modern laser range-finders with infra-red sights were given priority. Then, at the NATO May 1978 summit, a long-term defence programme (LTDP) was approved, together with improvement programmes projecting up to fifteen years into the future and grouped into ten key areas. These are:

1. *Theatre nuclear forces modernization* (see below).
2. *Readiness*, aimed at improving the alert times of standing forces, reserve units and civil support.
3. *Air defence.* The first of eighteen Boeing E-3A Sentry Airborne Warning and Control Systems (AWACS) was delivered to joint NATO control in January 1982. F-15 Eagle interceptors are now with US squadrons in Germany and the Improved Hawk missile screen with its NADGE (NATO air defence ground environment) radar net have been upgraded.
4. *Maritime improvement programme*, to correct 'serious deficiencies in combat capabilities'.
5. *Command control and communications programme*, aimed at achieving improvements in C^3 such as automatic data processing (ADP) systems at HQs and improved encryption and electronic security.
6. *Electronic warfare.*
7. *Reinforcement programme.*
8. *Reserve mobilization programme.* 7. and 8. are complementary. Planning is to increase arms stockpiles in Europe for 'reforger forces' which together with airlift improvements should give US forces in Europe the capability of moving five divisions in ten days together with sixty tactical air squadrons as against current capabilities of one division and forty TAC (Tactical Air

Command) squadrons in that time. Reserve mobiliz-
ation is NATO's 'companion piece' to improve the
European contribution. At the May 1980 NATO
meeting US delegates pressed for an expansion in
European reserves to free uncommitted US forces for the
Gulf-oriented RJDTF (Rapid Joint Deployment Task
Force).

9. *Consumer logistics programme.* This aspires to produce an
improved structure and better civil participation in
supplying military operations.
10. *Rationalization*, the search for standardization, inter-
operability and compatibility of systems and supplies
which is by now a traditional NATO goal.

The most important and immediately controversial of these ten
areas of initiative was theatre nuclear forces (TNF) modernization.

Theatre Nuclear Forces

US weapons in Europe have served to link the American nuclear
threshold much more closely to the defence of the continent but
their military efficacy in defence has been less clear because of
the problems of using these weapons without destroying by
so-called 'collateral damage' those being defended.

In the 1950s there was an intense period of technical
development by the US Atomic Energy Commission which tried
to forge the atomic bomb into a weapon that could be used on
a battlefield. This effort was paralleled by the Soviet Union and
two broad types of weapon were the result – short-range for use
against troops and long-range theatre weapons for use against
targets in the enemy rear.

The Soviet Union's first nuclear capacity was originally aimed
entirely at Western Europe, as far as they could reach. In the
1950s bombers such as the Tu-4 could hit the United Kingdom
with free-fall bombs but only the bigger Tu-95 and M-4 could
theoretically reach the United States. Apart from the brief
excursion of missiles into Cuba in 1961, the USA was
invulnerable. Europe certainly was not.

The first Soviet SS-3 and SS-4 medium-range ballistic

missiles (MRBMs up to 3000 km range) were deployed in the late 1950s, followed by the intermediate-range (IRBMs up to 5000 km) SS-5 in the early 1960s. At peak deployment in the mid-1960s, over 600 fixed launchers were pointing at Western Europe and 100 more were aimed at the Middle East and SE Asia. By 1968 about a quarter of this force was retargeted against the new ideological enemy, China. Soviet Frontal Aviation deployed new nuclear-capable aircraft such as the Su-24 in the 1970s and the long-range Tupolev Tu-22M *Backfire* bomber.

This was the situation until 1977 when the new generation IRBM, the SS-20, began to enter service. The head-count on deployment of this theatre system was not covered in SALT. (For dates relating to TNF weapons in Europe, see Chronology, pages 180-205.) The missile is mobile, and is fitted with three very accurate and independently targeted MIRV warheads. Each SS-20 unit is equipped with a triple warhead reload round. In January 1982, 265 SS-20s with 795 warheads were deployed facing NATO countries and base construction is still continuing.

In a similar fashion, first-generation battlefield weapons such as the comparatively crude FROG artillery rockets with ranges up to 50 km are being replaced by the SS-21 and SS-X-23 with ranges up to 500 km and much increased accuracy and payload.

The SS-20 in particular alarmed NATO planners. The missile's most dangerous property was its counterforce ability to knock out NATO's own tactical nuclear stockpile, eliminating the middle rung of the escalation ladder. There would be no means to make a 'limited' nuclear counterstrike in kind, the only possible response would be to use the heavyweight strategic arsenal of the United States.

Meanwhile this middle rung was being compromised anyway by the approaching obsolescence of NATO's own long- and short-range theatre nuclear forces. By 1977 US Navy Poseidon submarines still provided 400 warheads as a long-range theatre force but these were relatively inaccurate missiles unsuited for sniping at tactical targets; the same went for Britain's Polaris force. US strike carriers with nuclear-capable aircraft are highly vulnerable. The predominant NATO nuclear long-range theatre forces were always land-based aircraft and all stationed in Britain: 170 USAF F-111s and 56 ageing RAF Vulcans, their ability to penetrate Soviet defended airspace highly questionable by then.

For some European politicians this gentle decay coupled with the second round of SALT talks was highly alarming. The SS-20s and *Backfires* facing Europe were not to be controlled, just weapons that could fly between the two superpowers. Helmut Schmidt, the Chancellor of West Germany, made a discreet but influential speech in London in October 1977 with an implicit message for the Americans. The Soviet Union should be persuaded to abandon its Europe-targeted arsenal or it should be matched by theatre nuclear modernization.

The NATO summit of 1977 tackled the question of TNF modernization, responsibility to the study being given to the Nuclear Planning Group (NPG) which set up a working group in October 1977 known originally as Task Force 10 and later as the High Level Group. The NPG, first set up in 1963, is NATO's nuclear elite, and includes all member nations of NATO in its councils. In contrast to the United States where a rich and interactive community of think tanks, academic institutions, service, government and Congressional committees genuinely have their hands on defence policy-making few Europeans have actually been involved in it – only an outer circle of 150 and an inner circle of around 20 politicians, civil servants, soldiers and academics. Faced with a nuclear inventory fast approaching obsolescence and the buildup of Soviet power, this small circle of planners urged their political clients to embrace the latest products of American technology. This poisoned chalice contained the neutron bomb and the cruise missile.

Cruise

The cruise missile is a pilotless aircraft which flies under continuous power through the atmosphere to its target. The German Navy developed such weapons to be launched from Zeppelins against London in 1917, and the V-1, which performed the same function more effectively in 1944 for the Luftwaffe, was a cruise system. In the 1950s and 1960s both America and the Soviet Union developed cruise missiles such as the Mace and *Shaddock* but they were unwieldy and inaccurate and the US types were rapidly superseded by ballistic missiles in all but short-range roles. By the early 1970s new technologies opened up the system's potential once again. These were lightweight warheads, small high-efficiency turbofan engines with low specific fuel consumption giving long-range and modern guidance technology which, combined with satellite mapping, allowed the missile to match terrain contours (TER-COM) by using a memory stored in its onboard computer. Thus the missile arrived at its target with great accuracy and with little chance of being intercepted by current air-defence techniques. Cruise was not mentioned in the Salt 1 agreement of 1972 which covered ballistic missiles only. Here was an elegant new system which typified the superiority of American technical competence, and the more the Soviets tries to impede its development by embracing it within SALT 2 the more its reputation as a wonder weapon grew. (See page 215 for a description of the development and capabilities of US cruise missiles.) The US military wanted it and NATO caught the bug.

The apparent cheapness and flexibility of the ground-launched cruise missile (GLCM) seemed to offer the planners of NATO's TNF modernization a cost-effective way of offering some European-based response to Soviet theatre nuclear dominance. It was not as simple as that. Three factors conspired to ensure that the accession of new-generation theatre nuclear weapons would not be as straightforward as acquiring updated communications or anti-tank technology. The first was the public-relations fiasco over the 'neutron bomb' in 1976-8, the moral repugnance it caused in Europe and the rekindling of dormant European anti-nuclear sentiments. The second was the determination of the Soviet Union to exploit these sentiments for the maximum political advantage.

The third factor was the perhaps ironic proposition that a redress of the imbalance of nuclear power might actually serve to dilute the 'indivisibility of deterrence' by which the United States' core strategic arms were presumed to be available as a direct means of response to any direct attack on a NATO country. The problem was that flexible response had always been ambiguous, depending on which side of the Atlantic you stood. For the US, forward-based nuclear weapons were a complement to conventional weapons which could be employed up the rungs of the ladder and could be halted before the USA was touched. The Europeans in NATO, however, wanted to emphasize how quickly conventional war would turn into a full exchange.

The Neutron Bomb

The 'neutron bomb' is shorthand for a family of nuclear weapons, the basic research on which started in the 1950s. They emphasize or 'enhance' the prompt radiation yield in neutron or gamma rays of a fusion reaction and minimize the heat and blast effects. They were developed originally as an anti-armour weapon, the flesh-and-blood crew of a tank being the target and not the hardened, blast-proof vehicle itself. Military supporters of the system, which can be packed into a short-range artillery missile or a howitzer shell, see it as an essential redress to the Soviet tank preponderance in Europe while at the same time not necessarily being a nuclear weapon on a definable rung of the escalation ladder. Further, with a range of advanced 'discriminative' Soviet tactical warheads ranged against them, it would be the indiscriminate big bang NATO stockpile that would blast Europe to pieces. The actual limitation of enhanced-radiation-weapons effects and any special 'sub-threshold status' is highly questionable.

Detailed technical discussions about the glaring obsolescence of NATO's short-range tactical nuclear arsenal began in 1974, and in 1976 President Ford declared his intention of keeping the system under development. The weapon only made sense if it was forward-based in Europe, but its reputation as the 'capitalist bomb' which destroyed human life and left property intact made it highly controversial and politically unwelcome, particularly in West Germany and Holland. Europe did not want it and the agonising was a gift to Soviet propaganda.

President Carter became caught up in the moral dilemma and in March 1978 decided on setting aside production plans. Alarmed by this decision the German Foreign Minister, Herr Genscher, flew to Washington and the decision was altered yet again, all parties deciding not to decide until future Soviet activity justified another reversal. In August 1981 President

Reagan announced an unequivocal decision to procure the weapon.

December 1979

Thus the High Level Group had to decide on a policy which both accommodated the political and trans-Atlantic contradictions within NATO and was still militarily effective. Two missile systems were immediately available: the Pershing II IRBM with a high-accuracy, terminally guided warhead and range of probably near 1000 km; and the General Dynamic Tomahawk GLCM.

Pershing II lacked the range to hit deep into the Warsaw Pact's rear areas except from bases in Germany, and the influence of the Federal Republic was strong in the decision to have a mix of both systems. Half of the 7000 US warheads already in Europe, including those with the British Army of the Rhine and the Pershing Is of the Luftwaffe, were under dual-key control, with the nuclear warheads under American command. The system was clumsy and diplomatically embarrassing and the Germans were anxious for the new-generation missiles to be under exclusive US control, a prospect made more attractive by the American willingness to bear the financial cost. The Germans were also keen that they should share the responsibility with a non-nuclear power, a condition known as 'non-singularity', although some German military planners are keen to have Pershing IIs under German control. Britain was already a nuclear power, Norway and Denmark refused to have nuclear weapons on their soil and Turkey and Greece were too unstable. Italy decided to support the scheme but Belgium and Holland accepted only with extreme reluctance. Against this background Germany and the other European nations insisted that there should be a 'double-track' approach and a trans-Atlantic promise to start arms limitation talks with the Russians, urged on President Carter by Schmidt and Callaghan at the 1978 Guadeloupe summit. Thus in the spring of 1979 the 'Special Group' was set up in NATO to consider TNF modernization as a problem in arms control to move in parallel with the resolutions of the High Level Group. When the NATO ministers met again in Florida in April 1979 they agreed to set a deadline for announcing a decision by the end of that year, both to concentrate their own minds and because Presidential elections were coming up in Germany and the US in late 1980. Just as the Western planners were completing their report the Soviets made a pre-emptive move by offering to reduce Soviet missiles and conventional forces as part of wider negotiations. Red-starred tanks rolling eastwards on railway flatcars out of East Germany were seen on television screens all over Europe just before the December meeting. The 'peace offensive' brought results when the Belgians, Dutch and Danes began to argue for delaying the decision in order to give negotiations a chance. Great Britain's line, however, expressed through Defence Secretary Francis Pym, was the exact opposite. There was little, apparently, to lose – US nuclear weapons had been stationed in Britain for thirty years and had always been a prime target. In 1977 the number of UK-based F-111s had been increased without any political protest. Cruise would cost the British government a mere £10 million contribution to the infrastructure costs of basing and communications; the big bill would be picked up by the Americans.

The historic decision was announced on 12 December 1979 but it was far from being with the sought-after united front. The Belgians wanted another six months to decide whether or not to opt out; the Dutch wanted eighteen months in which to decide whether or not to opt in. For political reasons, final numbers of weapons and their allocation were left out of the original communiqué but they broke down as: 108 Pershing IIs and 96 Tomahawk GLCMs to Germany, 112 GLCMs to Italy, 48 GLCMs to Belgium, 48 GLCMs to the Netherlands and 160 GLCMs to Great Britain (originally scheduled to take 124 but offering to take 36 extra from the German allocation).

Disarmament Reborn

The decision to deploy cruise and Pershing II brought an instant reaction but not from Moscow – it came from the people of Western Europe themselves. As 1980 progressed with a grim series of pronouncements (see Chronology) from Moscow and from NATO leaders, Chancellor Schmidt began to talk darkly of 'Sarajevo'; it was an image that Europeans could instantly understand. The Americans believed 1939 not 1914 was being re-run, envisaging the rise of a ruthless military power which could not be appeased. Many Europeans, seeing an arms race completely out of control, began to do something about it rather than waiting until Middle-East potentates, playing the role of Austrian archdukes, provided the peripheral spark which would ignite Europe. Marching under a banner seemed more immediate than waiting for the sophistries of the 'double-track' approach to be explained – it was obviously going nowhere.

Diplomatic disarmament activities have all stagnated one by one. SALT 2 (which did not embrace Europe) went into limbo after Afghanistan, and US involvement in any serious attempt at arms control faded with the US Presidential election. After frantic prodding, most notably by the West Germans, and the obvious impact of the peace movement (Caspar Weinberger is reported to have attended the October 1981 rally in London in person), after ten months of sabre-rattling the US administration embraced the zero option to cancel modernization plans if all the SS-20s targeted on Western Europe were dismantled.

The state of the main East-West Arms talks in summer 1982 is as follows:

Strategic arms. President Reagan promised in November 1981 to resume strategic arms reduction talks (START). Began summer 1982.

Intermediate-range nuclear forces (INF). Negotiations opened in Geneva on 30 November 1981, recessed at the end of February 1982, resumed in May 1982.

Comprehensive test ban talks. Tripartite discussions between Soviet Union, UK and US to ban all nuclear explosions began in 1977. Last discussions were in November 1980; they have not resumed pending review by US administration.

Mutual and balanced force reductions (MBFR). Talks began in Vienna in 1973 in an attempt to reduce conventional forces in Europe. Bogged down in bureaucracy and verification problems ever since. Exchange of figures in January

1980 put air and ground manpower in central Europe as approximately equal (NATO - 991,000; Warsaw Pact – 979,000); but disagreement over mobilization of reserves.

Conference on disarmament in Europe. At 1982 Madrid meeting of the Conference on Security and Cooperation in Europe (CSCE) the West urged the Soviet Union to accept a French proposal for a European disarmament conference to negotiate confidence and security building measures. Little progress made.

Committee on disarmament. This forty-nation body meeting in Geneva is working on four separate international agreements covering chemical weapons, radiological weapons, so-called negative security assurances (that is, assurances about refraining from use of nuclear weapons) made to non-nuclear states and a comprehensive disarmament programme.

United Nations special session on disarmament. Opened June 1982.

The View from Moscow

The Soviet Union has shared the continent of Europe with the armed forces of its trans-Atlantic ideological enemy for forty years. There are thousands of nuclear warheads under American control capable of destroying the economic heartland of western and central Russia based in Western Europe and around its coasts.

Russia was invaded by Japanese, Germans, Austro-Hungarians and sundry others in the first decades of the twentieth century. The new Bolshevik state was attacked by British, Americans, Yugoslavs, French, Japanese, and Poles. Accompanying the German invaders in 1941 were the armies of Finland, Romania, Hungary, Slovakia, Bulgaria and Italy, joined by SS contingents from Spain, France, Holland and Belgium.

The Soviet leaders look west to a 'security zone' of truculent and surly buffer states which have to be economically underwritten and bought with cheap energy as well as garrisoned for their own protection. Farther out is the NATO front line bristling with high technology weapons and a highly trained and well equipped *Bundeswehr* with 3800 tanks now and 1700 on order (for Barbarossa the Germans assembled 1332; the Soviets lost 14,287 tanks in the first few months). Beyond that are three centres of nuclear decision-making, Britain and France, respectively Conservative and Socialist, embarking on major strategic arms modernization programmes, and the United States with a President pushing the economy to the limit to acquire the most sophisticated and most devastating strategic weapons available. To the rear is the huge army and adolescent nuclear power of China. To the south the turbulence of Islam, a suppurating police action against Afghan bandits and the uncertainties of an Islamic bomb. Third World clients have proved fickle and ungrateful, or, apart from the stalwarts of Cuba and Vietnam, have turned out to be losers.

For the Soviet leadership, the December 1979 decision and President Reagan's 'new chip on the table' was indeed the bad news that NATO intended it should be. In spite of the USSR's great strides of the 1970s, it was clear that renewed military superiority was within the West's grasp. Here was an incentive to bargain over 'Eurostrategic' systems at least, but first there would have to be a battle of numbers.

In September 1981 Soviet Defence Minister Dmitri Ustinov insisted in *Pravda* that parity already existed in Europe and pointed out the difference between American forward-based systems such as the F-111s (based in Britain), which can attack Soviet territory, and the SS-20 which cannot reach the USA but 'has been deployed for the sole purpose of reliably neutralizing these extra American strategic weapons in Europe which have not been covered by the SALT negotiations so far'. The argument went on: 'Furthermore, if the United States deploys qualitively new medium-range nuclear missiles in Western Europe reducing the warning time to 4.5 minutes' (which is ambitious even for the Pershing II) 'instead of half an hour, the available Soviet medium-range potential will obviously be insufficient to neutralize them and the Soviet Union will have to take corresponding countermeasures.' President Brezhnev in

November 1981 issued a strong warning that West Germany would become the target of 'vigorous counterattacks against suspected deployments of theatre nuclear forces because the new American missiles would be used as a first strike weapon'.

The Soviets were insisting therefore that parity existed even before cruise or Pershing II, counting in French and British forces and US Navy nuclear-capable systems afloat with the carriers of the 6th Fleet, but ignoring the naval *Backfires* and the *Fencers* and *Fitters* of Frontal Aviation and the Soviet SSBN fleet. The Soviets further cannot recognize any linkage between the firepower facing NATO and the defences facing China.

The View from Germany

West Germany is the front line. It is the point where the full conventional, nuclear and psychological weight of Soviet military power is brought to bear. Against the background of strategic arms limitation talks which did nothing to diminish the build-up of Soviet firepower facing Europe, Chancellor Schmidt moved in private to persuade the Ford administration to include them in SALT 2. Apparently Zbigniew Brezinski, President Carter's security adviser, told Schmidt 'it was none of his business', then, in London in October 1977, Schmidt went public, making a speech which set in motion the political process for NATO theatre force modernization – even though it evntually put the Social Democratic Party on the rack and brought hundreds of thousands of Germans of many political standpoints on to the streets in protest.

When President Brezhnev declared in a speech in East Berlin in October 1979 that the Soviets would be ready to withdraw some of their missiles from western Russia if NATO halted their plans, Chancellor Schmidt had to make a response and keep a dialogue open as the bigger East-West relationship deteriorated with Afghanistan, Iran, the Reagan Presidency and the rumblings from Poland all happening with a year. It was by this open line via Germany that the new US administration could signal its resolve for more confrontation or a renewed desire to bargain – it did both.

The Zero Option

The bellicose tub-thumping of the first months of the Reagan presidency not only rattled the Russians, it shook Western politicians and nourished Europe-wide peace movements. The Americans reacted angrily – it was the Europeans who had asked for theatre nuclear modernization in the first place. The systems were symbolic anyway as even if there were a genuine military requirement, cruise and Pershing II were obvious counterforce targets, and Pentagon analysts if anything preferred much more survivable SSBNs. The Americans could say that they had found the resolve and voted the cash to confront Soviet power at every level, whereas the Europeans were unwilling to pay even for conventional weapons. There could be no more free lunches.

The United States meanwhile was being condemned for supporting and paying for a doubtful programme which was a response to a European initiative in the first place. America was being paraded as more of a threat to the peace and security of Europe than was the Soviet Union. Now the NATO governments who had made the December 1979 resolution were changing their minds again, insisting on US-Soviet talks as a condition for 'allowing' the US to protect them with missiles on their soil.

'They ordered the pizza; when we delivered they told us they didn't want it,' was one US defence analyst's laconic reaction.

All this, however, made the US administration more open to the European imperative for arms control and the US came into the disarmament lane of the dual track in April 1981. When Chancellor Schmidt advanced the 'zero option' – no cruise, no Pershing and no SS-20s – the Americans were already softened up, and when the policy was publicly embraced by President Reagan in October 1981 it stole the thunder both of the Soviet Union (who had been offering partial reductions all along) and of the European disarmers both in governments and in the mass peace movements.

With talks already scheduled to start in Geneva in closed session in November 1981, President Reagan's zero option speech also included the 'readiness to open negotiations on strategic arms as soon as possible next year' (1982). It was just as well because without progress on strategic arms control there can be no real progress on nuclear arms control in Europe. This is because strategic weapons can be used over European ranges and because for a Muscovite there is no real difference between coming under attack from a missile launched from Wyoming and one from Cambridgeshire. Only the flexibility offered by global ceilings seems to offer the diplomatic lines of retreat for a compromise to be reached.

Theatre nuclear modernization had been advanced in the first place to blur the distinction between 'Eurostrategic' and long-range strategic weapons not as a means of fighting a limited war (Reagan's 'war confined to Europe' statement and Secretary of State Haig's 'warning shot' speech threw away this moral advantage). The Pershings and cruise would be there to *ensure* the ICBMs flew, thus, by the perverse logic of deterrence, to provide greater security; wouldn't the zero option undermine this?

It will be remembered the NATO dual-track decision had set up two planning groups to implement TNF modernization, the High Level Group and, to pursue arms control, the Special Group (renamed later the Special Consultative Group). As the SCG was pushing the zero option in October 1981 the High Level Group was taking a long hard look at 'threat assessment' and 'the functional requirements of NATO's theatre nuclear forces', in effect the nuts and bolts of nuclear defence without the politics. They concluded that the zero option did not work.

The recommendations drafted for the Geneva negotiators gave a shopping list of criteria by which bargains could be recognized as good or bad. They reportedly contained two implicit conclusions, however: that if NATO needs penetrating systems for the 1980s it can forget aircraft and needs the Pershing II.* The fight for the zero option is one within NATO itself even before the Soviets are drawn into the equation, or the desires of Europe's population are taken into account.

---

* The Pershing II programme is running into trouble. The first test over the missile's full range is now scheduled for June 1983 when a full production decision will have to be taken for an initial operating capacity by the end of that year. It looks unlikely.

2 • The Air War

Tactical combat aircraft are broadly expected to perform four functions. The primary one is air superiority or 'counterair operations', seeking out and destroying hostile air forces over disputed territory so that friendly air or ground forces can operate, while defensive counterair efforts detect and shoot down intruders or destroy their bases. Suppressing the enemy defences may be an important precondition of success and involves the use of specialized anti-airfield weapons, anti-radar missiles and electronic countermeasures. Air interdiction is aimed at enemy supply lines and logistic war fighting ability and deflecting or destroying enemy reserves. Close air support, the third function, aims precise and flexible firepower against enemy troops and armour in contact with friendly forces. Tactical air reconnaissance furnishes military data using manned aircraft, drones, satellites and other sensors to watch enemy activity, identify targets or provide post-strike assessments. Means of carrying out these four basic functions are reflected in the tactical doctrines, force structure, and in the weapons of both the Soviet and NATO air forces, although in different ways.

The Aircraft

A modern combat aircraft is a combination of systems which the airframe and powerplant are there to make mobile. The pilot in charge of this package of terrain-following radar, cameras, infra-red scanners, navigation-attack radar, inertial navigation, electronic countermeasures, electronic counter-counter-measures, weapons-computers plus bombs, missiles and guns is a highly sophisticated component himself, consuming years' and millions of pounds' worth of training.

The ever-increasing expense and technical complexity of modern combat aircraft and supporting personnel has led to two distinct strands of development. One has blurred the old distinction of fighter, bomber, ground attack and even trainer, and brought on the age of the multi-role aircraft such as the Tornado or MiG-23 which can be optimized by avionics or weapons fit for a single or mix of tactical roles. The other strand is the opposite, back to dedicated single combat types in a so-called 'high-low mix' which combines expensive high-performance aircraft with simpler and cheaper counterparts seeking to increase qualitative strength and operability levels.

US tactical airpower, shaped in the 1970s for service in the 1980s and 1990s, reflects this second strand. The F-15 Eagle with its fantastic power and performance was originally intended for air-to-air combat alone with the light F-16s, procured in greater numbers, making the running in fair-weather fighting over the battlefield. A-10 tank busters, slow and rugged weapons platforms, took over close air support duties, freeing the older F-4 Phantoms and F-111s for long-range interdiction strike operations.

This formula, with roughly 60 per cent at the simpler end of the spectrum, was based on the premise that air war in Europe would be nasty, brutish and short. Tactical combat aircraft would be 'attrited' at phenomenal rates and thus US airpower planners chose to rely on large numbers of comparatively cheap interceptors to win the counterair battle in air-to-air combat with the sheer mass fielded by Soviet Frontal Aviation, beating them by superior aircraft and weapons technology. That has changed with the comparable modernization of Soviet tactical air fleets, and US air defence procurement is once again looking for the most capable tools to command the skies no matter what the cost in money or serviceability requirements.

Serviceability and operability are vital components of air-power. It is no good happily calculating available force levels of multi-million-pound, high-technology, high-performance air-craft if a large proportion is grounded waiting for non-available skilled maintenance manpower or a vital component ware-housed in California. At any one time 40 per cent of the USAF's F-15 force is inoperable, waiting for or undergoing mainten-ance. All-weather capacity is regarded as an increasingly important requirement because the pace of land operations in Europe is not likely to be hindered by night or bad weather. Most modern NATO interceptors have the ability to take off and land at night or during bad weather and to complete air-to-air missions, and there are diverse development programmes to improve the all-weather performance of F-15s and F-16s in both the interceptor and strike role and a night-fighting A-10. Eventually, in the late 1980s, the US NAVSTAR satellite-based Global Positioning System will provide tactical aircraft with 'precise three-dimensional, all-weather position and velocity data without requiring potentially compromising trans-missions'.

NATO Airpower

Allied Command Europe has more than 3000 tactical aircraft operating from some 200 standard airfields with many more fuel, weapons, communications, electronic and dispersal sites under its control. On the Central Sector, Allied Forces Central Europe (AFCENT) has two subordinate commands – NORTHAG, supported by the 2nd Allied Tactical Air Force with its HQ at Mönchengladbach, including British, German, Belgian and Dutch units, and CENTAG which has the 4th Allied Tactical Air Force with its headquarters at Ramstein in support, including US, Canadian and German units plus a US Army Air Defence Command. The six-nation Allied Air Forces Central Europe was established in 1974 to provide a closer co-ordination of airpower in this crucial area.

AFNORTH with its HQ in Norway is responsible for the defence of Norway, Denmark and the Baltic approaches and controls Norwegian and Danish squadrons and two German air combat wings. AFSOUTH has an overall air command, AIRSOUTH, based at Naples, and the ACE mobile force has an attached composite air wing. United Kingdom Air Force (UKAIR), whose headquarters are at High Wycombe north-west of London, is directly subordinate to SACEUR.

United States tactical airpower is projected truly globally with twenty-seven active squadrons based in Europe, nine in the Pacific and one in Alaska. Thirty-eight squadrons of strike aircraft are based in the Continental United States under Tactical Air Command whose mission is to provide a combat-ready reserve capable of rapid worldwide deployment backed up by the US Air Force Reserve and Air National Guard. TAC's huge Fighter Weapons Centre at Nellis AFB, Nevada, provides a special facility for weapon testing and combat training and it is here that the 'Flag' series of simulated combat exercises are carried out. In 'Red Flag' exercises the so-called 'aggressor squadrons' of F-5Es provide realistic simulations of Soviet aircraft and tactics, complete with simulated ground threats.

Nearly a quarter of the USAF'S total tactical combat aircraft strength is allocated to US Air Forces Europe (USAFE) which controls the 3rd Air Force with HQ at Mildenhall, UK, the 16th Air Force with its HQ at Torrejon, Spain, and the 17th Air Force with its HQ at Sembach, Germany. In the event of conflict these would come under the control of Allied Air Forces Central Europe (AAFCE) whose Commander in Chief, an American General, is also commander of USAFE. USAFE is currently concentrating on introducing new aircraft, the F-15 Eagle and A-10 Thunderbolt and from January 1982 the first of 650 F-16 Fighting Falcons. USAFE has also embarked on a very large airfield-hardening programme with more than 600 concrete aircraft shelters complete and 200 more under construction. The force will be responsible for deployment of the Tomahawk GLCM from the end of 1983 and, significantly, is taking steps to equip its base security police with heavy weapons and tactical vehicles over a five-year period.

Through the early 1980s the second-generation jet combat of the RAF will be supplanted in operational squadrons by the long-awaited Tornado multi-role combat aircraft built by the Anglo-Italian/German consortium, Panavia. The Tornado F Mk 2 will eventually replace the Lightning and Phantom in the air defence squadrons of Strike Command and RAF Germany, and the Tornado GR Mk 1 will replace reconnaissance Canberras and strike Vulcan B2s and Buccaneers. The first operational Tornado squadron, No 617 'Dambusters', con-verted from Vulcans to GR Mk 1s in December 1981.

The British air defence conundrum is how to maintain a credible defence of the British Isles and meet maritime commitments on dwindling resources while putting enough into

W.F.N.—C

the Central Sector German front line. In 1982 Royal Air Force Germany, forming part of the 2nd Allied Tactical Air Force with its HQ at Rheindahlen near Mönchengladbach, fielded two squadrons of Buccaneers and four of Jaguars for the strike/attack role, one Jaguar and two Harrier squadrons for the attack/reconnaissance role, two Phantom interceptor squadrons, one Puma transport helicopter unit and a communications flight.

Normally only the interceptor and the five Rapier SAM squadrons are directly under NATO control but the warplan places the whole of RAFG under 2nd Tactical Air Forces Commander (who traditionally is also the RAF officer commanding RAFG) in the event of hostilities.

The force is based on four airfields, the 'clutch' of sites on the Dutch border at Bruggen, Laarbruch and Wildenrath, and Gütersloh to the east of the Rhine. There is also Gatow in the British sector of Berlin which is not used operationally. All operational airfields are heavily fortified positions; command centres are buried underground, ringed with barbed wire and protected by the missiles and ground combat formations of the RAF regiment now equipped with Scorpion tanks. Runways are chemically treated to blend visually with their surroundings, and the aircraft themselves are dispersed around the perimeter in hardened shelters often in woods. Groundcrew train intensively to keep operations supported while under chemical, biological or nuclear attack.

Capabilities of current NATO/French combat aircraft are summarized below:

BAe Harrier
(first flight: 1966)
Single-seat V/STOL strike reconnaissance aircraft able to operate from dispersed sites, forest clearings, roads, etc. 5000 lb bombload or reconnaissance pod. AV-8B advanced Harrier developed by McDonnell Douglas for US Marine Corps will be procured by RAF.
MAX. SPEED 1185 km/h. COMBAT RADIUS: 500 km. CEILING: 15,000 m.

BAe Sea Harrier FRS Mk 1
Maritime Harrier with new radar in revised nose. Equipped with Sidewinder air-to-air missiles for fleet air defence and can carry various strikeloads. Nuclear capability under development. Successful in South Atlantic fighting.
MAX.SPEED: 1185 km/h. COMBAT RADIUS: 1204 km.

Dassault Mirage F1
Main all-weather, multi-purpose fighter of French Air Force. Armed with Magic air-to-air missiles and up to 4000 kg of ground attack weapons. Will be supplemented by Mirage 2000.
MAX SPEED: 2350 km/h. COMBAT RADIUS: 1000 km. CEIL ING: 20,000 m

Fairchild Republic A-10A Thunderbolt II
(first flight: 1972)
Single-seat close support aircraft with massive tank-busting rotary cannon in the nose. Can carry up to 7250 kg of external attack stores, including laser-guided bombs, retarded bombs, area weapons, anti-tank cluster bombs, Maverick missiles etc.
MAX. SPEED: 717 km/h. COMBAT RADIUS: 1000 km.

General Dynamics F-16A Fighting Falcon
(first flight: 1974)
Very important and capable single-seat lightweight fighter with high-capacity radar and armed for air combat with rotary cannon and six Sidewinders or can carry 5400 kg of attack loads including cluster bombs and laser- and optically guided weapons. Selected as standard NATO fighter in 1976. In service with air forces of USA, Belgium, Denmark, Netherlands and Norway (plus Israel and Egypt).
MAX. SPEED: Mach 2 . COMBAT RADIUS: 925 km. CEILING: 15,240 m.

General Dynamics F-111 (first flight: 1964)
Variable geometry long-range two-seat fighter bomber. Latest F-111F version has Pave Tack laser designator pod and can carry wide range of nuclear or smart weapons.

EF-111A is ECM jamming conversion of F-111F. FB-111A is strategic nuclear bomber. Nuclear-capable.
MAX. SPEED: Mach 1.2. COMBAT RADIUS: 2500 km. CEILING: 18,000 m.

Hawker Siddeley Buccaneer (first flight: 1958)
Ageing naval strike aircraft reworked by RAF for low-level, land-based strike. Equipped with Pave Spike designator and LGM. Grounded by wing cracks in 1980. To be replaced by Tornados in 1983 in RAFG but will continue in maritime strike role with Sea Eagle missile. Nuclear-capable.
MAX. SPEED: 1038 km/h. COMBAT RADIUS: 3700 km. CEILING: 9145 m.

Hughes AH-64
Winner of advanced attack helicopter competition, 536 to be ordered for service with US Army by mid-1980s. Armed with Hellfire laser-seeking anti-tank missiles and 30 mm Chain gun plus advanced target designators and sensors.
MAX. SPEED: 309 km/h. COMBAT RADIUS: 300 km. CEILING: 6250 m.

Lockheed F-104 Starfighter (first flight: 1954)
Tactical strike and reconnaissance fighter never adopted by USAF for this role but NATO's front line from the 1960s onwards. In service with air forces of Belgium, Canada, Denmark, Germany, Greece, Italy, Norway, Netherlands and Turkey (plus Japan and Taiwan). Will be replaced by F-16. Nuclear-capable.
MAX. SPEED: Mach 2.2. COMBAT RADIUS: 1247 km. CEILING: 17,680 m.

McDonnell Douglas F-4 Phantom II (first flight: 1958)
Most successful Western postwar combat aircraft with over 5000 built. Adopted by the Royal Navy then RAF in 1968. Still a very capable multi-mission strike fighter which will be in front line service for many years to come.
F-4G is 'Wild Weasel' defence suppression version; RF-4E is reconnaissance version. Most versions nuclear-capable.

MAX. SPEED: Mach 2.2. COMBAT RADIUS: 1500 km. CEIL-
ING: 17,700 m.

McDonnell Douglas F-15 Eagle (first flight 1972)

Single-seat counterair fighter with secondary attack capacity.
Very fast and powerful aircraft designed to establish air
superiority, armed with multiple cannon and air-to-air missiles.
Strike Eagle prototype interdictor version can carry up to 10,885
kg of attack loads. In service with air forces of USA, Japan and
Israel; ordered by Saudi Arabia.
MAX SPEED: Mach 2.5. CEILING: 30,500 m.

North American F-100 Super Sabre (first flight: 1953)

Survivor of US 'Century Series' fighters, this single-seat
interceptor and fighter bomber still serves in dwindling
numbers with NATO Danish (to be replaced by F-16s) and
Turkish air forces. Some nuclear-capable.
MAX SPEED: 1390 km/h. COMBAT RADIUS: 1200 km.

Northrop F-5A/B (first flight: 1959)

Lightweight tactical fighter and reconnaissance aircraft, widely
exported in 1960s and 1970s including NATO air forces,
Greece, Netherlands, Norway, Canada, also Spain. Many other
air forces operate the aircraft.

F-5E Tiger II and F5G Tigershark are much more advanced
versions of basic design.
(F-5A) MAX. SPEED: 1488 km/h. COMBAT RADIUS: 314 km.
CEILING: 15,390 m.

Panavia Tornado (first flight: 1974)

Tandem two-seat multi-role combat aircraft of great importance
to NATO. Built by Anglo-Italian/German consortium and
designed to fulfil six principal roles: close air support, battlefield
interdiction, interdiction counterair strike (airfield attack), air
superiority, interception, naval strike and reconnaissance. Air
Defence Variant under development for the RAF with increased
capacity radar and ECCM, cannon, Sky Flash and Sidewinder
missiles. 212 Interdictor Strike (IDS) Tornados are in production for the German air force, 112 for the German Navy, 100 IDS

for Italy and 220 IDS for the RAF plus 165 Air Defence Variant. Nuclear-capable.
MAX. SPEED: Mach 2.2. COMBAT RADIUS: 1390 km.

Sepecat Jaguar (first flight: 1968)

Anglo-French strike/trainer. Single-seat tactical support aircraft with computer-controlled navigation and weapon-aiming, serving with RAF and French Air Force. Laser rangefinder and target-seeker in chisel nose (RAF only). Can carry up to 4535 kg of bombs, rockets or air-to-air missiles. Nuclear-capable.
MAX. SPEED: Mach 1.1. COMBAT RADIUS: 815 km. CEILING: 15,000 m.

Vought A-7 Corsair II (first flight: 1965)

Single-seat attack aircraft originally developed by US Navy but adopted by USAF. Only used by Reserves and Air National Guard but still represent part of NATO replenishment force. Also serves with air forces of Greece and Portugal. Nuclear capable. Carries up to 6,805 kg of attack loads.
MAX SPEED: 1,123 km/h. COMBAT RADIUS: 965 km.

Westland/Aerospatiale Lynx (first flight: 1971)

Anglo-French military helicopter. AH Mk 1 serves with British Army and can be armed with TOW anti-tank guided missiles. Lynx Mk 80s of Royal Navy effective in South Atlantic armed with Sea Skua missiles for attacking light surface craft.
MAX. SPEED: 232 km/h. COMBAT RADIUS: 240 km.

Frontal Aviation

Soviet tactical airpower is grouped under the command of Frontal Aviation, the *Frontovaya Aviatsiya (FA)*. Most of the sixteen Soviet Military districts have a tactical air army attached, and four more are assigned to the groups of forces in Eastern Europe. In the case of war, all would come under the Front-level ground combined-arms commander as integral elements of active fronts. Half of all the *FA* faces NATO, and a quarter is in the Soviet Far East facing China.

Frontal Aviation is divided into 16 Armies comprising 112

regiments and 7 independent squadrons assigned to the Groups of Forces outside the borders of the Soviet Union and to the Military Districts into which the Soviet Union is divided. An *FA* Army is variable in its size according to the importance of the area to which it is assigned. For example, the 16th *FA* Army assigned to the Group of Soviet Forces in Germany possesses approximately 1000 tactical aircraft, the 37th *FA* Army in Poland as a component of the Northern Group of Forces has some 350 tactical aircraft, while the 13th FA Army in the Leningrad Military District has less than 200 aircraft and the 5th in the Kiev Military District barely 100 aircraft. For organization purposes, the largest unit of the FA Army is the Division (*Divisiya*), and there are usually divisions devoted to air defence cover (*prikrytiye*), support (*podderzhka*) and air accompaniment (*soprovozhdeniye*), plus autonomous reconnaissance (*razvedka*) and transport (*transportnaya*) regiments. A division consists of three and sometimes more regiments (*polki*), each usually possessing three squadrons (*eskadrilii*) of 16–18 aircraft, including a reserve.

Frontal Aviation exists as part of the combined arms concept, able to apply offensive shock power on a large scale. Heavy emphasis has always been placed on battlefield air defence and the deployment of large counterair forces including interceptors, surface-to-air missiles and mobile rockets and anti-aircraft guns in profusion. US intelligence estimates indicate that within four days of mobilization NATO would face in the Central Sector 2100 fixed-wing tactical aircraft and 900 helicopters within 100 km of the Front Line, a further 1300 fixed-wing aircraft and 1100 helicopters within 200–400 km of the FLOT (Front Line of Troops) and yet a further 1300 fixed-wing aircraft and 200 helicopters within 400–600 km to the Soviet border. From the FLOT to a distance of 500 km within WP airspace about 2350 air-air fighters would be available to oppose any NATO penetration.

Most new Soviet aircraft in production, however, are designed for offensive counterair or ground-attack missions with much greater payload and range than their predecessors. In the past, NATO superiority in deep-strike capability was matched by Soviet medium-range ballistic missiles (allowing no room for conventional/nuclear distinctions). Now new aircraft such as the Sukhoi Su-24 *Fencer* present a much greater problem for NATO air defence and give Soviet planners much greater flexibility.

In a combined-arms attack short- and medium-range missiles could devastate known fixed NATO targets such as airfields, missile sites or radar centres early in a nuclear conflict. Soviet tactical aircraft released by effective land-mobile air defence systems from defensive commitments could be best used to attack moving targets with mobile nuclear systems as a priority, then sweep away defending aircraft over axes of armoured advance. Close support of Soviet armour itself would come as a third priority although new aircraft are under development for this role. Alternatively it could be enough for Frontal Aviation to embark on a counterair defensive alone in the opening phase of a battle for Europe, with SAMs sapping the enemy's strength before interceptors and then close support ground attack forces are committed. The Warsaw Pact's interior lines of communication give greater flexibility as does the ability of many Soviet aircraft to operate from dispersed natural airfields although ironically the introduction of more capable advanced combat aircraft is eroding this last advantage.

In the 1960s, the MiG-17, -19 and -21 were the *FA*'s front line air superiority fighters and the Sukhoi Su-7 gave some ground attack potential. There was very little deep interdiction capability, feeble electronic countermeasures, no advanced conventional munitions and poor range-payload and all-weather capability when compared with NATO types.

That has changed. New aircraft, new avionics, new penetration aids and a new generation of 'smart' munitions for the 1980s have transformed capabilities, backed by an intense electronic warfare effort and sheer numbers – 4800 fixed-wing aircraft, 3500 helicopters and 250 transports.

MiG-21 Fishbed-L (first flight: 1955)

Still an important type, 1300 MiG-21 all-weather interceptors remain in Soviet service although being replaced by MiG-23 *Flogger*.

MAX SPEED: Mach 2.1. COMBAT RADIUS: 900 km. CEILING: 18,000 m.

MiG-23 Flogger -A, -B, -C, E, -F and -G (first flight: 1967)

The variable geometry *Flogger-B* and *-G* are the *FA*'s primary single-seat air combat fighters armed with 23 mm rotary cannon and *Apex* and *Aphid* air-to-air missiles. Other marks are trainer or export versions.
MAX. SPEED: Mach 2.3. COMBAT RADIUS: 960 km. CEILING: 18,600 m.

MiG-27 Flogger-D (first flight: ?)

Developed from MiG 23 as single-seat ground attack fighter with redesigned forward fuselage incorporating armoured cockpit, laser rangefinder and target seeker. Can carry bombs, rockets, tactical nuclear weapons and AS-7 *Kerry* stand-off air-to-surface missile.
MAX. SPEED: Mach 1.75. COMBAT RADIUS: 960 km. CEILING: 18,600 m.

MiG-25 Foxbat -A, -B and -D (first flight: 1964)

Soviet 'superfighter' which turned out to be rather less formidable in close-up when pilot defected to Japan in 1976. Foxbat-A has very powerful radar and high standard of ECCM fit but little look-down shoot-down capability necessary to intercept low level intruders. *Foxbat-B*, most important model, is unarmed reconnaissance version. *Foxbat-D* has large SLAR (sideways-looking airborne radar) and no cameras. Advanced interceptor version under development known as *Foxhound*.
MAX. SPEED: Mach 2.8. COMBAT RADIUS: 1130 km. CEILING: 24,500 m.

Sukhoi Su-15 Flagon -A, -C, -D, -E (first flight: 1966)

Single-seat supersonic interceptor armed with radar and infra-red homing air-to-air missiles.
MAX. SPEED: Mach 2.3. COMBAT RADIUS: 725 km. CEILING: 20,000 m.

Sukhoi Su-17, Su-20 and Su-22 Fitter -C, -D, -E, -F, -G and -H (first flight: 1967)

Versatile multi-role combat aircraft. *Fitter-C* and *-D* important ground-attack types with laser designators and provision for tactical nuclear weapons, cluster bombs, napalm and AS-7 *Kerry* air-to-surface missiles.

MAX SPEED: Mach 2.17. COMBAT RADIUS: 630 km. CEILING: 18,000 m.

Sukhoi Su-24 Fencer

This two-seater aircraft was the first modern Soviet design specifically for ground attack and to carry a weapons officer in addition to the pilot. It has caused almost as big a stir in the West as the SS-20 missile by virtue of its advanced electronics, payload and range which allows it to reach Liverpool or Rome with a 1000 kg nuclear bomb and return to bases in East Germany. Because the *Fencer* represents both one of NATO's most formidable adversaries and a state of the art modern combat aircraft it deserves a closer look.

Fencer is a two-seat variable-geometry aircraft designed for long-range penetration missions. It is powered by two afterburning turbojets with a high thrust-to-weight ratio and is the first Soviet combat aircraft to have 50 per cent of its gross weight as fuel and warload, the same as comparable Western types. The overall design and material structure is advanced, making use of titanium, bonded materials, composites and printed circuit electronics. *Fencer* has a terrain-following radar, an attack radar used in conjunction with a laser rangefinder and weapon computer to release bombs much more accurately. As well as a Doppler navigation radar, the aircraft's inertial navigation system allows considerable ranges to be covered without ground reference. The pilot has an automatic flight control system, a map display and a head up display (HUD) which projects weapon sighting and other aircraft management data into the pilot's line of sight.

The aircraft is armed with twin 30 mm rotary cannon firing HE or armour-piercing rounds. Six external weapons stations can accommodate up to 8 tonnes of bombs and a 1000 kg nuclear bomb can be carried on the rear centre fuselage pylon. NATO expects at least 760 *Fencers* to be in service by 1987.

Counterair Operations

However advanced a modern combat aircraft may be, it is only as effective in action as the weapons it carries for the role it is intended to perform – such as stopping a tank, destroying an airfield or clearing the sky of hostile aircraft. Counterair operations employ not simply guns and missiles for use in aerial combat but also a range of specialized ordnance and electronic devices, all contributing to the struggle for air superiority.

Offensive counterair operations seek out and destroy competing air forces in hostile territory. The first imperative is defence suppression – the destruction of missile sites, the blinding of radars by direct attack by radar-homing missiles such as the US Shrike, or jamming and general dislocation of the defence. Secondly, hostile air forces are most vulnerable caught on the ground – a lesson from military history taught over and over again – and air operations can be blunted without physically destroying the enemy's aircraft themselves, which are likely to be dispersed in hardened shelters. The first act of enforcing the Falklands total exclusion zone on 1 May 1982 was a strike against the airfield at Port Stanley, first by a Vulcan bomber flying at high altitude and bombing by radar, then by low-flying Sea Harriers and finally by naval bombardment. The long runways on which many high-performance aircraft depend can be put out of action by such specialized weapons as the French Durandal and British JP 233 Airfield Attack Weapon which bury deep below the concrete crust of a runway before exploding. The F-15 with its tremendous thrust can take off from 2500 feet with an average load, but needs about 5000 feet of hard runway for typical combat operations. Lockheed are working on 'Project Axe' which is a monster airfield attack cluster munition mounted on a very accurate ballistic missile. Studies show the proposed force could close all 'WP hardened airfields with ten minutes', gaining air superiority at a stroke. VTOL aircraft such as the Harrier are more immune from counterair fixed-site attack, being able to operate from any flat site or forest clearing, although they require considerable wheeled logistic backup (now being supplemented by Chinook helicopters).

Ideally, offensive counterair operations would so disrupt the defence in the initial strike that no defensive challenge in the air itself would be offered. Defensive counterair efforts detect, identify, track and designate intruders then shoot them down or intercept them. Surface-to-air missiles, although effective in their own right, also degrade the accuracy of attacks on targets being defended and absorb some of the combat power of the enemy in defence suppression.

The primary weapons of airborne interception are the air-to-air missile guided by radar and weapons control computers on board the firing aircraft itself. The battle for disputed airspace begins as a battle for the electromagnetic spectrum with radars and other sensors attempting to acquire their target before the target can acquire them or jam them or hide from them in ground clutter or behind countermeasures. Acquisition is followed by identification, to make sure that the target is Foe not Friend (IFF), and then by target illumination.

The US Navy's Phoenix missile which arms the F-14 Tomcat represents part of a very capable (and very expensive) system which illustrates one end of air-to-air combat. The heart of it is the Hughes AN/AWG-9 Weapons Control System, able to detect airborne targets at ranges up to 195 miles according to their size, and to track twenty-four enemy targets at once and engage six of them simultaneously at varied altitudes and ranges. The AWG-9 illuminates the targets and guides the Phoenix missiles to them by semi-active homing (homing on to radiation reflected by a target illuminated by an external radar source). Close to the target, the missile's own radar takes over, providing its own illumination and active homing terminal guidance with an infra-red seeking subsystem. Each Phoenix missile costs more than a third of a million dollars and equips the US Navy's Tomcat fighters as a cost-effective protection for billion-dollar naval task forces. The only other air force able to afford the system was the Shah of Iran's.

Much more typical is the US AIM-9 Sidewinder series, more than a hundred thousand of which have been manufactured. These serve as the standard short-range dogfight missile of nearly every Western air force. The latest version has all-weather capability, seeks its target by enhanced performance infra-red which can distinguish an engine's heat emissions from other distractions and can cover eleven miles. These were the missiles used by Royal Navy Sea Harriers in the Falklands air fighting. (All-angle-capable AIM-9Ls.)

The Raytheon Sparrow (licence-built and developed in Britain as the Sky Flash) is another very important volume air-to-air NATO missile, arming F-4s, F-14, F-104s and F-15s and Tornados. It uses semi-active radar homing guidance. The latest AIM-7F version has advanced solid-state electronics which improve the weapon's 'look-down, shoot-down' performance (the weapon radar's ability to distinguish a target from ground clutter is a very prized combat asset) and has high resistance to jamming. The warhead produces a fragmented airburst lethal up to 400 yards from the detonation.

Air Intercept Missile Evaluation (AIMVAL) tests at USAF TAC's weapon-test facility at Nellis Air Force Base (AFB), carried out in 1977, pitted F-14 and F-15s armed with Sparrows against F-5Es of the aggressor squadron armed with AIM-9M all-angle-capable Sidewinders and simulating MiG tactics and capabilities. The rules demanded visual identification so the Sparrow's 10:1 range advantage was wiped out. The F-14s picked up the 'bogey' F-5s at twelve miles using TV enhanced-vision units and fired their Sparrows but had to remain on intercept course to provide continuous target illumination for the semi-active home missiles. The F-5s, now in range, fired their Sidewinders before they were themselves 'destroyed'. The F-15s, with no long-range visual identification devices, were also caught up in the mass aerial destruction which left very few theoretical survivors. Simultaneously, ACEVAL studies conducted to see how force levels influenced the battle found that the more aircraft involved, so the F-14 and F-15's technological advantage was eroded. In one-versus-one combat the F-15 Eagle's advantage in weaponry and its ability to 'energy manoeuvre' with its enormous power gave a 3:1 advantage. Once numbers went up beyond four, however, communications became overloaded, the two-man-crew concept disintegrated and skilled F-5 pilots devised lock-breaking manoeuvres to defeat the sophisticated radars hunting for them. As an aggressor pilot put it, 'Once we got into the knife-fighting portion, the F-15's kill ratio was distinctly less than 1:1. Overall, with no visual identification required prior to shooting, it was slightly better than 1:1; but once the fight matured, the Eagle died like everyone else.' The importance of short-range dog-fighting is reflected by the fact that modern combat aircraft retain gun armament, usually rotary cannon. Guns are more reliable than missiles and can be fired repeatedly during tight manoeuvres. Aircraft can also rapidly exhaust their missile load.

In 1978 the USA and Britain, France and Germany signed a Memorandum of Understanding to develop an important new 'family' of air-to-air weapons compatible with NATO aircraft operating in the late 1980s. The staff target for AMRAAM (advanced medium-range air-to-air missile) to be developed in the US was written by the NATO Air Forces Armaments Group, and will be a Sparrow replacement. ASRAAM (advanced short-range air-to-air missile) is being developed by an Anglo-German consortium.

Counterair operations are a means to a further end, the application of air power in support of ground operations. The new lethality of modern air-launched munitions is a factor of their accuracy and the way in which their chemical energy is released. Laser and electro optical techniques have created precision-guided munitions capable of being delivered to their target with great accuracy in all weathers and despite enemy electronic countermeasures. Precision-guidance research began during the Second World War and the infra-red and radar-seeking air-to-air missiles of the 1950s such as Sidewinder or Firestreak had a profound effect on air combat tactics. The Vietnam war, however, with its grisly superfluity of ground targets, brought forth a new technology and a new word – the 'smart' bomb. (Non-guided air-launched munitions are known as 'iron' or, less frequently, as 'dumb' bombs.)

Smart Bombs and Area Weapons

In Vietnam, massive raids by B-52s failed to block passes on the Ho Chi Minh trail and thirty fighter bombers were lost trying unsuccessfully to destroy the Thauh Hoy Bridge across the Son My river between Hanoi and Vinh. When laser-guided bombs became available two raids of four aircraft brought down the bridge without losses in early 1972. More than 20,000 smart bombs were dropped by the USAF and US Navy in the Vietnam war.

Laser-guided bombs (LGB) had their first successful trials at the US Armament Development and Test Centre at Eglin AFB, Florida, in 1966. Thus began the USAF's 'Paveway' project with Texas Instruments developing and manufacturing add-on laser-guidance kits for the US Air Force's standard high-explosive bombs. In this system a pencil-slim beam of laser energy is directed at the target from a 'designator' which may be mounted in an aircraft or in a remotely piloted vehicle or aimed from the ground. The seeker on the weapon homes in on the illuminated target and descends upon it with a hit probability more than a hundred times that of a conventional unguided weapon. The seeker is automatically directed towards the notional impact point by its annular vane. Laser energy reflected by the illuminated target is received by the seeker and all but the infra-red is filtered out. A photocell computes energy falling upon each one of four quadrants seeking balance, and the guidance system processes this quest for equality as steering commands to the control surfaces. When balance has been achieved, the seeker and now the whole weapon is pointing directly at the target.

Smart bombs reach their target under their own kinetic energy. The Maverick air-to-surface missile has a rocket motor to propel it to its target and was originally developed with TV guidance. On his TV monitor the pilot sees a picture transmitted from the camera in the missile's nose. The seeker is slewed to the target, the TV tracker is locked on and the missile is launched, its onboard guidance computer seeking the centre of the target and guiding the weapon all the way until impact. Later Maverick models are laser-guided with higher hit probability and bigger warheads. Laser guidance is also employed by the Hellfire helicopter-launched anti-tank missile, and the Copperhead artillery round which can be fired from a a 155-mm howitzer from ranges of ten miles to engage enemy armoured fighting vehicles illuminated by forward infantry.

The Royal Air Force employs American Paveway bombs (having abandoned development of its own LGBs) and the air forces of Australia, Greece, the Netherlands, Saudi Arabia, South Korea and Taiwan are reported to have been supplied.

Laser-guided cluster munitions known as Pave Storm are in development testing. The French missile and electronics industry has developed its own laser-guided munitions and LGBs are known to be entering service with Soviet Frontal Aviation. MiG-27 *Flogger* units are being armed with un-powered bombs and guided, powered weapons, and both will probably be carried by the Su-24 *Fencer* and 'Ram-J' anti-tank aircraft.

A profusion of laser designators has been developed by each of the US armed forces and by other NATO countries, including the remarkable Pave Tack turret installation for the F-111F, and F-4E Phantom. On a laser-illuminated battlefield, however, this mass of signals can be sorted out because it does not emit a continuous beam of light but rather a stream of pulses which can be coded and tuned to the seeker. Anglo-American interopera-bility trials of laser designators and smart weapons were successfully completed in 1980.

Many air-launched weapons in contrast are designed to spread their destructive power over a large area. They can use a component such as fuel-air or napalm, or they can spread their effects by dividing the total explosive weight into smaller packages called sub-munitions. Fuel-air explosives, which have been under development in the US for a long time, work by creating an aerosol cloud of fuel and air which is ignited to create an explosion with very high ground overpressures, useful for clearing minefields or, indeed, for crushing human bodies. The 'Daisy Cutter' or 'Big Blue 82' (BLU-82) is a cast-steel case full of ammonium nitrate, powdered aluminium and polystyrene soap. It produces an explosion described as the 'closest thing to a nuclear bomb' and, with blast overpressures of 1000 lb psi (per square inch), it shears off trees and smashes flat any objects on the ground to produce a wide circle of devastation.

Weapon tailoring designs munitions to perform specific attack roles, acting by blast or fire, by enhanced blast with longer pulse, fragmentation, armour piercing, anti-personnel, anti-concrete, earth penetration effects and so on. Several of these characteristics can be combined in cluster munitions (Cluster Bomb Units, or CBUs). The US CBU-24 750 lb cluster bomb contains 655 'Sadeye' sub-munitions, each one of which has a filler of TNT in which 600 steel shards are embedded, lethal to a range of 40 feet. The combination of three types of fuse can produce a mixture of air bursts, ground burst and delayed action bursts happening after the other Sadeye detonations have ceased and troops have come out of protective cover. The effects of a simultaneous CBU attack have been described as the equivalent of a well-aimed mortar barrage with 600 81 mm rounds landing at once.

Ground Force Air Defence

Even if counterair operations are successful, tactical air forces on interdiction missiles must still penetrate ground fire and missile (SAM) defences to engage forward or protected rear area targets. A US Army field manual states: 'no army can expect to win in battle unless its manoeuver formations operate under a cohesive extensive and mobile umbrella of air defence.' US doctrine for close air support or interdiction air attack requires abilities from pilots and aircraft to come in at high or low level but, in contrast to other NATO air forces, until recently placed less emphasis on very low-level attacks, depending rather on smart weapons, active defence and electronic suppression to protect air forces operating at intermediate altitude. European air tacticians tend to prefer fast and low approaches by two aircraft formations that do not need composite support from high-level counterair fighters or electronic warfare aircraft. US air forces, further, are very reluctant to suffer training crashes in Europe and thus to adopt high-risk, low-flying tactics.

The Soviets recognize that air defence is an essential part of combined-arms warfare, especially on the offensive, and emphasize that mobile protection should be afforded to units on the march. Soviet air defence forces, weapons and radars are designed, and combat doctrine expects them, to 'leapfrog' each other, providing a continuously effective shield for an advancing formation; and large numbers of tracked and high-mobility air defence systems are deployed to operate with tanks.

The recently introduced SA-8 *Gecko* SAM is designed to fulfil this concept operationally, launched from a high-mobility vehicle which has its own integral radar and is amphibious to cover river crossings. The ZSU-23-4 is a tracked, self-propelled, anti-aircraft mount with quad 23 mm cannon and integral radar and, therefore similarly, is a very important component of Soviet armoured operations, a mobile short-range counter-weight to much of the gunship and A-10 close-support airpower deployed by NATO on the Central Sector. The guns and the radar are stabilized and the system can engage aircraft while moving at 25 km/h. Advanced optical sights, a fire-control computer and a moving-target indicator make it very accurate. There are reported drawbacks, however: the radar-controlled guns have a tendency to fire inadvertently while the turret is traversing, the guns overheat and the radar cannot engage targets below 200 feet. Nevertheless, NATO tactical doctrine rates the ZSU-23-4 as a top-priority target to be neutralized by helicopters attacking with TOWs from extreme range from the flanks or by artillery fire before other tanks or APCs are engaged. These weapons represent only parts of an integrated system with mobile and static components, which is designed to cover threats at interlocking altitudes and ranges. If a long-range Fan Song radar loses a target in ground clutter (masking surface reflections), a Low Blow low-altitude radar will pick it up. In trying to evade SA-6 SAMs at altitude, attacking aircraft are driven into the killing zones of ZSUs or engaged by infantry portable SA-7 Grails which equip every Soviet rifle platoon; or they are straddled by the SA-9 medium-range SAMs fired from BRDM scout cars which, by Soviet combat doctrine, stand off a few kilometres behind the close-support ZSUs during a combined-arms attack.

Upgrading of NATO air defence was one of the main tenets of the long-term defence programme agreed in May 1978. Its most important standing components are the NADGE screen and Improved Hawk missile belt. The NATO Air Defence Ground Environment watches the skies from the Norwegian North Cape to Sicily, then turns through Thrace to Eastern Turkey, and its fully integrated and semi-automatic sites provide aircraft and missile warning.

Many improvements and enhancements have been made and planned since NADGE was completed in the early 1970s. Three-dimensional General Electric air defence radars became operational in Belgium in 1980, and two similar US radars were ordered the same year for use at Scottish sites as part of the UKADGE (United Kingdom Air Defence Ground Environment) improvement programme. Two improved radar sites nearing completion in Italy, and Norway ordered three dimensional radars from Hughes in 1981. The deep air defence of the German Federal Republic is closely integrated with the overall NADGE system of radars, communications and data processing centres. GEADGE (German Air Defence Ground Environment) is centred on the US Air Weapons Control Systems 412L with seven sites linked together by computer to the Combat Operations Centre and operated jointly by the US, Britain and West Germany. The whole is a very large defence complex which automatically performs the functions of aerospace surveillance, identification and defence weapons control on NATO's centre sector. If an aircraft intercept is ordered or a SAM launch commanded, AWCS 412L automatically computes and transmits the data necessary for an interception to be made. GEADGE itself is undergoing an extensive updating programme and is supplemented by other mobile low-level radars under German Army control.

The first Boeing E-3A Sentry Airborne Warning and Control Systems (AWACS) was delivered to NATO in 1982 and will provide early warning of attackers plus look-down air battle management capability. This force, NATO Early Warning Command, will be joined by the Royal Air Force's eleven Nimrod AEW (Airborne Early Warning) aircraft in the early 1980s. NATO's Air Defence Ground Environment Integration Segment (AEGIS) programme is designed to integrate further existing ground radar sites with the new AWACS and AEW airborne component with the controlled exchange of air surveillance data giving ground controllers, by the time the system is completed in 1985, the ability to watch targets detected and tracked by AEW radars at long range.

The Improved Hawk is NATO's standard air defence missile, the original version of which first became operational in 1959. Logistic shortages in the mid-1970s were corrected and all NATO Hawk batteries now have their basic load. In addition, each US Army Hawk battalion has extra maintenance crew and improved tactical data link equipment. The Patriot SAM, now in production for the US Army, is intended as a replacement for the Hawk; its firing platoon contains all the essentials for combat – the radar set, engagement control station, power plant and up to eight launching stations, each containing four missiles in transport/firing canisters. The Patriot's radar set performs all the surveillance, identification of friend or foe (IFF), tracking and guidance functions that require nine separate radars in the Hawk or longer range Nike-Hercules sytems.

Close-range anti-aircraft systems in service with NATO armies include the British Rapier SAM with its associated Blindfire radar (in service with the Royal Artillery and RAF Regiment) which has won many export orders including Switzerland and for the air defence of USAF bases in the UK, the Blowpipe man-portable missile and the elderly Bloodhound intermediate range SAM which is still operational in Britain and Germany. The French Crotale low-altitude ground-to-air weapons system consists of a surveillance radar vehicle controlling up to three combined launch and command guidance vehicles. The improved version of this system has been supplied to Saudi Arabia as the Shahine and South Africa as the Cactus.

There are several Western systems which mount short-range missiles or guns on high-mobility vehicles for close defence of armoured columns or other ground formations. The Euromissile Roland, jointly developed by France and Germany, is an important tube-launched missile which can be mounted on a range of armoured or soft-skinned fighting vehicles. In the US Army the Tracked Chapparral, which operates tactically in association with the 20 mm six-barrelled Vulcan air defence Gatling gun, will eventually be replaced by the DIVAD (Division Air Defence) Gunfighter built by Ford Aerospace. This tracked vehicle won the DIVAD competition in 1981 and uses two Bofors 40 mm guns under an advanced fire-control system firing prefragmented rounds each with 640 tungsten spheres for ripping through aircraft structures. The Gunfighter's search and tracking radar is developed from the fire-control radar of the F-16 aircraft. Similar high mobility anti-aircraft gun platforms are the French AMX-30 SA and the Gepard Flakpanzer based on the Leopard chassis with twin radar-controlled 35 mm guns, operated by Germany, Netherlands and Switzerland. The similar British Falcon project was abandoned in the 1970s but the tracked Rapier missile system, under development, should give some enhanced tactical air defence to Britain's mobile forces.

The recent emphasis on anti-aircraft weapons procurements in both East and West has been on fast reaction short- and medium-range weapons capable of tackling low-level aircraft and tactical missiles. Advanced man-portable weapons such as the US Stinger can engage anything from a supersonic jet to an assault helicopter, giving infantry soldiers real capability against fast and sophisticated combat aircraft, while such systems as the Gunfighter show the increasing and expensive overlap between air and ground warfare technologies.

Air defence does not simply act by destroying enemy aircraft, but rather by deflecting or degrading the accuracy of attacks. If precision-guided munitions and ECM go some way to restoring the attack power of aircraft, the very need to engage competent and sophisticated ground defences dilutes the forces available to get on with the real business of tactical airpower.

Aircraft versus Armour

A modern combat aircraft may cost up to ten times as much as a very expensive modern Main Battle Tank and have to press home its attack in the face of intense ground defence fire which can effectively deflect the accuracy of an attack made with unguided bombs or rockets. US Department of Defence studies showed that an aircraft which attacks a tank formation with cluster bombs under combat conditions has only a 50 per cent chance of destroying a single tank. Precision-guided weapons, however, are changing that equation as are a new generation of aircraft, fixed-wing and helicopters, specifically designed for close battlefield support and anti-armour operations.

Armed helicopters began as counter-insurgency lash-ups in Algeria and Vietnam in the 1960s but matured in the 1970s as purpose-built fighting machines for operations in the face of the most sophisticated enemy. They provide flexibility for the defence, being able to move rapidly from sector to embattled sector and employ 'pop-up, fire and evade' tactics literally scooting round woods and hills for cover – engaging armour and other ground targets with anti-tank guided missile and multiple cannon. The Hughes AH-64, under final development for the US Army, represents the latest generation purpose-designed anti-tank helicopter. Billed by its manufacturers as a 'total system for battle', the AH-64 carries up to sixteen Hellfire laser-seeking anti-tank missiles, which it can fire in ripples to engage multiple targets, together with rockets and a Hughes XM-230 30 mm Chain Gun in the nose. The machine is armoured to protect it from 12.7 and 23 mm anti-aircraft fire and is lavishly equipped with highly sophisticated systems including infra-red suppression, which reduces the heat signature from its own engines, Singer Doppler Navigator to improve its nap-of-the-earth terrain-contour-following flying, a Teledyne Systems-fire control computer, a Honeywell helmet sight for the gunner, a Martin Marietta pilot's night vision system and target acquisition and designation system incorporating forward looking infra-red sensors and laser-ranging and target-designation. This highly complex flying package of electronics costs more than $6 million.

The Soviet Mi-24 *Hind-D* has rocket pods, ATGMs (anti-tank guided missiles) and a multiple cannon, while the *Hind-E* is armed with four tube-launched laser-homing *Spiral* ATGMs and, like earlier *Hinds*, employs armour plate and titanium in critical areas for damage survivability. Assault helicopters, however, are slower and carry smaller payloads than fixed-wing attack aircraft and they consume vast quantities of fuel, ammunition and maintenance effort. The fixed-wing US Fairchild A-10 Thunderbolt II was specifically designed as an anti-armour airborne platform, able to survive a high degree of ground fire and is armed with laser-homing bombs, cluster bombs and the General Electric GAU-8A Avenger rotary cannon in the nose which is capable of firing 1350 30-mm rounds in ten bursts of two seconds each, and chewing up any tank by sheer weight of high-velocity metal. The Soviet Sukhoi design bureau is reportedly developing an aircraft similar in concept to the A-10, known by NATO intelligence as the Ram-J or Su-25.

3 • The Main Battle Tank and Its Enemies

'Nuclear weapons destroy, naval forces can blockade but only ground forces can retain or establish political power,' was the telling headline in a recent US armed forces journal. For all practical purposes 'ground force' still means armoured fighting vehicles and, in particular, it means tanks. The fears that led to NATO's concern with theatre and tactical nuclear force modernization were generated before the Soviets began to match the West's nuclear firepower – it was the Warsaw Pact's numerical conventional superiority, especially in tanks, that caused such alarm. Tanks have long enjoyed a special place in the Soviet Army, and showed no signs of falling from favour even in the nuclear age – in fact the opposite.

Soviet doctrine prizes their mass and hardness as being the only means of operating on a nuclear battlefield. According to a US DoD report of 1976, 'WP forces' current doctrine and training indicate a readiness for conducting war in Europe with theatre-wide, large-scale nuclear strikes. Their large armoured forces are postured to exploit these nuclear attacks with rapid, massive penetrations.'

In the mid 1960s the Warsaw Pact enjoyed a two-to-one numerical advantage in tanks deployed in the NATO Central Sector but the West was not too worried, content with its qualitative advantage, the fact that it would be fighting defensively, and their 50 per cent advantage in infantry anti-tank weapons. Since then, however, WP numbers and quality have grown dramatically. In 1968 five front-line Soviet Divisions replaced four Czech reserve divisions facing southern Germany. Secondly, as the Soviets modernized their own tank divisions with new-generation T-64s, T-72s and T-62s, older T-54/55s generally were redeployed into motor rifle divisions, and these have been re-engineered with modern target acquisition and fire-control systems. This quantitative growth is being followed by other WP armies with the East Germans close behind. Some projections put WP tank strength on the Central Sector as high as 18,000 by the mid-1980s, achieving a three-to-one local superiority.

Infantry Fighting Vehicles

The balance of Infantry Fighting Vehicles (IFVs), which give mobility, protection and firepower to infantry, has followed a similar pattern. In the mid-1960s the numerical balance was more or less equal, NATO having the more sophisticated equipment. The BMP vehicle, first introduced into the Soviet Army in 1967 and deployed in large numbers throughout the WP armies since then, has changed that. It is highly mobile, amphibious, resistant to chemical, biological and radiation hazards, has side-firing ports for its infantry squad's weapons and has a turret mounting a 73 mm low-pressure gun firing a rocket-assisted HEAT (high-explosive, anti-tank) round capable of engaging modern NATO tanks at 1000 metres range. With a 3000-metre-range ATGM and every third vehicle normally carrying an SA-7 air defence missile, the BMP is a hard-hitting combined-arms vehicle with no direct NATO equivalent.

The most capable IFV currently in the NATO arsenal is the West German Marder which has been retrofitted with Milan ATGMs and it now represents 80 per cent of the inventory on the Central Sector. The US M-2 Bradley IFV will be introduced in 1983 and will match the BMP's long-range anti-armour capability with a dual TOW heavy ATGM missile and a 25 mm chain gun, although it is still vulnerable to attack from high-explosive projectiles including light infantry-fired anti-tank missiles.

Indeed, so useful are IFVs, with so many roles and capabilities demanded of them, and now so complex that their costs are becoming near to those of Main Battle Tanks themselves. One solution NATO is examining is a double development path with a front-line IFV combining the survivability of a Main Battle Tank capable of defeating HEAT projectiles with a high-velocity gun and yet still carry an infantry squad. Motorized infantry operating in rear areas of wooded or urban areas would employ cheaper and less complex wheeled vehicles.

Main Battle Tanks

In the 1960s the NATO nations perfected and deployed sophisticated third-generation Main Battle Tanks such as the Chieftain, the US M-60, French AMX-30 and German Leopard I which outgunned and outmatched the Soviet equivalent T-54s and T-55s. A decade later, these systems have been technically matched by the T-62, and a fourth generation of Soviet tanks is now in the inventory in strength – the T-64 and T-72.

'Fourth-generation' technology means that the system incorporates certain features including a high-velocity, large-calibre smooth bore gun firing an APFSDS ('armour-penetrating, fin-stabilized discarding sabot') projectile, a laser range-finder and automatic loader, high power-to-weight ratio and special armour able to defeat HEAT rounds. The T-72 incorporates all these characteristics and total production from plants in the Soviet Union, Czechoslovakia and Poland is estimated to reach 22,000 by the mid-1980s with an even more advanced tank, the T-80, coming into follow-on production. This vehicle is expected to incorporate advanced armour and a new smooth-bore weapon firing ammunition with depleted uranium penetrators.

Two fourth-generation vehicles are entering service with NATO – the German Leopard II and the US M-1 Abrams. Advanced versions armed with the new German 120 mm gun, can defeat any known armour and their laser range-finders, ballistic computers and stabilization give high-precision target accuracy. Their Chobham composite armour can defeat a range of missiles and projectiles, allowing much freer movement on the battlefield; and their advanced powerplants and suspensions have doubled cross-country speeds. The M-1's integral thermal sight allows it to manoeuvre and engage targets at night or in the dark, a tactical capability which other vehicles do not even approach. However, the M-1 shows the strengths and the weaknesses of US weapons policy – the vehicle was under development for eighteen years. It costs $2.5 million, a price so big that President Reagan had to add nearly $1 billion to the budget so that the US Army could get its required 1289 M-1s over two years. The M-1's gas turbine consumes three gallons propelling the tank's 54 tonnes weight one mile. Only a huge C-5 Galaxy can airlift it and then only one at a time. In 1982 it was announced that it would be succeeded in production by the upgunned M1A1. With the very high costs of Main Battle Tanks and IFVs capable of operating with tanks, attention is once again concentrated on other ways to redress an armoured imbalance other than by trying to match it with yet more tanks.

Anti-tank Missiles

The anti-tank guided missile is now technically mature, having come of age in the 1973 Middle East war. After Soviet ATGMs deployed by the Egyptians had proved particularly effective, the Soviets, with their enormous investment in armour, conducted a careful study of their own tanks' vulnerability and concluded: 'The battle between armour and anti-tank missiles has now shifted to the scientific research laboratories, the proving grounds and industry ... obviously the traditional method of improving the survivability of tanks – by increasing the thickness of the armour – is far from being the only solution and probably not the best one to the problem' (*The Armed Forces of the Soviet State*, 1975). Indeed, it was not the only solution, but composite Chobham-type armour was developed successfully in Britain in the mid-1970s to defeat the existing ATGMs with high-explosive warheads. The Soviets have been working on advanced 'combined armour' since the early 1960s and the Soviet Defence Minister was able to claim that the new-generation T-64 and T-72 were 'invulnerable to attack from ATGMs' – US TOW and Dragon missiles cannot penetrate their frontal armour.

New-technology ATGMs with advanced guidance systems grew up alongside, but they are still very vulnerable when deployed by infantry in the open. NATO exercises have demonstrated that dismounted infantry firing man-portable ATGMs such as the Milan and Dragon can suffer 90 per cent casualties in unprepared positions from artillery fire.

The efficiency of ATGMs is a factor of their manoeuvrability, rate of fire, guidance system and penetrating power. The first generation flew comparatively slowly and needed sizeable wings to remain airborne. They were 'manual-command, line-of-sight systems' (MCLOS) requiring the operator to track the target continuously and guide the weapon directly through trailing wires. The second-generation 'semi-automatic-command line-of-sight systems' (SACLOS) require the operator merely to keep his target in the command system's aiming mark, while electronics do the rest. Laser-seeking missiles launched from helicopters such as the US Hellfire or Soviet *Spiral* require ground or air laser designation to mark their targets but there are no comparable ground systems operational yet.

Milan (France/Germany)
Missile d'Infanterie Legère Anti-Char, light wire-guided SA-CLOS system, equips France, Germany and UK infantries, and many others
RANGE: 25-2000 m

Carl Gustav M2 (Sweden)
Infantry recoilless gun firing HEAT shell
RANGE: 1000 m
PENETRATION: 400 mm armour
Shot down a helicopter and damaged Argentinian corvette during first Falklands battle.

RPG-7 (USSR)
Standard man-portable, short-range anti-tank weapon of the Warsaw Pact
RANGE: 500 m
PENETRATION: 320 mm armour

Snapper (USSR)
Wire-guided, vehicle-mounted MCLOS
RANGE: 370 m
PENETRATION: 356 mm armour

Swatter (USSR)
Radio-guided MCLOS
RANGE: 3500 m
PENETRATION: 500 mm armour

Sagger (USSR)
Compact wire-guided MCLOS; man-portable or vehicle-mounted
RANGE: 3000 m
PENETRATION: 400 mm armour

Spigot (USSR)
Man-portable, wire-guided MCLOS
RANGE: 2000 m
PENETRATION: 500 mm armour

Spandrel (USSR)
Vehicle-mounted SACLOS comparable with NATO Milan
RANGE: 4000 m
PENETRATION: 500 m

HOT (France/Germany)
Heavy-vehicle- or helicopter-launched SACLOS; good short-range performance
RANGE: 75 m - 4 km
PENETRATION: 800 mm armour

Swingfire (UK)
Long-range heavy MCLOS system; in service since 1969
RANGE: 4000 m
PENETRATION: Powerful hollow charge able to defeat very heavy armour

Dragon (USA)
US Army's standard infantry ATGW; wire-guided SACLOS; in service since1975
RANGE: 1 km
PENETRATION: 600 mm armour

TOW (USA)

Heavy anti-tank weapon, crew-portable or vehicle-mounted; tube-launched, optically tracked, wire-guided SACLOS (TOW 2 under development to deal with new Soviet armour)
RANGE: 3750 m
PENETRATION: 800 mm armour

Anti-tank missiles do offer substantial advantages to the defence and have longer range than tank guns, but there are considerable drawbacks. They have a much slower rate of fire than tanks, and they have far bulkier ammunition; a missile-launching vehicle, for example, carries one-sixth the ammunition load of a tank. The use of infra-red trackers on SACLOS systems requires a thermal imager six times more expensive than the launcher when firing through battlefield smoke. Most important of all, existing warheads will not penetrate 'Chobham' armour.

Chobham, or composite, armour is a plate sandwich based on nylon and titanium with granular material in the middle, designed to disperse the penetrating effects of modern anti-tank missile warheads and degrade the penetrating power of high-velocity weapons.

Anti-tank guns and missiles can defeat armour in several ways. High-velocity tank guns fire solid-shot, armour-piercing projectiles which can either be spin- or fin-stabilized. The 'discarding' system, in which a higher calibre expendable sheath covers the shot itself, allows much greater kinetic energy to be applied by the gun to the smaller calibre core made of very hard metal such as tungsten carbide or depleted uranium. A reference to a HVAPFSDS round means 'high-velocity, armour-piercing, fin-stabilized discarding sabot', and a HEAP round is a further refinement, a 'high-explosive, armour-piercing' round, designed to explode inside a target having pierced its armour defences.

Composite armour, although still vulnerable to high-velocity weapons, was designed to defeat the range of warheads deployed on low-velocity weapons such as anti-tank missiles. The most important system is the HEAT round ('high-explosive, anti-tank') which employs a shaped charge of explosive which is detonated offset from the armour surface and, acting like a rocket motor in reverse, blasts a superheated jetstream at 20,000 m/s through the metal and into the tank's interior. The HESH round, another low-velocity system, has a 'high-explosive squash head' which crumples on impact, making a large contact area before exploding and blasting off scabs of metal from the interior armour face into the target vehicle at high velocity.

Anti-tank Firepower

There are further ways of engaging tanks other than by line-of-sight, high-velocity tank guns or by guided missiles. The Warsaw Pact has doubled the effectiveness of its conventional artillery firepower in the 1970s with 5000 pieces of artillery and 1000 multiple-bombardment rocket launchers now deployed in the Central Sector compared with NATO's figures of 2400 and 1000 respectively. The Soviets have been introducing more and more self-propelled artillery which offer the dual advantage of mobility and protection against gas or nuclear-radiation effects on the battlefield. There are several comparable NATO and French self-propelled weapon systems under development, and new, very capable towed artillery pieces are already in service, such as the Anglo-German FH-70 and the US M-198, but the main development imperative in the West has been to make the munitions which these launchers fire more lethal, all the way up to tactical nuclear weapons. For example, new types of ammunition for the SP 155 mm cannon have been developed to increase the utility of indirect artillery fire on a battlefield swarming with tanks and infantry-fighting vehicles – the 'dual-purpose, improved, conventional munition' (DPICM), 'cannon-launched guided projectile' (GLGP) and 'family of scatterable mines' (FASCAM).

The effectiveness of these new and highly expensive munitions is very dependent upon the means of locking on to the target, and on the fire control of the systems directing them. This is even more important when applied to the US Army's newly developed concept of deep engagement – hitting the rear echelons of WP forces at well beyond the 'forward edge of the battle area' (FEBA), breaking up the cohesion of the attack, and relieving the 'target-servicing load', as it is somewhat primly called, on the direct line of sight weapons engaging the enemy head-on. The US Army is working on the SADARM ('sense and destroy armour') project; and the very ambitious joint US Air Force/Army programme known as Assault Breaker is under high-priority development.

Assault Breaker

The name of this US programme is very pointed: the various projects it embraces are designed to counter very strong enemy armoured formations without resort to nuclear weapons. It is a joint services programme under control of the US Defence Advanced Research Projects Agency (DARPA). The parallel short-range SADARM programme uses anti-tank submunitions that can be fired from 8-inch howitzers or MLRS (multiple launch rocket systems). The SADARM round, after reaching the target area, ejects three canisters over the targets which descend by parachute. A sensor in the canister scans an area with a radius of 75 metres and, if it detects a vehicle, fires an armour-penetrating warhead at its roof. The project was first tested successfully in 1979.

The ground-launched missile component of Assault Breaker is testing two systems, the T-16 and T-22, the first a modified version of the Patriot SAM and the second a development of the Lance tactical missile. They are designed for launch at up to 150 km range into an electronic 'basket' area above a company-size tank formation, where they each dispense enough 'smart' submunitions to guarantee knocking out six tanks. Target-acquisition and the steering of the electronic basket are activated from an aircraft equipped with Pave Mover radar. The first successful tests of the T-22 and T-16 were in Spring 1981. An air-launched system is also being studied in which up to twenty-two T-16s could be carried by a B-52 giving a theoretical capability to destroy over 300 enemy tanks.

The USAF's WAAM ('wide area anti-armour munitions') programme is studying three concepts. The first is the anti-armour cluster bomb which is released from an aircraft making a low pass. A large number of submunitions employing self-forging fragment warheads is dispensed over an elongated ground pattern and can act as mines if not immediately effective.

The ERAM ('extended range anti-armour mine') enhances this concept, each submunition incorporating a sensor which will project it into the air again from the ground if a tank comes within 150 metres. The most advanced WAAM concept is the Wasp, a miniature missile capable of its own target-acquisition and tracking. A swarm of Wasps could be released from an aircraft which, because of the missile's 'lock-on-after-launch' capability, could stand off out of range of the armoured formation's air defence. Further, the aircraft does not have to visually identify a target as each missile will have a terminal guidance-seeker to locate and identify an enemy tank independent of the launch aircraft.

Mines are a traditional enemy of the tank and their technology has also advanced – they can be activated by magnetic or vibration influence and can be rapidly dispensed over wide areas by aircraft or tube launchers. Aircraft, fixed-wing or assault helicopters, armed with precision-guided munitions and rotary cannon remain the tank's deadliest enemy (see page 85).

In this battlefield criss-crossed by precision-guided anti-tank-missiles, strewn with mines and swarming with helicopters and 'smart' munitions, how can the Main Battle tank hope to survive? It does so by continuous technical improvement of its armour and agility and by integrating air defence systems within its military formations. Once high technology tanks break through the crust of a high-technology defence, however, they become the fast-moving, paralysing spearheads that cut Europe open in 1940. It is this contingency that NATO could not cope with – being swamped by sheer numbers, trying to handle tens of thousands of mobile targets at night or in bad weather conditions – in theory, at least, more than 30,000 tanks and Infantry Fighting Vehicles, 6000 artillery pieces and rocket launchers protected by over 4000 SAMs and mobile air-defence guns. This is the fear that engendered the decision to develop and deploy tank-killing neutron warheads for artillery or missile delivery which will string a nuclear tightrope across a rearward defence line.

Soviet Main Battle Tanks

(Speeds are overland, armour frontal maximum)

T-54/55
Weight: 36 tonnes
Speed: 50 km/h
Main armament: 100 mm firing HVAPDS, 3-4 rpm
Muzzle velocity: 1400 mps
Armour: 130 mm
Systems: retrofit laser range-finder, NBC hardening

T-62
Weight: 37 tonnes
Speed: 50 km/h
Main armament: 115 mm smoothbore firing HVAPFSDS, 4 rpm
Muzzle velocity: 1600 mps
Armour: 100 mm
Systems: NBC hardening, retrofit laser range-finder

T-64
Weight: 35 tonnes
Speed; 50 km/h
Main armament: 125 mm smoothbore firing HVAPFSDS, 4-6 rpm
Muzzle velocity: 1750 mps
Armour: 210 mm
Systems: laser range-finder, passive night vision, NBC hardening, autoloader

T-72
Weight: 41 tonnes
Speed: 60 km/h
Main armament: 125 mm smoothbore firing HVAPFSDS, 4-6 rpm
Muzzle velocity: 1750 mps
Armour: 220-240 mm combined
Systems: laser range-finder, passive night vision, NBC hardening, autoloader

NATO Main Battle Tanks

M48A3 (USA)
Weight; 47.17 tonnes
Speed: 48 km/h
Main armament: 90 mm firing HEAT
Muzzle velocity: 1220 mps
Systems: NBC, infra-red searchlight, laser range-finder

Chieftain Mk 5 (UK)
Weight: 55 tonnes
Speed: 48 km/h
Main armament: 120 mm gun firing APDS
Muzzle velocity: 1370 mps
Armour: 120 mm (estimated)
Systems: NBC, infra-red searchlights, fire control system, laser range-finder

M1 Abrams (USA)
Weight: 53.390 tonnes
Speed: 50 km/h
Main armament: 105 mm (120 mm smoothbore from 1984) firing APFSDS
Muzzle velocity: 1370 mps
Armour: composite
Systems: NBC, passive night vision, thermal imager, laser range-finder, computer fire-control

AMX-30 (France)
Weight: 36 tonnes
Speed: 35 km/h
Main armament: 105 mm firing APFSDS
Muzzle velocity: 1525 mps
Armour: —
Systems: NBC, infra-red searchlight

Leopard 1 (West Germany)
Weight: 40 tonnes
Speed: 65 km/h
Main armament: 105 mm
Muzzle velocity: 1400 mps
Armour: 70 mm
Systems: NBC, passive night vision equipment, laser range-finder

Challenger (UK)
Weight: 62 tonnes
Speed: 60 km/h
Main armament: 120 mm firing FSAPDS
Muzzle velocity: 1400 mps
Armour: composite
Systems: NBC, passive night vision equipment, laser range-finder

M60A1 (USA)
Weight: 48.9 tonnes
Speed: 48 km/h
Main armament: 105 mm firing FSAPDS
Muzzle velocity: 1400 mps
Armour: 120 mm
Systems: NBC, infra-red searchlight, laser range-finder, retrofit ballistic computer, thermal imagers etc.

Leopard 2 (West Germany)
Weight: 55 tonnes
Speed: 72 km/h
Main armament: 120 mm firing APFSDS
Muzzle velocity: 1800 mps
Armour: composite
Systems: NBC, infra-red searchlight, fire-control computer, laser range-finder

4 • Chemical and Biological Weapons

In February 1982 the United States announced its intention of resuming the manufacture of chemical offensive agents for the first time since 1969, rejoining a chemical arms race from which the Soviet Union had never withdrawn.

Chemical agents are compounds which are intended for military use to incapacitate, kill or seriously injure men through their physiological effect. Any country with a chemical industry could manufacture them, although storage presents problems. Since the First World War they have been used by technically advanced troops against guerrillas or other insurgents but never on European battlefields. They were not used during the Second World War although stockpiled.

They have only one target – the human body; military equipment and weapons can still function even though contaminated. There are different sorts of chemicals, grouped according to their effects and methods of operation. They enter the body by one of three routes: through the lungs, the gastric tract or through the skin.

Chemical agents are distinguished from biological weapons, which cause disease in humans, plants or animals, and from toxins, which are poisonous chemicals initially isolated from natural sources which may include micro-organisms. There are over thirty known viruses, micro-organisms and toxins suitable for use as weapons. The UN Convention of April 1972 that prohibits the manufacture and stockpiling of biological and toxin weapons was signed by 109 nations including those of NATO and the Warsaw Pact. Moreover a major provision of the Convention charges signatories 'never in any circumstances to develop, stockpile, acquire or retain microbial or other biological agents or toxins of types and in quantities that have no justification for prophylactic, protective or other peaceful purposes, as well as weapons, equipment and means of delivery designed to use such agents or toxins for hostile purpose or in armed conflict.'

Thus 'defensive' research continues, and in April 1979 a reported explosion in a military compound of Sverdlovsk in the Urals led to a release of pulmonary anthrax spores into the atmosphere, reawakening fears that the Soviet Union was engaging in the quantity production of biological agents. The Soviets put the outbreak down to contaminated meat and accused the CIA of fabricating the whole thing.

Bacillus anthracis possesses characteristics that make it an ideal instrument of biological warfare. It is the most hardy, the most easily produced and the most easily disseminated disease-producing organism for use against humans. In its pulmonary form, anthrax has a mortality rate approaching 100 per cent. Anthrax spores remain in the soil for decades and the Scottish island of Gruinard – site of dispersal experiments for 'Anthrax-B' in 1941 – has been barred from the outside world ever since.

No such treaty restrictions apply to the manufacture and stockpiling of chemical weapons. The Soviet Union has a very large stockpile, and the US is going to rebuild its store. Britain destroyed its stockpile in the mid-1950s, leaving only France in Europe with a reported offensive capacity. The US capability has dwindled since July 1974 when the USA and the Soviet Union issued a joint communiqué reaffirming both countries' interest in an effective international agreement which would exclude chemicals from their warfare arsenals. After that, US research and money went into binary munitions, a system by which two singly inert chemicals are mixed in action to produce a nerve agent, rather than into maintenance of the old stockpile. Several times the House of Representatives turned down more money but finally it relented in June 1981, voting enough to build a binary munition plan at Pine Bluff, Arkansas, capable of turning out 155 mm artillery shells and 'Bigeye' chemical bombs from mid-1984 onwards.

It is impossible to divine actual Warsaw Pact offensive intentions although great emphasis is put on chemical warfare defence and civil defence. Actual stock levels are equally contentious, although reports suggest that the largely obsolete US stockpile rests at 42,000 tons and the Soviet stockpile, 350,000 tons. The US cites a total strength of 4700 troops assigned to chemical warfare, while the WP armies have specialist units totalling up to 100,000.

Soviet Military Chemical Troops are an integrated part of combined-arms warfare, with a range of agents and delivery systems available for different tactical requirements. Each tank and motorized rifle division has a chemical defence battalion with thirty-two decontamination vehicles. Many tanks and infantry fighting vehicles are pressurized to be able to fight on a contaminated battlefield (as are NATO's) although individual protective clothing is not as comprehensive as NATO equivalents.

Protection against chemical agents can be afforded by a pressurized vehicle or bunker with filtration systems to keep the agents out or by an individual NBC suit with a filtering respirator to provide protection against absorption by inhalation. NATO protective clothing is an all-over suit with a permeable skin and a charcoal interliner to protect the skin against blister and nerve agents. Warsaw Pact clothing is made of impermeable rubber. Special electro-chemical detectors provide early warning of the presence of agents, but the current US M8 alarm apparently can only detect vapour, not liquid persistent agents.

After exposure, men and equipment must be decontaminated by using an oxidizing agent on the body such as Fuller's earth, and vehicles must be washed down with soapy water. An injection of a mixture of trimedoxime, atropine and benactyzine as soon as symptoms are recognized (BAT-TAB and Nemical-5 are NATO and WP standard-issue antidotes) is an immediate therapy for nerve-agent victims.

All this NBC 'hardening' protects military forces but not civilians. The ratio of civilian to military casualties in a limited European nuclear war has been put at 8 to 1. With the use of chemical agents, that climbs to 20 to 1. The USAF bases in Europe have had contingency plans for chemical attack for some time and that, of course, includes those in East Anglia. Indeed, Great Britain has been advanced by US planners as the obvious site for the forward basing of Pine Bluff's reborn chemical 'deterrent'.

5 • Electronic Warfare

War now on land, sea or in the air aims to bring together a series of pre-planned automated sequences concentrating devastating force in time and place. The whole depends on an electronic command-and-control network which instructs, informs and animates the components, which themselves depend on electronics for their individual concentrations of destructive power. The electromagnetic spectrum is now therefore as important an arena for war as land, sea and air themselves. It can only become more so.

An electronic order of battle began emerging during the Second World War and has evolved since into a very, very major military consideration today. Electronics, for example, represent a third of the value of the USAF's equipment costs. The 1982 USAF Research and Development budget allots $270 million of its $960 million total to basic electronic research, which is more than for weapons, aircraft or propulsion. USAF Systems Command already looks after 40,000 computers and 250,000 other 'black boxes'. The new industrial giants of weapons technology are the electronics companies. Loral, for example, makes displays, threat-warning and jamming electronics for the US Air Force, Army and Navy and enjoys business partnerships with Racal/Decca in the UK, Philips in Belgium, Dornier in Germany and AEL in Israel. Ten years ago Loral was a one-product company which made a loss of $3 million. Between 1976 and 1981 the company trebled its sales to $213 million and made a $21 million profit.

The October 1973 Middle East war made the importance of electronic warfare (EW) very clear. An integrated air defence system supplied by the Soviet Union shielded the Egyptian aircraft while Israeli aircraft felt the effects of successful communications-jamming even before they took off. Almost one hundred aircraft fell to SA-6s, ZSU-23 radar-guided multiple cannon and man-portable, heat-seeking SA-7s in the first six days of the eighteen-day war. In Israel's June 1982 invasion of the Lebanon, Syrian SA-6 missile defences were neutralized by a concentrated ECM offensive. Expendable unmanned drone aircraft were sent into the Bekaa Valley to ascertain the frequencies and signatures of the SAM's radars and seekers. This electronic intelligence (ELINT) was interpreted and programmed into EW jamming aircraft which were then able to blanket air defence frequencies, confounding the missiles.

The overwhelming characteristic of the technology of EW is the rapidity of change. A typical advanced component stays out in front for a few years and then is superseded just as microprocessors have transformed consumer and industrial electronics. The glut of information produced by these systems and their complexity cannot simply be grafted into flesh-and-blood armed forces, however advanced their technical manpower base. The US armed forces have drawn together to concentrate resources. In June 1980 the Department of Defence set up the Joint Electronic Warfare Centre with the Commander of USAF Electronic Security Command as its first director, and the multi-million-dollar Very High Speed Integrated Circuit Programme (VHSIC) is a tri-service project.

At the same time the implementation of some very advanced physics, for example in laser and particle beam research, has lengthened development cycles and pushed up costs still further. In the case of systems such as the B-1B, Trident and MX which are extremely 'EW-intensive', development and procurement cycles are over a decade, and the costs are only predictable as being bigger than the figure last thought of.

The military electronics industry is charged with making practical battlefield tools. Electronics of every kind are already integral to essentially every aspect of modern warfare and modern weaponry, and these systems have to be made comprehensible, durable and interoperable with other systems. Concepts developed for one medium are applicable to another, shipboard ECM sets such as Raytheon's 'fleet defence umbrella' go up in helicopters and F-16 fighter radars end up in anti-aircraft tanks. Depending on the particular weapons systems, one or more of the following EW capabilities will be incorporated: avionics; engine status/control/display; onboard computer; navigation – inertial, doppler, radio, stellar; radar, target acquisition, tracking and display; fibre-optic flight controls; weapons management; ECM; ECCM (electronic counter counter-measures); communications systems power supply, servo control; self-diagnosis; battlefield display mapping.

The electronic battlefield stretches under the ocean and into space. It begins with systems which can detect events many thousands of miles away and ends with a radar which can track a sniper's bullet. Early-warning radars, satellites and space-track systems span the globe looking for distant events and communicating almost instantaneously through global telecommunications systems. At sea, surface warships or submarines can make satellite-informed attacks against targets over the horizon. Anti-submarine forces, aircraft, ships and submarines themselves cast electronic and acoustic nets through the oceans.

Strategic missiles and bombers strive to penetrate defended airspace, dispensing decoys and radar-confounding emissions while other specialized aircraft join in the chorus of jamming or physically attack enemy electronic installations with radar-seeking missiles.

On the land battlefield, men in their tanks and personnel carriers peer through the gloom with sophisticated imagers and mark their targets with lasers. Reconnaissance aircraft strive to detect the passage of the enemy from their heat signature, summoning tactical aircraft to attack the enemy with smart munitions. Antennas bristle, monitoring enemy communications for a glimmer of their intentions, while communications nets patch this electronic battlefield into the analytical and control power of distant computers.

A new concept of electronic warfare has emerged to strike at the core systems that make this electronic battlefield intelligent. It has been called 'signals warfare' or 'radio electronic combat' but is now known by the US Air Force as C^3CM – Command Control and Communications Countermeasures – and blends aspects of EW, destructive weapons deception and intelligence. The idea is to attack the command and control structure of the enemy (and on the way learn how to defend your own) by identifying the nodes and key interchanges of the target C³ system and preplan their destruction in a systematic attack using a balance of physical and electromagnetic means. Your own system can be defended by using a spread of the electromagnetic spectrum, fast frequency-hopping, error coding, hardening or making mobile the command facilities, double routing and dispersing command and control nodes. A superior level of technology should deny these advantages to the enemy.

The increasing integration of electronics into the basic design of weapons systems and the proportion of costs has stimulated vertical integration within US and European defence industries and given the military electronics companies a bigger slice of the cake. It has also accelerated the trend for the established aerospace giants of American industry to establish or buy out electronic warfare-oriented subsidiaries. They include Boeing, General Dynamics, Fairchild Republic, Grumman, Lockheed, McDonnell Douglas, Northrop, Rockwell International and Vought. Close behind come the EW system-specialists, between twenty-five and fifty companies usually already established as divisions of diversified corporations – single or multi-division entities within Westinghouse, Textron, Teledyne, RCA, Raytheon, Martin-Marietta, IBM, ITT, Hughes, GTE, General Electric, Ford, TRW and Eaton AIL. Sanders, E-Systems and Loral (mentioned above) are fast-growing first-division independents. Then there is the next hundred company-dense layer of problem-solvers integrating with the systems-specialists, including ATI, Bendix, Control Data, Edo, General Instrument, Schlumberger, Hazeltine, Litton-Amecom, Motorola, Norden, Sperry-Univac, Varian and Watkins-Johnson. Over 200 subsystem and component houses share the next level of the aerospace electronics business, often acting as centres of technical innovation.

Competing for a share of the estimated $4.192 billion worldwide EW market (1981 figure growing at 10-15 per cent) are the electronic industries of Europe. Japan is conspicuous by its absence, being forbidden by its constitution to export military equipment. Great Britain has British Aerospace, Plessey, Racal-Decca, Marconi and EEV. Belgium: MBLE (Philips). Germany: Wacker, Siemens, SEL, AEG-Telefunken. France: Thomson-CSF, Enertec. Italy: Selenia, Elettronica.

The Netherlands: Philips and Hollandse Signaalapparaten. Spain: CECSA. Sweden: Datasaab. Israel: Telkoor, Tadiran and Israel Aircraft Industries.

In mid-1981 after the Reagan defence budget increased, a Wall Street investment consultancy picked out its hot defence shares for the mid-1980s. They were Loral and Sanders (EW systems), Itek (lasers), Milacron and Analog Devices (robots) Quantronics (microelectronics) and Nuclear Metals (advanced materials).

The Language of Electronic Warfare

EW: Electronic Warfare—use of a wide range of electronic systems and subsystems to conduct active or passive measurement of an enemy's offensive or defensive electronics capabilities, attack or defend against those systems, and reach tactical or strategic mission objectives using personnel and/or weapons that include ground forces, ships, submarines, aircraft and missiles.

ELINT: Electronic intelligence gathering—the activity of monitoring, measuring, identifying and analysing hostile electromagnetic radiation of any kind, across the electromagnetic spectrum from DC to light.

ECM: Electronic countermeasures—tactical or strategic operational methods of using electronics technologies to deceive, disrupt, jam or negate the effectiveness of opposing electronics systems and techniques.

ECCM: Electronic counter-countermeasures—way to defeat ECM used against one's own electronics systems, to acquire genuine targets despite the ECM interference, and eliminate the disruptions either in attack or defence.

ESM: Electronic support measures—typically 'passive' (non-radiating) receiving systems that listen to hostile electromagnetic signals, store and process them, and add them to the known or likely electronics systems deployed by the enemy so that the presence, identity and capability of the threat can be established.

SIGINT: Signal intelligence—information obtained about a radiating element, usually a communications function, based on the transmitter characteristics. Computers are used to determine the precise characteristics of the emission or signal to characterize the technology being employed.

COMINT: Communications intelligence gleaned from analysing voice and data communications, plain or encrypted. COMINT includes computer-based cryptographic analysis, or code breaking, that enables an adversary's communications traffic, orders, instructions and other data to be intercepted and understood rapidly.

C³I: Command, control, communications and intelligence – the electronic 'nervous system' of a battlefield or region, up to and including the global arena.

JAMMING: One of several forms of deceiving, blocking or blinding electronic devices, such as those used to search (e.g. radar), launch and guide weapons, identify friends or foes (IFF) or perform interception by fighters or other means. Typically, active 'noise jammers' radiate signals that may also, in some systems, be aimed or focused on a search radar to obliterate a target return on the radar screen. 'Standoff jammer' aircraft such as those carried in specialized aircraft (EF-111A for the US Air Force, EA-6B for the Navy/ Marines) suppress enemy electronic/missile defences beyond the physical range of the threat. Deception jammers receive search-radar signals and send back, instead of a 'target' echo, a signal that may be delayed to misplace the target location on the radar screen. Expendable passive jammers include 'chaff' to create 'phantom' radar signals simulating real targets. Expendable active jammers work similarly, by creating false targets that look as real as an aircraft or missile warhead to attract enemy weapons. Heat-seeking missiles, either air- or ground-launched, may use infra-red (IR) detectors that lock onto hot jet effluxes or exhausts, but they may themselves be jammed by IR jammers used to attract the weapons. Communications jammers are used to inhibit an enemy's C³I. Both sides use all these possible jamming techniques.

RWR: Radar warning receivers that monitor hostile radar illumination, analyse and identify the threat.

COMPUTERS: In EW, high-speed digital signal processors used to analyse and prioritize threats to the vehicle or system (aircraft, ship, submarine. tank or land installation). This analysis may be done in essentially 'real time' for immediate response. Large-scale scientific computers may be used in the laboratory to establish detailed understanding of the capability and potential of an electronic threat. On-board, militarized (ruggedized) computers to airborne, shipborne or other specifications are frequently supported by 'libraries' within their permanent memory, containing known electronic threats.

ANTENNAS: Structures used to transmit or receive electronic signals: in transmission, the final exit point from the vehicle or system; in reception, the first arrival point. Shapes may be flat, circular, dish-shaped or fan shaped, they may be fixed, rotating or 'nodding' or they may be electronically steerable or aimable for maximum performance.

ELECTRO-OPTIC (EO): Electronic systems or devices working in the visible or near-visible portions of the electromagnetic spectrum, such as lasers and IR components. These systems can be used for target tracking/illumination, or to 'blind' or deceive similar devices in use by the enemy.

6 • The Military Uses of Space

Space is a fundamentally important military arena. In spite of the 1967 treaty which forbade the placing of weapons of mass destruction in orbit, about three-quarters of all earth satellites ever launched have been for military purposes. Although satellites are probably not yet weapons platforms themselves, they are vital to inform, monitor and control the weapons of destruction that still wait on earth.

A military power needs a space programme or at least access to one if it is to join the big league. A relatively 'simple' system such as a cruise missile needs space-derived data to pinpoint its target and give it its accuracy. The superpowers are reluctant to allow intruders on their patch. It was a Soviet Cosmos satellite which reportedly detected South African preparations for an apparent nuclear test in the summer of 1977, and the USSR informed the Americans. A US Vela surveillance satellite reported a flash consistent with a nuclear explosion soon afterwards.

Military satellites broadly fulfill five functions: they provide global communications, early warning of long-range attack, surveillance of events on the ground or electronic intelligence, weather reconnaissance and navigational references. The breakdown of Soviet launches in 1980 (overleaf) shows the relative importance of each function.

Military satellites are not permanent features of the heavens but 'fly missions' as an aircraft would do, only the missions are longer. Soviet photo-reconnaissance satellites, for example, are placed into low-earth orbit, fly twelve- or thirteen-day missions and then return to earth, ejecting capsules which are recovered with their photographic information. New-generation Soviet and the Big Bird American surveillance satellites can transmit data digitally by radio or eject it in parachute capsules from orbit.

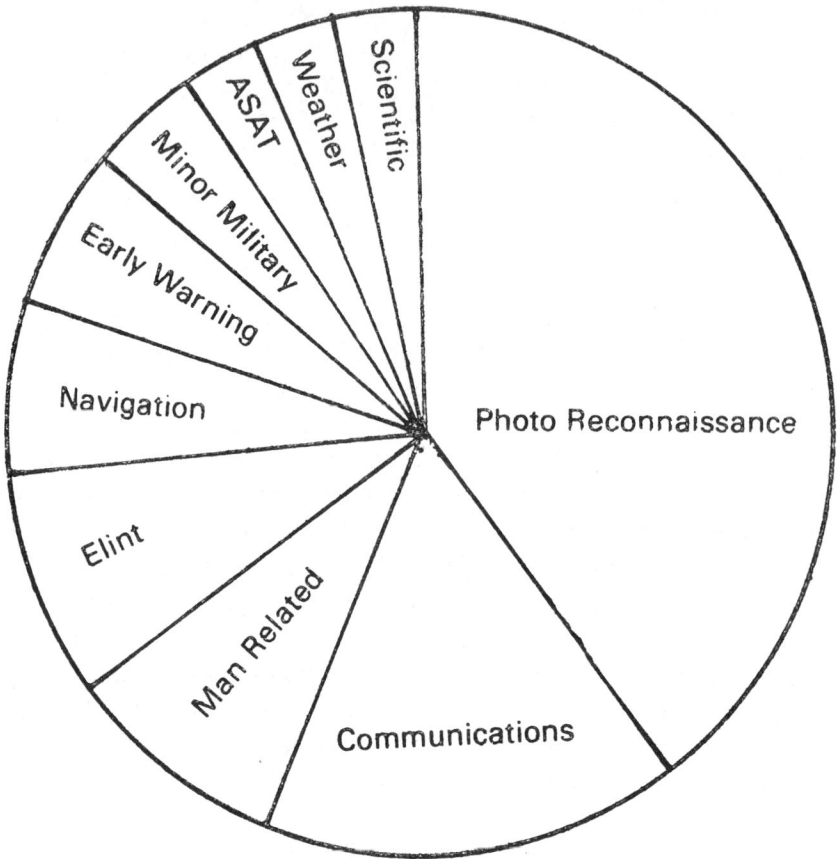

Soviet Satellite Launches, 1980

A typical mission was launched from the Soviet centre at Plesetsk near Leningrad on 12 November 1980 just as the US Rapid Deployment Force was conducting joint operations with the Egyptians near Cairo. Twenty-four hours after launch, Cosmos 1221 passed over the area to return again the next day 80 km further west, bringing its information back to earth in the Soviet Union two weeks later as the exercises were ending. Similar launches were made to monitor British and Argentinian movements in the South Atlantic.

Navigation, communication and early-warning satellites are more permanent features and hence are usually placed in geostationary orbits, at an altitude and velocity where the orbit will match the earth's rotation and thus the satellite will stay over

the same point on the surface of the earth. These networks
require careful building and replacement as the orbits decay or
the equipment wears out. This is the military significance of the
Space Shuttle, able to place systems in orbit and tend them
afterwards, thus superseding traditional rocket-launch systems
(although so far it shows no sign of doing this cost-effec-
tively).

Communications Satellites

US Navy Fleet Satellite Communications System (FLTSATCOM)
Built by TRW, five satellites (one back-up), each with thirty
speech/twelve teletype channels. First launched February 1978.
Used by Britain during Falklands crisis.

Defence Satellite Communications System Phase II
TRW contract for US Air Force communications system. Total
of at least 16 operational satellites. First launched November
1971.

LEASAT
Hughes contract for Geostationary World Wide communi-
cations system for US armed forces based on four large satellites
occupying geostationary locations over the USA, the Atlantic,
Pacific and Indian Oceans. Designed to be launched from the
Space Shuttle and become operational in 1982.

Satellite Data System
US communications system for SSBNs in polar regions.

NATO 3
Geostationary communications satellites linking US and European NATO commands.

AFSATCOM
USAF satellite C³ system for strategic forces.

Tacomsat 1
Provides tactical communications between US forces in the field using small transmitters. First launched 1969.

Molniya 1
Soviet communications satellite, first launched 1965. High elliptical orbit designed to provide the longest possible communications sessions between Moscow and Vladivostok.

Molniya 2A
Updated version. Current operational system consists of four pairs of *Molniya* (lightning).

1 and 2A circling the earth maintaining stationary ground tracks and thus predictable communications coverage of whole of the Soviet Union, linked to the Orbita ground station net. *Molniya 3* is the latest version, able to accommodate colour television and new communication frequencies.

Skynet IV
UK communications satellite, Skynet I launched 1969, 2B geostationary over Seychelles 1974. Still operating in 1979. BAe began development of replacement in 1981.

Reconnaissance Satellites

Lockheed/USAF 467 Big Bird
First launched in 1971, this large satellite is capable of high-resolution photography of ground objects and events and can eject its findings for mid-air 'snatch' recovery or process the information and relay it by radio as digital data. Its orbit takes its cameras within range of every point on earth twice in every twenty-four hours. Big Birds are launched at four to six monthly intervals and have a lifetime of approximately 180 days.

Key Hole KH II
CIA intelligence-gathering satellite first launched in 1976. Flies in higher orbit than Bird Bird and has a life of around one year.

Agena D

Satellite launched in large numbers able to accommodate variety of payloads and equipped with a restartable engine to enable it to change its orbit in space. Has carried wide range of US military surveillance equipment.

Cosmos

Soviet military satellite series, first launched in 1962. Cosmos reconnaissance satellites are launched about thirty times a year, from bases at Plesesk and Tyuratam, the Soviet equivalents of Kennedy Space Centre and Vandenberg AFB, and most eject capsules after eight or thirteen days. Some have an ability to manoeuvre in orbit for precision target coverage and, like their US counterparts, there are 'search-and-find' and high-resolution systems working together.

Without the facilities for aircraft-based worldwide ocean suveillance, much reliance is placed on satellite systems. Two satellites are launched within a few days of one another, each carrying a powerful radar to locate surface ships. A small nuclear reactor provides the power. After completion of a sixty- to seventy-day mission at a low orbit or 250 km, the satellite reactor is fired into a higher orbit. In 1978 Cosmos 945 crashed in the Canadian Northwest contaminating a wide area with radioactive debris. Since 1976 an advanced reconnaissance satellite has been developed which is thought to be a development of the Salyut space station.

Early Warning

IMEWS/USAF 647

'Integrated missile early-warning satellite' provides early warning of hostile ICBM launches by means of an infra-red 'telescope'. High-resolution cameras can transmit pictures of missiles to a ground station in Australia which relays them to NORAD. Replacing IMEWS is a new system called Rhyolite, placed in geosynchronous orbit over Asia which can pick up and transmit data from Soviet or Chinese missile tests. Secret Argus satellites intercept and retransmit Soviet and Chinese telephonic and radio microwave communications.

Vela
Nuclear-event detection satellites launched from 1964 onwards.

Soviet early-warning satellites
The first is believed to have been Cosmos 159 launched in 1967 with one each year following until 1977 when three were launched.

Weather and Navigation

Block 5D Defence Meteorological Programme
Designed to provide high-quality meteorological data to US services worldwide. First launched in 1976; twenty-one by 1981.

Transit
Original US Navy system operational in 1965 to provide navigational fixes for SSBNs, accurate to 160 m. First of three Nova satellites, advanced version of Transit, launched in 1981.

Navstar
Eighteen satellites placed in three sub-synchronous orbits with six satellites per ring will provide the US military services with a Global Positioning System (GPS), able to provide a fix of three-dimensional position accurate within 10 m and precise timing and velocity reference. Six Navstars in orbit by 1981, total by 1985. Key to the system is the use of atomic clocks, three of which are installed on each satellite, accurate to within one second over 36,000 years. May be used with D-5 SLBM targeting.

Meteor
Soviet weather satellites. First launched 1969; three to four per year since then. Soviet navigation satellites are in the Cosmos

series, the first becoming operational in 1971. Above five are launched per year.

Anti-satellite Warfare

Systems placed in orbit therefore are vital to the functioning of strategic weapon systems and indeed to the military and political decisions of governments at the highest level. It follows that anti-satellite (ASAT) techniques are under high-priority development. The US had a limited ASAT capability by the mid-1960s and a decade later embarked on two new research programmes, one for an anti-satellite missile launched from an aircraft and the other for a 'hunter-killer' satellite which closes with its target in orbit. The US First Tactical Fighter Wing will be operational as a satellite killer unit by 1984.

The Soviet Union began testing a hunter-killer ASAT system in 1967 and continued experiments through the 1970s. In February and March 1981, Cosmos 1234 twice successfully intercepted its target Cosmos 1241, using an explosive fragmentation warhead to disable its target on the second attack.

Lasers

Lasers have long had military applications for range-finding and target illumination, and now they are used in communications. The USAF's Lasercom programme is showing the promise of producing a system which can deliver more information in pulses of light in one second than the US Mail gets through in a week, and the Shuttle is scheduled to take up satellite P80-1 with a Lasercom experiment in 1983. The US Navy's Blue-Green project is a satellite-based laser system for communicating with submerged submarines well into its development cycle.

Fundamental research has been going on for a long time into the use of lasers as weapon systems themselves that would revolutionize tactical and strategic attack as well as defence in the atmosphere and in space. According to the US Department of Defence the Soviets have a high-energy laser programme three times the size of America's and could have ground-based systems operational by the mid-1980s, with ship, aircraft and space-mounted versions by the end of the decade. The Soviets say just the same thing about the Americans.

Laser satellites in high orbit are predicated as the ASAT weapon of the 1990s – and, by extension, as a means of ballistic missile defence, able to smite an incoming ICBM with a high-energy beam and destroy it by exploding its fuel or its warhead safely outside the atmosphere.

In 1973 the USAF destroyed a target drone with a high-energy laser, and soon afterwards the US Navy brought down a TOW missile with a chemical laser developed jointly with DARPA. These were beams directed from ground installations requiring enormous inputs of energy and cooling efforts. The US Air Force Weapons Laboratory at Kirtland AFB, New Mexico, working with DARPA, has built the NKC-135 ALL (Airborne Laser Laboratory) based on a Boeing KC-135 airframe and able to aim and 'fire' a laser beam from mid-air. The first air-to-air test in June 1981 failed to bring down its target, a Sidewinder missile, but the second test a few weeks later was regarded as 75 per cent successful. The NKC-135 ALL will join a new high-energy laser facility at White Sands Missile Range in late 1982 when testing will be renewed.

Significantly, much effort is going into protecting satellites from laser attacks by giving them 'stealth' qualities and equipping them with sensors which detect if they are being illuminated with laser energy.

7 • Seapower

Traditionally the exercise of seapower has been divided in two – first, to win control of a disputed area of ocean by destroying the enemy in battle or by scaring him away; and then, having won control, to exercise it to further other military or policy ends such as attacking the trade of an enemy or projecting power to support friends or attack the enemy's periphery. The rules today are the same but the means of playing have changed.

The naval war in the South Atlantic was not fought between warships (apart from the torpedoing of the *General Belgrano*). It was fought by air forces seeking to destroy the British warships which were exercising 'seapower' by landing troops and equipment and providing air support for land forces, but which had themselves not yet won 'sea control' by clearing the enemy from the skies. It was a very high risk operation.

Winning sea control is no longer a duel between capital ships but an interlocking battle above, on and under the sea requiring composite forces of special-purpose ships, missiles, aircraft, submarines and satellites. Computers and electronics dominate modern warship technology just as they do war on land or in the air, and have given surface warships a chance of survival even in the age of the nuclear-powered submarine. Long-range guided weapons, powerful radars and fast-slewing close-in weapon systems can engage aircraft, air-launched munitions, even sea-skimming missiles and are backed up by electronic counter- and counter-countermeasures. For engaging submarines there is a range of weapons and sensors discussed below.

A submarine, however, can despatch an aircraft carrier with a salvo of cruise missiles launched from over the horizon unless the carrier and its consorts can detect the predator first or unless last-ditch defences work. One ballistic missile submarine can carry enough MIRV warheads (140 on a Poseidon boat) to wreck the economy of a superpower and slaughter millions of its citizens. The composite seapower that the technology of modern naval weapons demands is therefore tilted very much towards the submarine, either bringing it aid and comfort or hunting it down. Nowhere is this demonstrated so effectively as in the force structure and operational doctrine of the Soviet Navy.

The Soviet Navy

Fleet Admiral Sergei Gorshkov has been Commander in Chief of the Soviet Navy since 1956 and has supervised its expansion from a coast defence force to a world power with complete continuity of purpose. All use of the sea by the state is integral – navy, merchant marine and oceanography interlock – and economic competition serves long-term political ends. Fishing fleets gather intelligence and merchantmen replenish warships.

Soviet naval power is bottled up by geography, ice impeding ports every winter except in the Black Sea. Routes out funnel through bottlenecks such as the Kattegat at the mouth of the Baltic, the Channel and the Greenland-Iceland-UK (GIUK) gap, all of which reduce search-areas for NATO's anti-submarine forces. The Bosphorus and Gibraltar pinch off each end of the Mediterranean and the islands of Japan screen exits via the La Perousse Strait. These historic constraints were to be swept aside and turned to advantage.

In the first phase of expansion the emphasis was defensive, aimed at American aircraft carriers which brought nuclear-capable air groups within range of the homeland. Then from 1960 onwards, when Polaris first went to sea, the emphasis shifted to anti-submarine warfare. With the advent of a Soviet SSBN fleet itself, the emphasis shifted from coast defence to sea-based deterrence and power projection. Ballistic missile submarines comprise the primary instrument and most other naval forces contribute to their efficiency and security to seek out the enemy's equivalents. According to Gorchkov's own *Seapower and the State*, full-scale fleet-against-fleet confrontations are secondary to submarine warfare as are large-scale initial attacks on sea lines of communication, and the whole doctrine is based on the precept that the transition from peace to war at sea will be very rapid.

The hardware of the Soviet Navy reflects this strong emphasis on submarine warfare. It currently operates some 377 submarines including 180 nuclear-powered, and a third of the force is fitted to fire anti-ship cruise missiles. The first nuclear-powered submarines, the *Novembers*, laid down in 1958, were designed as hunter-killers and reflected the realization that the most effective way of stalking and destroying an enemy submarine was from another submarine. The distinction should be noted between ballistic missile submarines (which are mobile floating batteries of silos) and attack submarines which engage in warfare on the oceans. In 1962 the first of the gas-turbine-powered *Kashin* destroyers appeared, classed as a large anti-submarine ship, but by then the US had changed the rules by deploying the 2500-mile-range Polaris A-3 and thus extending enormously the amount of ocean in which enemy SSBNs could hide. The task of searching the Atlantic while NATO looked on was beyond the powers of Soviet surface ships.

The solution was more submarines with range and endurance enough to wait around the enemy's ports of departure and stalk their prey to the patrol area or seek them out in the deep ocean. The *Victor* class, armed with torpedoes, was designed for this purpose and was rapidly followed in 1968 by the *Charlie* class able to engage submarines or attack surface ships with twenty-mile-range cruise missiles launched from beneath the water. In fact they were specialized aircraft-carrier killers. While the US Navy was depending on carrier aircraft for offensive seapower the Soviets were investing heavily in the ship-killing ability of the cruise missile.

Meanwhile new surface ships appeared in the late 1960s – the *Moskva*-class helicopter cruisers and the *Kresta* II cruisers – but these warships were still extensively configured for anti-submarine warfare. Then increasingly ambitious Soviet exercises showed these new ships being employed as a composite force deploying for surface engagements with cruise missile submarines as the first line of attack followed by air, then torpedo and surface ship missile attacks; but this did not seem relevant to the avowed primary task of dealing with enemy ballistic missile submarines.

In 1972 the answer appeared, the *Delta* I class SSBN armed with SS-N-8 missiles with a range commanding targets in North

America without the need to move far from its bases in Murmansk or Kamchatka. Now it was NATO hunter-killers which would have to penetrate the potentially increasingly formidable Soviet ASW (anti-submarine warfare) screen, and the geographical advantages that had previously obtained were reversed, the GIUK and the Japanese Straits once Soviet-controlled becoming outer defences and not contested passages.

The tempo of construction continued unbroken through the 1970s with radically new classes of surface warship being introduced but still with an emphasis on anti-submarine warfare. In May 1975 the *Kiev* was commissioned, first of a class of four, heavily armed with missiles and with *Hormone* ASW helicopters and Yak-36 *Forger* VTOL aircraft embarked. In May 1980 the first Soviet nuclear-powered surface warship, the 25,000 ton battlecruiser *Kirov*, began sea trials. Her main armament is a group of twenty SS-N-19 anti-ship missile launchers, and defence against air and missile attack is provided by twelve SA-N-6 launchers. Long-range sonar, five *Hormone* helicopters and twenty-five-mile-range SS-N-14 ASW cruise missiles provide a powerful anti-submarine capability. The first of the 8000-ton, steam-turbine-powered *Sovremenny* class appeared in 1980, its emphasis being on surface attack, while the gas-turbine-powered *Udaloy* class, the first of which also appeared in 1980, has eight SS-N-14 missile launchers and is clearly specialized for the ASW role. Available evidence suggests that the *Udaloy* will become a standard ASW platform with a large number built and deployed through the 1980s.

Yet another cruiser class is under construction at the Nikolayev yard on the Black Sea; at 13,000 tons, it is larger than the *Udaloy* and *Sovremenny*s built at Leningrad and Kaliningrad. US intelligence calls this ship *Black-Com 1* and expects it to function like *Kirov* as a multipurpose command ship capable of leading a naval battle group and providing it with enhanced air-defence and surface-strike capabilities. The second *Kirov*-class cruiser now under construction reportedly has laser armament for close-in defence against sea-skimming missiles. Western intelligence is also predicting the appearance of a 75,000-ton, nuclear-powered aircraft carrier with up to sixty fixed-wing aircraft embarked (probably navalized MiG-27 Flogger Ds) sometime in the late 1980s.

The decade also saw tremendous investment in submarines themselves. In 1970 the Sudomekh yard at Leningrad completed the first *Alfa*-class submarine and although this first was scrapped, six of these nuclear-powered, advanced-attack submarines have been built making extensive use of titanium in the hull construction to give a diving depth of 3000 feet (914 m), and they have a claimed submerged speed of 44 knots. In the same period the *Echo-I* class was modernized, and the *Victor I* class was superseded by the *Victor II* and *III*, all adding to the nuclear-attack submarine inventory. The programme of conventional-attack submarine-building was also kept up, the relatively large 3000-ton *Tango* class replacing *Foxtrot*.

At the other end of the scale Russian shipyards in 1980 produced two leviathans, the first of the *Oscar* class, a 15,000-ton nuclear-powered submarine with twenty-four tubes for SS-N-19 400 km-range anti-ship cruise missiles, and the 30,000-ton *Typhoon* ballistic missile submarine to be armed with twenty SS-NX-20 SLBMs.

The large Soviet attack submarine fleet, both nuclear and conventionally powered, and many armed with long-range cruise missiles, represents the ocean-going equivalent of the very large conventional landpower piled up on the NATO Central Sector and brings similar pressures to bear when aimed against trade, highly vulnerable oil tanker routes, offshore energy-gathering infrastructures and the military link between forces in the United States and in Western Europe. Like large and flexible landpower, it gives the Soviet High Command a range of options including a nuclear one. Many weapons for fighting the war at sea are nuclear-tipped, such as depth charges, anti-ship missiles and mines. The use of such weapons at sea, where only ships and sailors are incinerated, has a much lower threshold than the use of nuclear weapons on a battlefield with a million people up the autobahn. (One recent development is the research into neutron weapons for use at sea.) This is one arena where 'limited nuclear war' strategies begin to look dangerously attractive. Sinking the enemy's tanker fleet should not invite the same level of response that an attack on refining installations ashore using intercontinental ballistic missiles might bring.

NATO/Warsaw Pact Navies, 1982 (total global deployment)

Category	WARSAW PACT			NATO		
Aircraft Carriers	Soviet Union	ASW	4	US	Attack	13
				UK	ASW	2
				France	Attack	2
				Italy	ASW	1
Cruisers	Soviet Union	Large	1	US	AAW	37
		Missile	8	France	AAW	1
		ASW	17	Italy	ASW	2
		Command	2			
Destroyers	Soviet Union	AAW	60	US	AAW	27
	Poland		1		ASW	43
				UK	AAW	11
				France	ASW	6
					AAW	12
				West Germany	ASW	3
					AAW	4
					Missile	5
				Netherlands	AAW	4
				Italy	ASW	2
				Greece	ASW	12
				Canada	ASW	16
				Turkey	ASW	12
Frigates	Soviet Union	ASW	26	US	AAW	10
	Bulgaria	ASW	2		ASW	58
	GDR	ASW	2	UK	ASW	42
				W. Germany	ASW	6
				Netherlands	ASW	9
				Portugal	ASW	7
				Belgium	ASW	4
				Norway	ASW	5
				Denmark	SS.M	2

Corvettes

Warsaw Pact	Type	No.		NATO	Type	No.
Soviet Union	Missile	20		Norway	ASW	2
	ASW	66		Denmark	SSM	3
				Portugal	ASW	10
				Greece	ASW	4
				Turkey	ASW	2
				Italy	ASW	16

Submarines

Warsaw Pact	Type	No.		NATO	Type	No.
Soviet Union	SSGN	45		US	SSN/SS	68 5
	SSG	16		UK	SSN/SS	11 16
	SSN	46		France	SS	21
Bulgaria	SS	4		W. Germany	SS	24
Poland	SS	4		Norway	SS	11
				Denmark	SS	6
				Netherlands	SS	6
				Canada	SS	3
				Portugal	SS	3
				Greece	SS	11
				Turkey	SS	15
				Italy	SS	12

Amphibious Warfare Ships

Warsaw Pact	Type	No.		NATO	Type	No.
Soviet Union	Medium	83		US	Large	61
GDR	Medium	14		UK	Large	2
Poland		23			Medium	5
				France	Large	10
				Greece	Medium	1
					Medium	10
				Turkey	Medium	5
				Italy	Medium	2

TOTALS

	Warsaw Pact	NATO
Aircraft Carriers	4	18
Cruisers	28	40
Destroyers	61	157
Frigates	30	143
Corvettes	86	37
Submarines	199	212
Amphibious Warfare Ships	120	96

Note: In any naval order of battle a large percentage of warships will be on long or short term refit. AAW: anti-aircraft warfare. ASW: anti-submarine warfare.

Anti-submarine Warfare

From the above it will be seen that the conduct of anti-submarine warfare follows two streams: the hunt for the SSBNs which seek silence and solitude, and the hunt for the attack submarines which must stalk and engage their foes in battle. Strategic ASW is the most contentious and relies largely on passive means.

Over many years the US Navy has worked on seeding the oceans with fixed, passive, hydrophone arrays (underwater microphones), and annually spends several hundred million dollars on improving systems for surveillance and, most important, *interpretation* of underwater activities. The latest system is called SOSUS (Sound Surveillance System) and guards approaches to the USA and the entrances to the Atlantic via the Greenland-Iceland-UK gap. This system feeds information to the US Navy's Anti-submarine Warfare Centre Command and Control Systems (ASWCCCS) along with inputs from another network called CAESAR and standing patrols using SURTASS ('surveillance towed array') systems which are long arrays of passive sonars towed at slow speed over designated sweep areas. DARPA is funding an undersea surveillance programme which relies on concentrated computer power to unscramble the cacophony of the oceans (caused by seismic upheavals, marine life and churning of ship propellers) and isolate the extremely weak acoustic announcement of a submarine's passage at very long range.* Submarines can further 'hide' behind the sea's shifting gradients of temperature, pressure and salinity. The DARPA project uses very long linear acoustic arrays and satellites to provide links for transmitting data in real-time (absence of delay between the event and reception of data at another location) to an Acoustic Research Centre in California where what is claimed to be the world's most powerful computer has demonstrated the technique.

More research is pursuing the detection of the signatures of

* The relative silence of a submarine is a prized military asset. Soviet submarines tend to be much noisier than their US counterparts although a nuclear submarine can never be completely silent because it has to constantly circulate coolant through its reactor even when stationary.

moving submarines which leave thermal and ultra-violet radiation disruptions in their wake and trails of dying micro-organisms. Radar at exceptionally high frequencies can dimly recognize submarine signatures *above* the oceans. Some sources report that the Soviets, who cannot yet hope to impose ASW barriers between US submarine bases and the open oceans, have designated part of their SLBM and heavyweight ICBM force to attack SSBN support facilities and likely patrol areas in the open ocean with saturation attacks.

Tactical ASW

Successful tactical anti-submarine operations depend on forces that can find, fix and destroy undersea predators before they can get their shots in. Active sonars ('sonar' from sound navigation and ranging which works by emitting a beam of high-intensity sound and interpreting the echoes) can be mounted on surface ships, towed arrays, buoys, helicopters and submarines. Towed array sonars which can detect submarines at long range and be operated without too much speed loss are changing the nature of tactical ASW and have rendered classes of traditional escort ships obsolete at a stroke. Shore-based and carrier aircraft carry magnetic-anomaly detectors, radars and other sensors, and drop sonobuoys to widen search areas. The US Navy's Lockheed Orion P-3C is an airframe virtually built around a computer and in its Update II configuration has infra-red detection systems, sonobuoy reference systems, magnetic-anomaly detectors, extensive analysis and communications equipment and cameras, and is armed with nuclear depth-bombs, mines and torpedoes. Less specialized aircraft such as USAF's B-52 bombers can carry out long-range ASW reconnaissance and mine-laying. Helicopters are very useful ASW platforms and can pack a heavy fit of sensors including 'dunking' sonar, electronics and weapons into their airframes.

The most effective non-nuclear anti-submarine weapon is the torpedo which searches for, acquires and then attacks its target. If it misses the first time it can make multiple attacks. The most effective offensive ASW torpedo in the US Navy's arsenal is the heavyweight Mk 48 (which is being further developed to deal with deep-diving, fast targets, such as *Alfa*-class submarines, in a programme called ADCAP) and can be wire-guided in active, passive acoustic and non-acoustic modes, and is aboard US Navy attack and strategic submarines for self-defence.

The strategic importance of anti-submarine warfare has been the imperative for successive British governments to approve very large sums for the development of anti-submarine torpedoes. The British Sting Ray lightweight torpedo designed for launching from helicopters, aircraft or surface ships in a wide range of sea states and speeds is claimed to be unique because its onboard sonar and powerful digital computer enable autonomous acquisition of the target in very shallow or very deep water and before it had completed its operational trials the weapon was rushed out to equip the Falklands task force. The automatic-homing system has built-in resistance to decoy targets and countermeasures. It's very clever but the UK Ministry of Defence admits that the twenty years' development and procurement Sting Ray programme may cost £800 million. Naval Staff Requirement 7525 has produced a new British development programme for a heavyweight torpedo capable of dealing with *Alfa*-class submarines similar to the US Mk 48 ADCAP improvement programme.

Mine Warfare

The US Captor programme combines the actively homing ASW torpedo with static mines. Captors can be laid from ships or aircraft to create barrages and are designed to release automatically a Mk 46 torpedo on activation by a transmitting submarine. The programme, however, has not been an unqualified success. Indeed, the US Navy ran down virtually all its shipborne mine countermeasures forces in the 1970s, preferring to rely on helicopters (seven of which were lost in the Iran hostage operation). Currently deployed US mine technology is 1950s vintage, relying on aircraft and submarines for sowing. The Soviet Navy possesses a very large stockpile of mines which can operate in deep-water shipping lanes (US types are limited to depths above 600 feet). Nuclear mines can be deployed by both sides in strategic areas. The US Navy has embarked on a 21-ship mine countermeasure (MCM) ship-building programme to counter the Soviet deep-water mine capability and a new class of mine-warfare vessel combining the features of the mine-hunter and minesweeper, but it is still trailing other NATO navies in emphasis on MCM.

Airpower at Sea

The aircraft carrier is the heart of the US Navy and the basis of its offensive capabilities. In 1965 there were twenty-five US carriers (not counting amphibious assault ships), reduced to thirteen active carriers with twelve air wings to put in them in 1982. One carrier is under construction (the unnamed CVN-71) with commissioning scheduled for 1987. Five carriers are in reserve, two of which are worth resuscitating. The Reagan administration intends maintaining this force at current level by extending the lives of existing carriers and building a fifth and even a sixth *Nimitz*-class carrier for commissioning in 1989-92 (at a price tag in 1982 of $3.5 billion), replacing *Midway* and *Coral Sea*.

US Navy Carriers (Year commissioned in brackets)

Atlantic/Med: 2nd/6th Fleets		*Pacific:* 3rd/7th Fleets	
CVN Eisenhower	(1977)	CVN Enterprise	(1961)
Nimitz	(1975)		
		CV Constellation	(1961)
(Building)		Kitty Hawk	(1961)
Carl Vinson	(1984)	Ranger	(1957)
CVN- 71	(1987)	Midway	(1945)
CVN- 72	(1989)		
CVN- 73	(1992)	Coral Sea	(1947)
		(used for contingencies)	
CV John F. Kennedy	(1968)		
America	(1965)		
Independence	(1959)		
Saratoga	(1956)		
Forrestal	(1955)		

Currently, four out of twelve US carriers with fifty fighter attack aircraft embarked on each are permanently forward-positioned, two with the Sixth Fleet in the Mediterranean (one is available for Atlantic operations) and two with the Seventh fleet in the Western Pacific, with one of the pair periodically patrolling the Indian Ocean. The two PACOM (Pacific Command) carriers, however, moved to positions off the Persian Gulf in November 1979 to cover Iran and ône has been there ever since. The *Nimitz* departed the Sixth Fleet in January 1980 to bring the PACOM force back to two, leaving one carrier in the Mediterranean. The carrier-based aircraft of the US Navy (about 700 fighter-attack combat aircraft) can project power and bring military pressure to bear at long range, supplementing USAF or Marine Corps squadrons in many of the circumstances of land warfare. The Soviet Navy with its fifty Yak-35 VTOL fighter/attack aircraft embarked aboard *Minsk* and *Kiev* cannot compete at sea, but the land-based Naval Air Arm and, particularly, the growing number of long-range Tu 22M *Backfires* equipped with stand-off cruise missiles represent a rapidly growing maritime airpower capability.

The Royal Navy's Airpower

Sea-based airpower can be used to establish local sea control by deflecting enemy air or submarine attacks on the fleet; or it is a means of taking strike power to a distant enemy. The Royal Navy had to perform both these functions with insufficient means in the south Atlantic fighting of the Falklands crisis. When the leading elements of the task force set out in April 1982, the flagship *Hermes* was only a short time away from her projected date with the breaker's yard and it had only just been announced that *Invincible* would be sold to the Australians when the second and third of her class, *Illustrious* and *Ark Royal*, became operational in the mid-1980s. The *Hermes* in her long life had been converted from a fleet carrier to a commando carrier to an anti-submarine carrier and finally, in 1980, to a hybrid ASW/VTOL carrier equipped with Sea King helicopters, a 'ski-jump' flight deck and five Sea Harrier vertical-take-off aircraft. The old ship with her pre-sold new sister would have

Fleet Defence in Depth

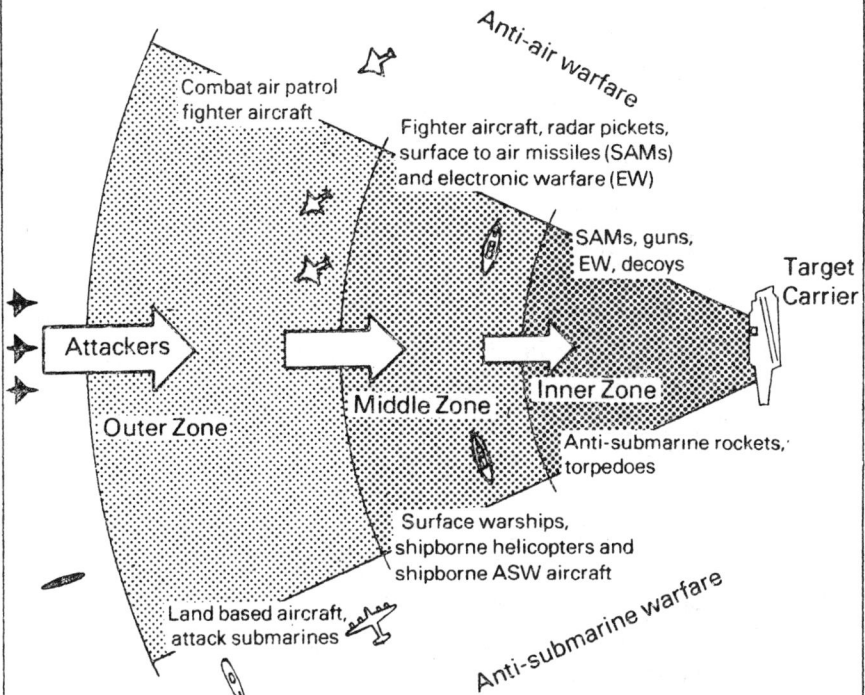

Anti-air warfare

Combat air patrol
fighter aircraft

Fighter aircraft, radar pickets,
surface to air missiles (SAMs)
and electronic warfare (EW)

SAMs, guns,
EW, decoys

Target
Carrier

Attackers

Outer Zone

Middle Zone

Inner Zone

Anti-submarine rockets,
torpedoes

Surface warships,
shipborne helicopters and
shipborne ASW aircraft

Land based aircraft,
attack submarines

Anti-submarine warfare

Anti-air weapons envelope

AEW (Airborne early warning)

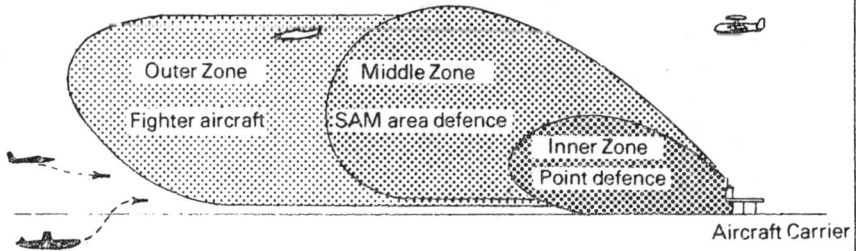

Outer Zone
Fighter aircraft

Middle Zone
SAM area defence

Inner Zone
Point defence

Aircraft Carrier

to fulfil both roles of sea-based airpower – protecting the fleet from air and warship attack and providing air cover for land operations – and do both with an untried and unconventional weapon system, the Sea Harrier.

The Sea Harrier, armed with Sidewinder AIM-9L missiles directed by Ferranti Blue Fox radar, proved itself able to compete and win against aircraft with twice its speed, such as the Argentinian Air Force's Israeli-built Mirage IIIs in air-to-air combat and yet undertake low-level ground attack missions successfully, including repeated attacks on the airfield at Port Stanley.

The *Hermes* was only still operational almost by accident. Delays and political shifts with the *Invincible* programme meant that she was run on and given a refit in 1980 to accommodate the five Sea Harriers and ski-jump. Under political pressure the Royal Navy had abandoned the building of new strike carriers in 1966 and envisaged the demise of fixed-wing flying by 1972. In fact the last of the line, the *Ark Royal*, with the great strike power of her thirty Phantom and Buccaneer aircraft, carried on until 1978. Meanwhile an earlier project for a 'through-deck cruiser' (the strange name was to avoid any embarrassing affinity to 'aircraft carrier') was resurrected to be armed with anti-submarine helicopters and anti-aircraft missiles. Meanwhile the promise of the yet unflown Sea Harrier offered a means of keeping the Navy in the business of fixed-wing flying and, after several changes of policy and demonstration of the advantages in range and payload offered by the new 'ski-jump', the new class of warship was redesigned to accommodate the new vertical-take-off aircraft. The name 'through-deck cruiser' gave way to 'command cruiser' and by the time of the Falklands crisis any vestiges of embarrassment about calling the ship an 'aircraft carrier' had disappeared completely. Indeed, the greatest embarrassment belonged to Defence Minister John Nott who had so recently announced the sale of *Invincible* to the Australians for £175 million.

Sea War Now

This section postulates an attack by cruise-missile submarines against an aircraft carrier at the heart of a composite battle group. Eight high-explosive cruise missiles are estimated to be necessary to sink a *Nimitz* class carrier but one nuclear-tipped missile would be enough. The *Charlie* class carries eight launchers for the SS-N-7 system, an anti-ship cruise missile with a 65 km range. It is launched from underwater, breaks surface, and flies at high subsonic speed under autopilot in the cruise phase, using active radar homing in the terminal attack phase. It is tipped either with a 500 kg high explosive warhead or a 200 kt nuclear weapon.*

The target fleet defends itself by deploying weapons in depth in three distinct zones. In the outer zone, which should extend beyond the maximum range of cruise missiles, friendly aircraft and attack submarines patrol for predators. Fleet air superiority fighters such as Phoenix missile-armed Tomcats fly standing air patrols heading off enemy reconnaissance and watching for maritime strike aircraft, while an early-warning aircraft from the carrier such as the US Navy's Grumman E-2C watches for intruders at long range and directs operations.

In the middle zone, destroyers hunt for submarines with towed array sonars and long-range, passive-hull sonars, and helicopters join in with their sonobuoys and dunking sonars. Carrier-borne ASW aircraft such as the Lockheed S-3A Viking drop sonobuoys and prepare for attack with depth bombs and homing torpedoes.

Informed of enemy dispositions by satellite surveillance and computerized data flow, a group of enemy attack submarines move into the outer zone to launch their cruise missiles against the fleet's high-value targets. While two submarines engage the screening ships, one slips through the net and fires a salvo of eight SS-N-7s from a range of 30 km at the carrier. The missiles break surface and enter the middle defence zone at high subsonic speed. The fleet's Standard, Terrier and Tartar shipboard surface-to-air missiles can tackle medium-intensity missile attacks, but because of radar restriction cannot tackle sea skimmers. And batteries on two or more ships may concentrate

* The Exocet missile that gutted HMS *Sheffield* has a warhead of 165 kg high explosive.

fire on one group of multiple targets, letting the rest leak through.

The target ship and its escorts' electronic countermeasures suites are now taking over, providing early warning, identification and the directional bearings of incoming, radar-guided cruise missiles while computers analyse the information by comparing the 'threat' radar emission with memories of hostile and friendly emitter characteristics. They can automatically put defensive measures into effect, firing the Mk 33 RBOC (rapid bloom off board countermeasures) system which projects a cloud of chaff from an array of mortars (metal strips simulating the ship's radar characteristics) or infra-red decoy flares. The equivalent British Corvus system was used extensively in the Falklands sea-air fighting and the expedient was adopted of flying helicopters stood off from ships, like the cape of a matador, to confuse the terminal seekers of sea-skimming missiles.

US carriers carry the Hughes AN/SLQ-17 Naval Electronic Countermeasures suite which is designed to operate in a very crowded electromagnetic environment, and detect and track up to fifty missiles of different types. It can interpret and track potential launch platforms beyond the ranges at which the missiles lock on to the target and, under attack, it takes an electronic image of the target ship as it is sensed by the threat's guidance radar. It then offsets the radar image so that the weapon guides itself to a false ghost image stood off from the real ship.

Seconds are left for point defence systems to work guns and missiles. Rapid-acceleration Sparrow missiles in eight cell-launchers provide a short-range defence system for US and NATO navies, and the Royal Navy's Seawolf missile, now entering service, can automatically engage sea-skimming missiles attacking at Mach 2 in all weathers and sea states.

Very last-ditch defence on US warships is provided by the Phalanx close-in, multiple-weapon system whose radar tracks both the oncoming cruise missile and its own rotary cannon projectiles, bringing them together in the microseconds left to defend the ship, and this is the system installed on HMS *Illustrious*, the *Invincible*'s brand-new sister-ship.

8 • The Defence of Great Britain

By the beginning of 1982 the Conservative government of Great Britain had persuaded its own parliamentary supporters that its radical new defence policy was correct. The Soviet Union remained the perceived enemy and Trident missiles, to be acquired from the US, would continue the independent nuclear deterrent aimed at Soviet targets. The cost of Trident, however, would eat into the capabilities of the Royal Navy. British conventional forces would concentrate ever more tightly on north-west Europe and its maritime periphery.

Suddenly, in April 1982, Great Britain was at war with Argentina, fighting for South Georgia and the Falkland Islands 8000 miles away in the South Atlantic. A naval task force was put together; a carrier already sold to another navy, a flagship overdue at the scrapyard, car ferries, freezer trawlers, container ships and luxury cruise liners were assembled at high speed and despatched south into the unknown. The Americans called it 'the last nineteenth-century war' and in many ways it was – except for the nuclear submarines, communications satellites and the array of deadly weapons which gave this sub-imperial fleet its very modern strikepower. Britain's stitched-up fleet brought the deep-laid trends of twenty-five years to a juddering halt.

Great Britain acquired an operational capacity with nuclear weapons just after the Suez fiasco of 1956 demonstrated the perils of old-style power projection. The Sandys Defence White Paper of 1957 seized on the mood: it scrapped conscription and a mass army, planned to reduce forces in Germany, foresaw an all-missile air defence and championed the independent nuclear deterrent. Missiles were in and manpower was out.

Subsequent defence planning to 1964 was a retreat from this

position, although the emphasis on nuclear deterrence was increased. It was no longer quite so independent – the Holy Loch agreement of 1960 established a Polaris submarine base under US control in Scotland and the Nassau agreement of 1962 tied the British deterrent into US planning and technical, support and communications systems.

In 1964 the Labour government, who had promised to renegotiate the Nassau agreement, looked at the costs, liked what they saw and showed no real slackening of the nuclear commitment, but began to shed further the periphery of world roles and bases while retaining some home-based forces able to intervene at long range. The Conservative 1970-4 government, although instinctively warmer to imperial echoes, accepted the slimmed-down Labour inheritance without demur. By 1974 the concentration on the defence of the United Kingdom, its maritime approaches and Germany was almost complete. The Royal Navy had all but withdrawn from the Mediterranean and intervention forces had been wound down. There were troops in Ulster, Hong Kong, Belize in Central America, and small garrisons on Gibraltar and the Falklands. Great Britain's commitment to NATO had changed from its being simply one of the options of a global defence posture to being the central rationale; but the country could still find enough for significant air, ground and naval forces, tactical and strategic nuclear forces and continue an ambitious secret plan to modernize the front end of the Polaris missiles in the so-called 'Chevaline' programme.

There was, throughout, a deep-laid consensus on both conventional and nuclear forces because defence was not in the political front line as it had been in the early 1960s and because successive governments were just about able to adjust desired capabilities to available resources – as these dwindled and real unit costs increased, the long shopping list of capabilities could be crossed through one by one. The Falkland Islands had a tiny garrison of sixty marines and it seemed this must surely soon go the same way as other far-flung outposts of empire.

Available resources are set by economic performance, the cost of equipment (and to a lesser extent manpower) and how far a government thinks it can go. The new Conservative government of 1979 certainly had the will. It announced its decision in July

1980 to procure the Trident missile with US agreement, and its commitment to the NATO Long Term Defence Improvement Programme was undiluted. Meanwhile economic performance was sliding just as the cost of weapons was racing ahead of inflation, but now, on a dwindling basis of resources, the old option of shedding peripheral commitments had been used up. The core commitment to NATO itself was under attack and the result was the most radical Defence White Paper since 1957 (again delivered by a Conservative government) and the breakdown of the long political consensus on defence.

The primary reason is money. From 1973 to 1979 British defence budgets were relatively stable, but then they increased by 4.6 per cent in 1979-80 in response to the original NATO commitment to increase real spending by 3 per cent per year. In the past, the three services consumed roughly equal shares reflecting the planners' quest for balanced forces, and the maintenance of the nuclear strategic force in fact consumed less that did the reserve and auxiliary forces (1.5 per cent of total expenditure in 1980). However, the cost of military equipment was all the time rising ahead of inflation. In the breakdown of spending over this period, manpower, spares and research and development went down while equipment inexorably advanced. In the statement on the Defence Estimates published in June 1982, the new thinking of *The Way Forward* was propounded further, in spite of the Falklands crisis. In this document the cost of nuclear strategic forces rises to 2.3 per cent, and equipment overall to 46 per cent (40 per cent in 1980).

The increasing sophistication of modern weapons means that 'defence inflation' is on an escalator of its own and everybody involved in defence procurement tends to adjust to its rapacious logic. Unlike other government departments, nearly half of the Ministry of Defence's budget goes on equipment bought from industrial firms, spending over £3000 million with the top forty companies, and it is in these procurement programmes that spending has soared.

From 1978-9 onwards the MoD has spent well over its original cash limits: £634 million in 1980-1 and over £300 million in 1981-2 – more than the UK's annual hospital building programme. Along with 'defence inflation' (6 to 10 per cent above the national figure, according to the 1982 Defence Estimates) the MoD regularly plans to order more than is covered in its cash limits because of the assumption that equipment will be delivered late. This 'block adjustment' is a defence against the Treasury's restriction against carrying expenditure forward. However, in 1980-1 the spare capacity caused by the recession meant that government orders were suddenly being delivered on time; and along with the equipment, industry tendered its bills, exposing the Ministry's over-budgeting.

Cancellation of contracts also costs money. Since 1974, twenty-nine terminated development contracts have cost £150 million including the MBT-80 Main Battle Tank, the Skyflash II AAM, the Hawkswing helicopter ATGM, GWS-25 Sea Wolf radar, the GWS-31 Sea Dart radar and the naval 1030 Stir radar.

The Sting Ray lightweight anti-submarine torpedo was the heavyweight spending champion while the Chevaline project was clocking up huge cost overruns in secret (£750 million over original budget). The Ministry of Defence commissioned an internal report on overbudgeting and in November 1981 the Commons Public Accounts Committee demanded that changes be made.

Changes had been in the wind for over a year. Francis Pym was moved from the Ministry of Defence in January 1981 to be succeeded by John Nott and within two months the junior defence ministers were instructed to prepare major cost cuts. The procurement of Trident, agreed with the Americans in 1980, was untouchable but, unlike Polaris, it was to be treated as part of the Navy budget. It may have represented no more than $3\frac{1}{2}$ per cent of the *total* budget projected over fifteen years (nearly 20 per cent of the *equipment* budget), but the absolute sum matched the amount required of the Admiralty to come out of its ten-year spending plan – £7.5 billion. The second casualty of the cuts was Navy Minister Keith Speed who resigned in May 1981.

On 25 June Nott delivered the sixth defence review since 1945. It was called *The Way Forward* and was more radical in its implications than any of its predecessors. It set out proposals for a 3 per cent increase in annual defence spending, reaching £13,750 in 1985-6 in spite of zero growth in the overall economy. But underlying this were internal predictions of a much greater inflationary surge in defence costs in the medium and long term. Capabilities would have to match resources but savings would have to come from reshaping regional defence itself – from the strategic deterrent, the naval forces for the protection of the eastern Atlantic, the British Army of the Rhine and RAF Germany on NATO's Central Sector, something would have to give.

The Royal Navy took a body blow. Only two of the *Invincible* class aircraft carriers, the major surface ASW units would be retained (it was announced in early 1982 that *Invincible* would be sold to Australia) and the number of surface escorts would be cut from fifty-six to forty-two by 1985 with a concomitant reduction by four of fleet auxiliaries. The number of Type 42 destroyers was frozen at fourteen with no more major refits. This reduction in the fleet put the Naval dockyards, the British government's biggest industrial enterprise, next in line. The dockyard at Chatham will close in 1984, Gibraltar will go, there will be a 'very deep reduction' in work done at Portsmouth, and five other shore depots will close down.

Increased strike power was to be placed below the water. The number of nuclear-attack submarines was to rise from twelve to seventeen in 1990, armed with the American Sub-Harpoon anti-ship missile and a new, heavy, anti-submarine torpedo for which Marconi won a development contract against the US firm Gould in September 1981. By the time the total is reached, however, HMS *Dreadnought*, *Valiant* and *Warspite* will have reached the end of their hull lives* and, with the one submarine yard, Vickers at Barrow, engaged on Trident, replacements will be impossible. Cammell Laird could reactivate its nuclear berth but only one reactor per year could be supplied. Orders are also to be placed for a new conventionally powered submarine, the Type 2400 which will enter service at the rate of one a year from 1988.

Because the modern air- and submarine-launched-missile threat to surface warships requires composite fleet operations, the surface units of the Royal Navy would have to operate in

---

* At the beginning of 1982 HMS *Dreadnought* was laid up at Chatham. The hull life of a submarine is not determined by age alone but by the number of deep dives the vessel has made.

their war roles under the air umbrella of the US Navy, within the range of shorebased RAF aircraft or in low-threat areas. The lack of such an umbrella including Airborne Early Warning (AEW) was sadly felt in the Falklands fighting. The Royal Navy's primary military tasks are anti-submarine support of the US Strike Fleet in the Atlantic (where the *Invincible* class would operate), the defence of trans-Atlantic shipping (where other surface escorts would operate), submarine search and strike (in areas where the Soviet Navy enjoys superiority, such as the Norwegian sea or the Greenland-Iceland-UK gap, the nuclear-attack submarines would be committed) and shallow-water ASW and mine countermeasures. The Royal Navy is concentrating efforts in this last arena on a new generation of small ASW frigates, the Type 23 using towed array sonars, and a new medium helicopter, the E.101. Point defence for these surface units against anti-ship cruise missiles will be provided by Sea Wolf missiles and the Sea Guard gun system.

The loss of *Invincible* meant that there would only be two squadrons of Sea Harriers, and *Hermes* would go in 1983, but the RAF would gain enhanced maritime strike power with 34 Mk II Nimrods armed with Sting Ray ASW torpedos and Buccaneers and eventually Tornados would be armed with the new Sea Eagle air launched anti-ship missile.

Rhine Army was to be restructured to change the British Corps from four to three divisions made up of nine brigades with one brigade stationed in Britain although linked to the Corps order of battle. 55,000 troops will continue to guard 65 km of NATO's Central Sector eventually equipped with more Milan missiles, more Improved Blowpipe man-portable SAMs, Tracked Rapier SAMs and 240 Challenger tanks, enough to equip four armoured regiments plus re-engineered Chieftains.

A replacement for the RAF's Jaguar strike trainer was dropped although procurement would continue of 33 Boeing Vertol Chinook heavy lift helicopters and 60 AV-8Bs advanced Harriers jointly built by McDonnell-Douglas and BAe.

Tornado

Half the RAF's entire annual equipment budget is taken up by the Tornado programme. The Tornado, jointly built with West Germany and Italy, is a tandem two-seat multi-role combat aircraft designed originally to fulfil six principal roles with one single airframe. The RAF developed a requirement for a more specialized air defence variant (ADV) with advanced avionics and cannon and missile armament. The GR Mk 1 is the RAF designation for the interdictor strike version and the ADV is called the Tornado F Mk 2.

Britain is buying 385 Tornados, 220 GR Mk 1s and 165 F Mk 2s in a £10 billion programme phased over twelve years. A plan to change the ratio from 200 to 185 in order to strengthen Britain's fragile air defences was abandoned at the end of 1981 because each F Mk 2 is about £3 million dearer. Meanwhile air defence would hang on five Phantom and two Lightning squadrons with two Phantom squadrons to be retained instead of being replaced by Tornado F Mk 2s. Hawk trainers with missile armament VC-10 tankers, and the UKAGDE (United Kingdom Air Ground Defence Environment) improvement programme will provide support. Meanwhile the Vulcan force which the Tornado GR Mk 1s will replace began its phased run-down at the end of 1981, but when a West German initiative to slow down deliveries by 25 per cent was made at the same time it met a UK Treasury cost-cutting exercise coming the other way. The result was an extension in the Tornado delivery programme to 1988.

Training also suffered. The RAF is given a 'fuel year' allocation beginning on 1 March which has fallen in real terms since 1977. It costs £6000 per hour to fly a Phantom so the rate of cash consumption is obvious. Training in RAF Germany has apparently fallen to a level which is having an effect on operational efficiency and the number of hours actually flown is kept secret.

Trident

The Way Forward considered very little sacred except the modernization of the strategic deterrent. In 1982 Britain's long-range nuclear force consists of four *Resolution*-class SSBNs launched between 1967 and 1968, each armed with sixteen

Polaris A-3 missiles tipped with three RVs (re-entry vehicle) with a yield of 200 KT each. As with the US Navy's Polaris boats, two crews are assigned to each *Resolution* to assure maximum seatime with Port and Starboard crews (13 officers and 130 men) exchanging at the end of a three-month patrol.

After a final series of test launches off Florida and underground tests in Nevada, the Chevaline Polaris front-end improvement programme will phase in a new warhead from 1982 onwards with a new penetration-aid-equipped, manoeuvrable, post-boost vehicle able to disperse six 40 KT-yield RVs over impact points spanning 70 km. The Polaris missiles themselves are being re-motored and the submarines equipped with new navigation and fire-control equipment to sustain their effectiveness through to 1990.

In July 1980 it was announced that the British government intended to acquire from the United States a replacement system, the Trident SLBM, then beginning to enter service with the US Navy complete with its MIRV system but fitted with British warheads. The capital cost of a four-boat force with sixteen missiles each was estimated at £5000 million at 1980 prices, spread over fifteen years and broken down as 12 per cent for a hundred missiles bought 'off the shelf' from Lockheed, 30 per cent as submarines, built in British yards with British reactors and propulsion but incorporating US fire control, weapons systems including tactical self-defence weapons accounted for 16 per cent, shore facilities 12 per cent, and warhead design and construction 30 per cent. Of the total, 70 per cent would be spent in the UK.

In September 1981 President Reagan suddenly speeded things up when he announced the administration's intention to procure to all intents a completely new missile for the US SSBN fleet, the Trident D-5, then in the early stages of development by Lockheed's missile division. The D-5 will have great range and power: 11,000 km (6000 miles) carrying fourteen RVs with 150 KT-yield warheads each and a CEP (circular error probability) of only 120 m. The US Navy has also developed the Mk 500 MARV (manoeuvrable re-entry vehicle) for eventual deployment on the missile.

With the C-4 production line now due to be shut down in the mid-1980s and supplanted by the D-5, the British government

felt it had to switch. This would not be Nassau rewritten –
Polaris was then acquired at bargain rates – but a cripplingly
expensive capital-spending programme in real prices which the
shift in the dollar-sterling exchange rate from 1980 did not help.
The £500 million price tag had leapt to over £7000 million by
the D-5 decision alone, the submarines costing an estimated
£500 million more.

There is a twist. Because D-5 comes later, so will the bill, and
'only' £300 million will have been spent by the latest date for the
next general election in May-June 1984.

Meanwhile a cosmetic attempt has been made to engage
British firms on the project (although some feel they would do
much better to bid direct with Lockheed rather than work
through the proposed project liaison office). Testing of the
warheads started in early 1982 at the Atomic Weapons Research
Establishment at Aldermaston. These warheads are similar to
those which would have been carried on the C-4, and the plans
are to tip the D-5 with eight, not the fourteen it is capable of
carrying.

Work is also well advanced at the RN's Director General
(Ships) Department at Bath on the design of the four 14,680-ton
displacement SSBNs which will each be smaller than the US
Navy's *Ohio* class but twice the displacement of the *Resolution*
class. The diameter of the missile compartment will have to be
similar to the *Ohio*'s to accommodate the larger D-5.

Plans have also been laid for the extension of the RN
Armament Depot at Coulport on Loch Long, Scotland, where
the Polaris missiles are stored. A new nine-mile road will be built
and the site massively expanded from 300 to 2600 acres to run
Polaris and Trident in tandem. The whole facility is due to be
ready by 1989-90 and it is envisaged that RNAD Coulport and
the submarine base itself at Faslane will employ a total of 5500
uniformed and civilian staff.

Both Coulport and Faslane are far up a river approach which
would be very vulnerable to mining. At a time of tension some
say extensive British mine countermeasures forces would be
required to ensure that there was no threat from mines both to
the RN bases and to the US submarines and their depot ship
farther down the Clyde at Holy Loch, even though these sea
lochs are very deep.

What is Trident for? In military terms it delivers to its targeters many more warheads with much greater accuracy than the Polaris system it will replace – four submarines with sixteen Polaris with three RVs each (two SSBNs on patrol at any one time) becomes four submarines with sixteen Trident D-5s with eight RVs each. Two submarines therefore could deliver more than 250 highly accurate counterforce-capable warheads. The D-5's range extends the patrol area (and thus places to hide) of nuclear submarines into the Indian Ocean and South Atlantic and will still be capable of hitting the Soviet Union. Thus Trident increases 'survivability', its advanced re-entry vehicles will counter predicted development in Soviet anti-ballistic missile technology and it also delivers a silo-busting first-strike capability (on a limited scale) to the British centre of decision.

In political terms, Trident is to continue Britain's nuclear deterrent into the twenty-first century with the Soviet Union as the perceived enemy. Linking Trident to British jobs is a political expedient. However, after announcing the decision to procure the D-5, Defence Secretary John Nott announced a different rationale – that Trident was an insurance policy against NATO's breaking up, not exclusively a military contribution to its firepower. 'In the last resort we are an island, a sovereign state, and we must ultimately be responsible for our own defence, and it must be under the Prime Minister's control,' said Nott.

The Nassau agreement stated that 'British forces [the Polaris force] will be used for the purposes of international defence of the Western Alliance in all circumstances.' However Harold Macmillan ensured the insertion of the vital rider, 'except where Her Majesty's government may decide that supreme national interests are at stake.'

A decision to launch Polaris could only be made by the British Prime Minister, with the participation of at least one member of the Chiefs of Staff; and a senior civil servant and military officer are always accessible with the necessary codes. Each boat carries a selection of target tapes which are chosen and inserted on direction from London. If an order to launch came, the missile would take fifteen minutes to launch, two senior officers 'voting' by double-key to fire the missile. The boat can launch on its own but its captain and his launch officers can only consider this when they have reason to believe from monitoring communications that the British command centre has been devastated.

Now this highly complex exercise in long-range communications, command and control requires a global net to make it work. Only integration with US deterrent planning provides this – British weapons are assigned to their targets within the US Single Integrated Operational Plan (SIOP), drawn up at Strategic Air Command's HQ at Offutt AFB, Nebraska, by the Joint Strategic Targeting Planning Staff in conjunction with a five-strong British liaison team. This plan is kept updated by intelligence from US reconnaissance satellites.

The only way at present of communicating with submerged submarines is by very low- or extremely low-frequency transmitters (the US Navy is working on a satellite-borne laser system). The British VLF transmitter is at Rugby, the station in Canada may no longer be available nor is Simonstown, South Africa. The US satellite and shore communications net is therefore a vital component of Britain's seaborne deterrent and the operation of its naval forces, as the Falklands crisis demonstrated when operational orders were routed through US bases on Ascension Island and via US Navy Fleet communications satellites.

Trident D-5 is a high-technology programme early on in its development-life with all the ups and downs that that implies; and there are no guarantees that the British warhead development programme will come any closer to budget than did Chevaline. Britain will not have an operational Trident force until the mid-1990s. In the period until then, reliance will be on unbroken US commitment and technical co-operation will be conducted through the US contractor's liaison office.

The technology, the targeting information and the necessary communications techniques are not, therefore, the ultimate responsibility of a single sovereign state. Trident delivers a great deal more destructive power into the hands of Britain's leaders but in no sense can it be regarded as entirely within their competence, nor can it be if serious strategic arms negotiations get anywhere. What Trident and the coming of cruise missiles (which will be under US control although based in Britain) have done politically is to emphasize that British unilateral disarmament is not the true issue. It is the country's role as the forward base of US nuclear systems and as the surrogate operator of US strategic systems which matters.

Trident has broken the long political consensus on defence. The Labour Party is committed to immediate cancellation; the SDP-Alliance has said the same thing although not so clearly. Its opponents say it could break the Anglo-US military axis and when, rather than if, it is cancelled, leave the country shorn of conventional weapons programmes. Within the Conservative Party John Nott has had to fight hard to persuade such doubters that the inevitable deterioration of conventional capabilities in Europe and at sea was worth fixing Moscow with a glassy nuclear stare until the year 2020.

Part Two
Total War

9 • The Doomsday Web

Nuclear fission is the splitting of the nuclei of heavy atoms such as Uranium. Nuclear fusion is the combination of light atoms such as those of hydrogen isotopes. In both processes part of the mass of these elements is converted into energy. The old atomic bomb relied on fission for its power, the thermonuclear bomb perfected in the early 1950s works by fusion.

To trigger a fission reaction it is necessary to put together a mass of the U235 isotope of uranium or the P239 isotope of plutonium large enough to ensure that high-energy neutron particles in the material do not escape from the surface of the mass but strike other atoms within the material, causing them in turn to release more neutrons and set up a chain reaction of ever-increasing intensity. This is called the critical mass and is understood to be around 25 lb of Plutonium 239 and 100 lb of Uranium 235.

This mass has to be held together against its own disruptive forces for the chain reaction to take place. The first atom-bombs fired slugs of uranium into each other using high explosive and this was supplanted by a system in which a hollow sphere of fissile material is compacted together into a supercritical mass by a surrounding layer of high-explosive 'lenses'.

Only a fission reaction can generate the very high energies and temperatures of 80 million°C required to trigger the fusion reaction of the deuterium and tritium isotopes of Hydrogen into Helium. High-energy lasers which could produce an alternative means of triggering are under high-priority and highly secret research.

Tritium can only be kept stable at a few degrees above absolute zero. To create workable fusion munitions US and Soviet weapon scientists devised the same solution, a fission trigger surrounded by an envelope of Lithium 6 which is

1 MT airburst at 6500 feet

1.8 seconds after detonation

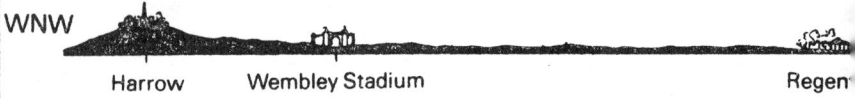

WNW

Harrow   Wembley Stadium

Regen

11 seconds after detonation

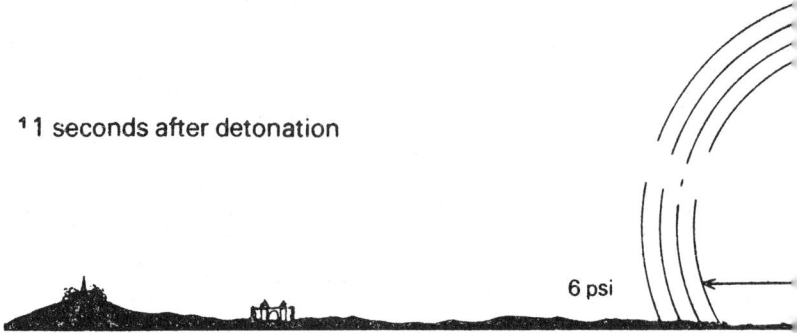

6 psi

37 seconds after detonation

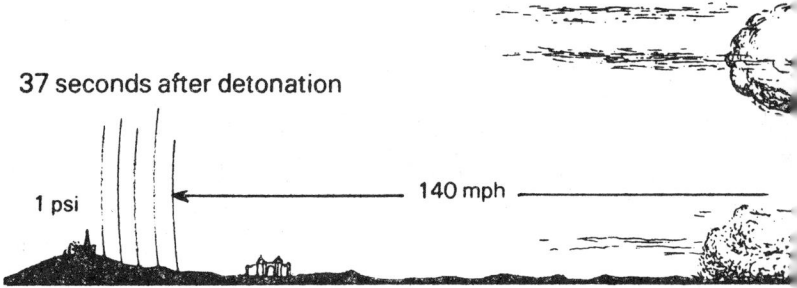

1 psi   ← 140 mph ———————

110 seconds after detonation

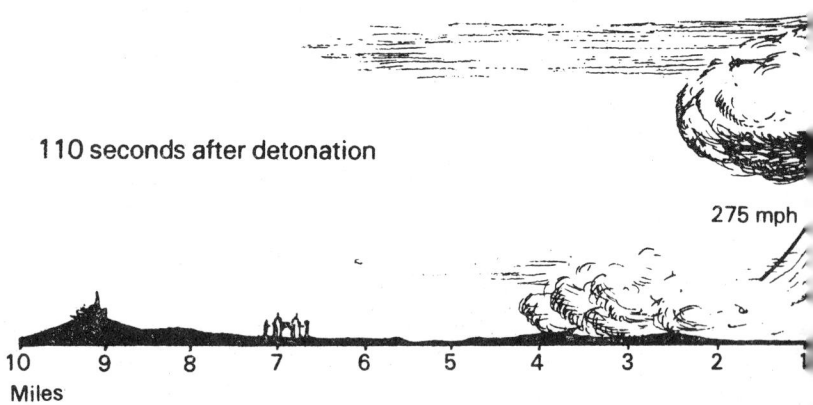

275 mph

10   9   8   7   6   5   4   3   2   1
Miles

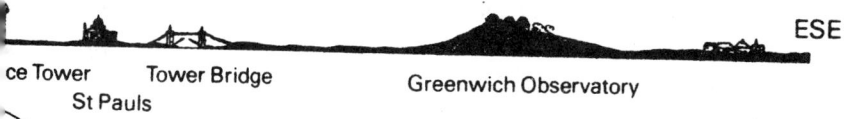

ce Tower   Tower Bridge   ESE
St Pauls   Greenwich Observatory

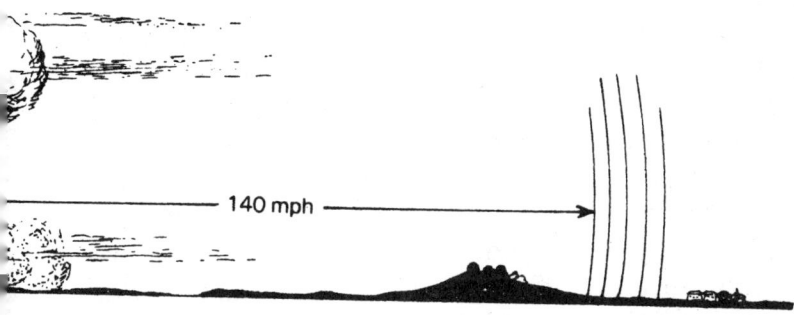

140 mph

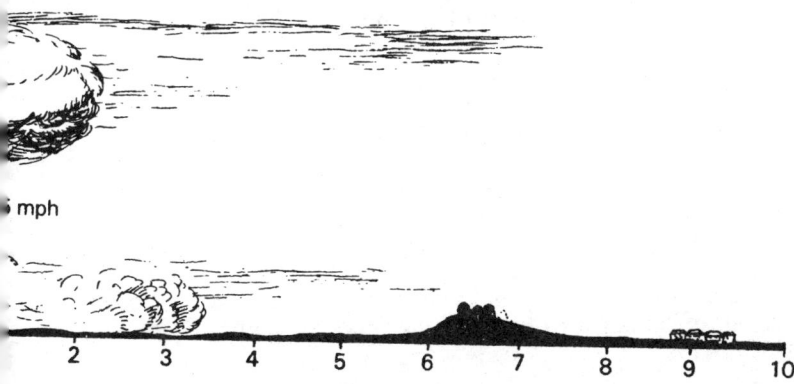

mph

2   3   4   5   6   7   8   9   10

converted into tritium by the fission reaction's neutron bombardment. The very powerful thermonuclear explosion is the result.

The effective destructive power of nuclear weapons is a function of accuracy of delivery, energy yield and reliability. Their energy yield is expressed as the equivalent weight of trinitrotoluene (TNT) that would have to be exploded in one place to create the same effects. The smallest nuclear weapon in the US arsenal is the W-54 special atomic demolition munition with 0.1 KT (100 tons of TNT) yield. The biggest is the B-53 heavy bomb with a yield of a 9 MT (9 million tons of TNT). A device tested in the atmosphere by the Soviet Union in 1963 yielded 58 megatons. A 1 MT warhead does not have destructive effects a thousand times greater than a single kiloton – the area of destruction increases by the cube root of the yield – thus many small weapons spread their effects over a wider area than a single very large weapon.

The immediate effects of a nuclear explosion are blast, heat, radiation and an electromagnetic pulse. 50 per cent of the total energy is released as blast, 35 per cent as heat, 5 per cent as prompt radiation and 10 per cent as long-term residual radiation.

The heat flash comes first. A one-megaton burst releases an initial pulse carrying 1 per cent of the total thermal energy. Two seconds later comes a ten-second pulse containing a third of the weapon's total power which will cause a disabling, second-degree burn at 14 km from ground zero, and burn out the retinas of anyone unfortunate enough to glance at the fireball at 25 km. Heat is not very effective against dispersed armoured forces, nor against hard targets. It is apocalyptic when used against cities, flashing conflagrations that could join into a firestorm that would rage for eight hours at 800°C, dry-roasting and asphyxiating human beings in underground shelters, however deep.*

---

* Whether or not a nuclear burst would start a firestorm is conjectural. The RAF Bomber Command-ignited firestorms of the Second World War such as Hamburg depended on a combination of climatic conditions and the use of blast bombs *first* exposing wooden structures and interiors of buildings upon which were rained thermite incendiaries acting at 5000°C for up to ten minutes. Five out of six failed to set anything properly alight. There was no firestorm at Nagasaki.

Blast comes next at supersonic speed following the pulse of heat. The blast wave carries half the weapon's total energy and, in an airburst, extends in two spheres from the point of detonation and in an echo from the ground reflection, which merge a little over a mile out. A one-megaton explosion will induce overpressure of 50 psi half a mile from ground zero. After eleven seconds the thermal pulse is past but the blast shock front is still travelling out now 5.1 km from ground zero at 6 psi accompanied by 160 mph winds whipping up fragments of brick and glass and propelling them with all the lethal effects of a cluster bomb. A surface wave of 1 MT will slightly reduce the remote-blast damage from the reflected wave but will gouge out a crater in dry earth 400 m wide and 43 m deep.

The fission contribution to the yield (the atom bomb component of a thermonuclear weapon) and the height at which the explosion takes place determine the level of its immediate radiation effects and subsequent fallout.

Fallout

Fallout is the name for residual radiation emitted from fission products and radioactive debris precipitated after the immediate effects of the explosion have passed. With bombs of one megaton and upwards the area of prompt radiation is the same as those affected by blast and fire – people in the way will be killed three times over. As bombs get smaller, the proportion of radiation to blast and heat gets bigger – this is the principle of the enhanced-radiation neutron bomb designed to irradiate lethally a tank interior through twelve inches of armour plate. When the power is so small that lethal radiation outdistances the area of lethal blast, then the affected area is down to under a mile in radius.

A one-megaton burst pushes out a lethal 1000 REM (roentgen-equivalent-man) dose of gamma rays and neutrons to 1.8 miles, falling off rapidly to 100 REM at 2.2 miles. Meanwhile, as the fireball rises, the 'prompt' radiation at ground level falls to zero, but as the cloud cools, the stable isotopes formed after the fission of the Uranium 235 core begin to form. In a ground burst they condense on dust or earth particles and fall to the ground relatively quickly, localizing the radioactive fallout contaminated area. If released from an airburst, they condense as minute droplets and are carried into the upper atmosphere, to fall to earth eventually in cigar-shaped plumes formed according to the prevailing winds and weather conditions.

The very finest particles are carried up high into the atmosphere. Those that enter the troposphere travel round the world in about twelve days and stay mainly in the same hemisphere. Stratospheric particles may stay aloft for several years.

The radioactive isotopes produced by an explosion have varying half-lives (the time required for the decay of half the radioactivity). The radiation dose from fallout decays at $T^{-1.2}$ where T is time. This means that the intensity of radiation after a nuclear explosion will decline by ten for every sevenfold increase in time.

Following a one-megaton ground burst with a wind of 15 mph, the cigar-shaped fallout plume containing enough precipitation to expose an unprotected individual to a cumulative dose of 300 roentgens in the first seven days will be 150 miles long, 20 miles wide and contoured in intensity according to proximity to the explosion or affected by local hot spots caused by rain.

A dose of 450–500 rads (100 ergs of energy absorbed by 1 gram of the human body and roughly equivalent to one roentgen) is enough to kill half of those exposed to it. Whatever the kind of radiation – X rays, gamma rays, alpha or beta particles or neutrons – the injury to biological tissue is produced by electrons already in the tissue absorbing energy from the incoming radiation. The consequences for the individual cells depend on the actual energy received by the cell's sensitive components, the nucleus and the genetic material – the chromosomes and genes. The tissues most sensitive to radiation are lymphoid tissue, bone marrow, spleen, male testes and gastrointestinal tract. The higher the dose, the greater is the damage; but if the exposure is spread over weeks or more the body can tolerate higher doses because cellular recovery is taking place even while irradiation continues. Animals will be similarly affected and the ability of crop seeds to germinate may be destroyed. Crops grown on contaminated soil will accumulate the longer lived isotopes such as Strontium-90 and Caesium-37 which also build up in the teeth and bones.

The hostage cities can be crushed by nuclear weapons like a doll's-house under a giant's foot, and unprotected survivors of the initial blast and flash caught in the footprint of fallout will die of radiation sickness.

The Soviets intend to evacuate their cities and put their government machine underground. The Carter government had such a scheme, the 'Crisis Relocation Plan', but after the painful experience of Three Mile Island in April 1979 when officials were faced with moving 630,000 people downwind from a malfunctioning nuclear power plant proposals to use private cars to evacuate threatened cities looked highly questionable. The Swiss intend to have a blast-and-radiation-proof shelter for everyone in the country by the end of the century. The British have built a shelter system for central and local government officials – for everyone from the Sovereign to chief librarians who will act as guardians of culture. The urban population is instructed to stay where it is and hide under the stairs.

Electromagnetic Pulse

The electromagnetic pulse (EMP) of a nuclear detonation spans the period of the prompt gamma and neutron radiation and covers a frequency spectrum up to several hundred megahertz, inducing very high currents and voltages in cables and metal structures. Power lines, telephone cables, TV and radio, computers, anything connected to a power line or antenna, in fact, would be burnt out and give a severe shock to anyone in contact with such a collector. The area effected by EMP varies with the height of the burst. A one-megaton surface burst would produce an intense pulse above ground zero and out to the 2 psi zone. However, an air burst high in the atmosphere could disrupt telecommunications and destroy data-handling computer facilities over a huge area a thousand miles or more in radius. The implications for command and control facilities and their ability to manage a 'limited' nuclear war are clear. NATO has embarked on a massive 'shelterized' communications system and the US is doing the same for its strategic and tactical forces, making large-scale use of EMP-resistant fibre optics.

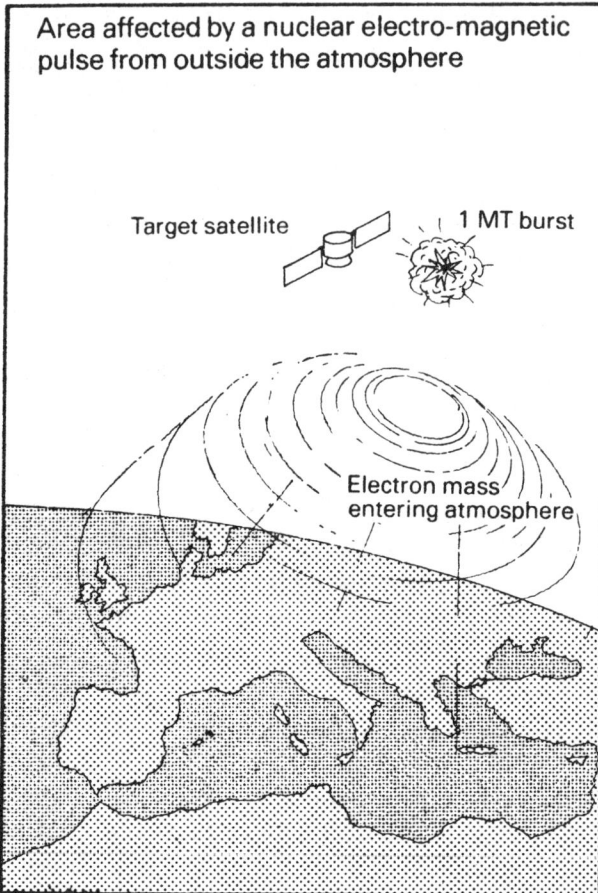

Area affected by a nuclear electro-magnetic pulse from outside the atmosphere

Target satellite   1 MT burst

Electron mass entering atmosphere

Counterforce

'Trashing' cities is what Mutual Assured Destruction was all about and, as will be seen from the next chapter covering the development of nuclear strategy, was the policy of the United States for a long time and is still the only option open to the comparatively small British retaliatory Polaris force.

In the 1970s, however, new technologies opened up for the USA and the Soviet Union an alternative to the city-busting strategy. The technological change was in the accuracy of delivery systems, and the new alternative was called 'counterforce'. 'Counterforce' is a new coining for an old military intention. It means attacking the weapons of your opponent, not his social structure. When the Luftwaffe attacked the airfields of Fighter Command in summer 1940 they were waging counterforce war, trying to destroy the RAF in combat or on the ground so that a seaborne invasion would be unopposed from the air. When they switched to 'countervalue' attacks on British cities they lost the battle. Counterforce targeting policy poses a difficult moral dilemma as in nuclear terms the logic can only really apply to a first strike. A Soviet attack on the United States would invite response by the surviving US 'counterforce' weapons on empty silos and deserted bomber bases. The policy further shakes the structure of nuclear deterrence, as we shall see, as it opens up 'war fighting strategies' with winners and losers.

The accuracy of a weapon is measured in terms of the radius of a target-centred circle within which half the warheads from such a delivery system are likely to fall and is called the Circular Error Probable (CEP). If the guidance system of a V-2 had been placed on a missile with intercontinental range, the CEP would have been more than fifty miles. The General Electric Mk 12A warhead employing the NS-20 guidance system on the MX missile is designed to have a CEP of .05 nm.

All missiles have a launch point and a point of impact. An ICBM is a small space rocket – it uses enormous amounts of chemical energy in the early stages of flight (the boost stage) to propel its payload into the required ballistic trajectory like the shell from a gun. In a MIRV missile the payload is a post-boost vehicle (PBV), a small spacecraft with its own guidance and motors with which to make course corrections. The PBV (or 'bus') carries the individual re-entry vehicles (RVs) and releases them to fall in the required pattern or 'footprint'. It is a matter of mathematics to devise a trajectory and powered adjustments to the flightpath to reach that target with precision over whatever range. The basis of missile guidance is inertial navigation, an assembly of very accurate gyroscopes which stabilize a gimballed set of very accurate devices measuring acceleration. An integrated clock gives a continuous reading of velocity and a second time integration gives a readout of present position relative to that at the start.

That system can be further refined. The Trident II can employ stellar-inertial navigation which takes mid-flight star shots which are compared with a map held in its computer memory to correct course deviations (integrating at launch with the submarine's own navigation and launch-position-fixing system). The US satellite Global Positioning System will provide an artificial celestial reference point with the accuracy of an atomic clock for further mid-term reference. The air launched cruise missile takes the technology even further – the inertial guidance system (which drifts off course by 900 m per hour) is updated by a terrain contour mapping system and its onboard computer. Up to thirty maps of areas en route to the target can be stored, and these are selected and compared with results from the missile's ground-scanning radar altimeter. At the target itself Scene Matching Area Correlation compares received images of the target with previously programmed information and last-minute adjustments are made. Circular error probability over any range is estimated at 100 m and could be as low as 30 m. These super accuracies are dependent on the precision-mapping that reconnaissance satellites have brought about.

Reliability is the next factor, as might be expected with all this precision equipment being hurled around at huge accelerations. Modern Soviet reliabilities are rated at 80 per cent and US a little better. Thus missiles can fly between continents, land with great precision and generate crushing devastation. In short, they can be aimed not just at the cities of an enemy or hit the sprawling economic infrastructure – they can attack the rival ICBMs in their silos.

Minuteman silos are hardened up to 2500 pounds per square inch (the amount of pressure needed to destroy them). Brick houses explode outwards at 5-10 psi. Submarines (because they operate at ocean depths) are resistant to about 1000 psi although the violent shaking associated with underwater bursts would fracture internal systems. The SALT agreement prohibited size increases in silos in excess of 32 per cent. Pentagon studies on boosting silo protection to 5000 psi showed a necessary increase in dimensions of four times. Thus it is possible, given the CEP, the overpressure yield at impact, the reliability factor and the estimated 'hardness of the target', swiftly to calculate the amount of force necessary to smash the enemy's fixed-site weapons (their positions known and precision-mapped by satellite). More than one missile would be necessary per target, although this introduces the problem of 'fractricide' when the blast, heat and electromagnetic pulse of the initial explosions divert other missiles in the salvo. (This is what the window of vulnerability [see page 177] protagonists in the United States were so alarmed about and why the way the MX missile will be based and not what it is intended to do at the other end is such a big political issue in the United States.)

Two short-term solutions were advocated: launch on warning (LOW) and launch under attack (LUA). The first depends on enough early warning – and the ability of computers to predict impact points – to get the ICBMs out of their silos before they are destroyed – to 'use 'em or lose 'em', as the USAF coyly put it. At best they would have thirty minutes. Launch under attack is self-explanatory. There were further proposals to build in a command disarm link into ICBMs (which, once launched, fly irrevocably to their targets) to add to the decision-making time. LUA and LOW lead to a combination of hair-trigger reflexes and all-out retaliation based on the virtual electronic roulette of early-warning and command-and-control systems all working properly and must be highly vulnerable to accidental triggering (see chapter 15 for a table of nuclear accidents).

Because of its second-strike constraints, US nuclear forces must be on a higher level of readiness and alert than their Soviet counterparts. The US cannot choose when they fire their missiles; they must come under attack first. The Soviet ICBM alert rate is lower than the US's 98 per cent, and slightly more than 10 per cent of their older SSBNs are at sea although the proportion is slightly higher for the *Yankee*-class, and long-range aviation bombers are not on constant alert. Fifty per cent of US Navy SSBNs should be on patrol at any one time, averaging sixty days on patrol and thirty days in port. Transit time to patrol area is between two and ten days.

Ballistic missile submarines (which will be joined in the mid-1980s by patrol submarines carrying land-attack, sea-launched cruise missiles) offer the highest rate of survivability because they hide in the oceans of the world – hence anti-submarine warfare is a very important component of strategic defence.

Nuclear submarines are designed to run deep, run quiet and come to the surface as infrequently as possible. Their navigation systems therefore are very much like those of a missile's, with inertial reference updated by stellar or satellite positioning. Communication is the problem – the US Navy relies on satellites, shore transmitters and an airborne system called TACAMO ('take charge and move out') mounted on twelve EC-130Q aircraft trailing wire antennae five miles long to make emergency communications with submarines up to thirty feet below the surface via VLF (very low frequency) radio. A proposal to built an ELF (extremely low frequency) transmitter 158 miles long is under investigation. It could make one-way communications with deeply submerged submarines even under the polar ice cap. It would, however, take fifteen or more minutes to transmit a three-letter message – 'not a system for sending ball scores to submarine crews,' one official said in 1979. In June 1981 Admiral Powell Carter, communications director of US Navy strategic and theatre nuclear warfare, revealed that there is no 'voting' system for launches in the US SSBN fleet as there is with bomber and missile silo crews who need coded correlations from outside sources to remove interlocks. In certain circumstances each of the thirty-nine submarine commanders can arm and fire his weapons without coded instructions from the national command authority – even though such a launch would require the co-operation of practically the entire crew.

Command and Control

Overall control of the United States armed forces is vested in the National Command Authority (NCA). In the event of the incapacity or inaccessibility of the President, the authority to order the launch of nuclear weapons can reportedly pass through a chain from President to Vice-President to Defence Secretary to Deputy Defence Secretary to Chairman of the Joint Chiefs of Staff. When President Reagan was shot in March 1981 his coded war card in the so-called 'football', designed for use during an emergency when the President would be without secure voice communications, was 'lost' for two days. Vice-President Bush was aboard an air force jet without full C³ facilities so the nuclear mantle passed to Secretary of Defence Weinberger (in spite of

Secretary of State Haig's insistence on television that he was in charge) who raised the readiness of the US forces from condition five to RedCon four on the five-point scale of readiness conditions.

The NCA works through the National Military Command System (NMCS) which consists in turn of a National Military Command Centre and Alternate National Military Command Centre plus the National Emergency Airborne Command Post, a fleet of six Boeing E-4B aircraft operated by SAC, interlocked by a complex network of telecommunications, data processing and satellite systems. Every operational order for US forces round the world travels via the thirty plus computer complexes and communication nodes of the World Wide Military Command and Control System. Within the WWMCCS is the core Minimum Essential Emergency Communications Network generating signals on the entire spectrum of radio frequencies in an effort to ensure that C^3 messages reach strategic bomber, missile and SSBN forces. MEECN patches into the USAF's AFSATCOM communications satellite system, the Defence Satellite Communications system and the US Navy's Fleet Satellite Communications (FLTSATCOM). A very large investment is going into the short- and long-term development of these systems. At RedCon two the National Command Authority gets up in the Airborne National Command Post or goes underground in the Blue Ridge Hill bunker. SAC's battle staff is already aloft and in touch with the EC-135s of the Airborne Launch Command System, able to re-target and fire 200 Minutemen from the air. NORAD (North American Aerospace Defence Command) is buttoned up under 1000 m of rock in Cheyenne Mountain. Inside the Presidential E-4B there are six compartments, the NCA suite, conference room, briefing room, battle staff work area, communications control centre and rest area, and the aircraft is hardened against thermal flash and the effects of the electromagnetic pulse. Communications equipment includes a super-high-frequency antenna in a dorsal bulge stabilized to keep it aligned with a MEECN communications satellite. A five-mile-long trailing antenna generates communications with submarines on extremely low frequencies.

The ABNCP programme is designed to enable the US to execute its Single Integrated Operational Plan (the SIOP), drawn up by the Joint Strategic Target Planning Staff even if an enemy attack has sundered ordinary communication nets and destroyed command centres. The whole thing is designed to retain a fine touch on the controls yet ensure the inevitability of a response. Thus beneath the Pentagon facing the 'Big Board' is at all times a one- or two-star General on a six-hour watch, sitting in the so-called 'cat-bird seat'. He can order SAC into the air and put ICBMs on alert and send SAC to their 'positive control' or first recall line. The man in the cat-bird seat communicates with the airborne control aircraft called Looking Glass which can stay aloft for up to 100 hours. An important point is this – after a first strike some military men think the politicians of Congress would surrender. A one-star air force General would not.

A proportion of the Minuteman force carry 'Universal Attack Order' communications satellites which beam out launch orders for all-out attack once committed. Further, the fear of 'decapitation', of knocking out the decision-making brain and leaving the massively armed limbs inanimate, is the background to long-term fundamental research into producing a computer system placed in orbit which can implement the SIOP.

The granting of the global power of life and death to an artificial intelligence in space may be man making god in his own image but it is only a technical refinement of current preoccupations. Immense resources of talent and treasure have spun this terribly clever web round the world. The story of how we got here may provide some clues as to how it might be disentangled.

10 • A Brief History of Nuclear Strategy

(Dates of treaties, the introduction of weapon systems and related events are given in the Chronology.)

When in the autumn of 1981 General Alexander Haig revealed before Congressional hearings that NATO had plans to fire a nuclear 'warning shot' in the early stages of a war in Europe, the US Secretary of State was dipping into the locker containing the thousands of 'resolutions', 'gameplans' and 'scenarios' devised by defence planners since the advent of nuclear weapons. According to Defence Secretary Caspar Weinberger, Haig was citing a leftover from the 1960s and not an operational plan. According to other sources, Haig the ex-Supreme Allied Commander knew just what the Joint Chiefs had up their sleeves whereas Weinberger the civilian did not.

Nuclear strategy is neither fixed immobile nor is it amenable to short-term political initiatives, but nuclear weapons have an unusual characteristic. Fissionable material once manufactured stays with you. The pressures within the military system to apply this material to more and more systems are strong – strategic, tactical, anti-submarine, air defence and so on. More and more requirements are generated and the availability of new weapons and delivery capabilities strongly influences doctrinal decisions – not the other way round.

The blast, fire and radiation of a nuclear weapon are as deadly to life and life-supporting endeavours whether they are released from a bomb dropped from an aircraft or arrive by sea-launched cruise missile. What does change is the means of delivery and the counter to those means. The technology of nuclear delivery systems and defence against them has been one of the biggest engines of scientific research in the Soviet Union and the West since the beginning of the nuclear age, and it has taken concomitant political, economic and industrial will to keep those programmes in the highest state of funding and activity. For a democracy the enormous capital cost and ever-lengthening development leadtimes of effective delivery systems – which can span the lives of several governments – put their procurement and funding at the very forefront of peacetime policy making, or, as in the case of Britain's secret Chevaline Polaris-improvement programme, remove them from the democratic process altogether.

This dialogue between capability and policy does not yet even include the perceived intentions of any opponent. President Carter's Secretary of Defence, Harold Brown, expressed it thus: 'Whether strategy or technology comes first is debatable...yet, if we examine how our strategy got to be where it is, clearly technology had a big part in getting us there...it is easier to produce military hardware than it is to know what policy to follow.'

The problem is that new hardware may open up a range of possibilities unperceived by the policy that sought their acquisition. Because technology can deliver a sophisticated new capability such as multiple warheads, ballistic missile defence or radar-evading 'stealth' bombers, it can and has given strategic advantages which, rather than 'increasing' the security of the possessor, can become destabilizing incentives for attack – or alternatively to bargain.

So far bargaining has been the result, not general war. Because of thirty-five years of constancy in the fundamental relations of the nuclear superpowers, the basis for armed ideologies to confront each other with weapons of mass destruction, the political framework by which each other's cities are constantly threatened with annihilation, has been taken for granted. Thus the story of military nuclear strategy compressed into this chapter and its accompanying chronology is one of tunnel-vision concern for the minutiae of military technology. It is a depressing story.

The Age of Assured US Ascendancy, 1945-60

In spite of the explosion of a Soviet atom bomb in 1949 and the Russian development of thermonuclear weapons in the 1950s, for fifteen years from 1945 to 1960 the United States enjoyed a period of unchallengeable military superiority. At this happy time's zenith in the mid-1950s, the Eisenhower administration defined the 'New Look' in strategic doctrine. It emphasized strategic nuclear power as a cut-price way of achieving US security. Tactical nuclear weapons in Europe were able to contain Soviet conventional power and even went some way to balancing the budget as nuclear weapons gave 'more bang for the buck' (maximum safety at minimum cost as Eisenhower originally defined it). This was a policy of pure deterrence depending on the ability of the United States to inflict massive retaliation on the Soviet Union. 'Counterforce' was uppermost in the targeting orders of SAC's fleets of B-47s and the new B-52s, with US Air Defence able to keep Soviet bombers in check, preserve US cities and pave the way for forward-based US airpower to strip the Soviet Union of its military capability.

In the Eisenhower period there was no doubt who would win. Along with a very competent long strategic arm, tactical nuclear weapons were developed in a crash programme and liberally deployed in Europe from the mid-1950s onwards – mines, rockets and artillery with intermediate-range ballistic missiles such as Thor and Jupiter stationed in the UK, Italy and Turkey, and Mace and Matador cruise missiles in Germany backing up B-47 jet bombers. Europe was bristling with offensive and battlefield nuclear weapons while the continental United States, in spite of the 'bomber gap' scare of 1955, was relatively secure.

For Great Britain, in contrast, it was a period of assured anxiety expressed by the development of an independent nuclear weapons programme (A-Bomb in 1952; H-Bomb in 1957), very ambitious jet bomber programmes, home-grown intermediate-range ballistic missiles, peak civil-defence spending and the birth and ascent into political credibility of the Campaign for Nuclear Disarmament. The UK remained all the while the forward base of the USAF's Seventh Division, Strategic Air Command.

The Soviet Union, meanwhile, more or less leapt the first generation of nuclear delivery systems, developing a few relatively unsuccessful long-range jet bombers armed with free-fall bombs and, later, primitive cruise missiles, and concentrated massive resources on rocketry and the leap into space. The successful placing in orbit of Sputnik I in 1957 was as much a blow to US feelings of security as the Soviet H-Bomb had been in 1953. Meanwhile the relentless buildup of Soviet conventional forces in Europe continued and a start was made in building a general-purpose navy under the tutelage of Admiral Gorshkov. As early as 1955 this navy was experimenting with missiles launched from submarines.

The rocket that put Sputnik into orbit, the SS-6, was a true ICBM technically capable of hitting the United States from Arctic Russia. The development of the follow-on, first-generation operational ICBMs, the SS-7 and SS-8, was sanctioned in 1957-8 with plans for deploying more than 225 launchers. It was clear that the Soviet Union was embarking on a strategic missile programme both on land and at sea far superior to that planned by the United States and that, in spite of the US development of experimental submarine-launched missiles – the second-generation, solid-fuelled Minuteman and Polaris missiles under development and the introduction into service of the first-generation liquid-fuelled Titan and Atlas ICBMs – the period of assured US supremacy was drawing rapidly to a close. With the Soviet Union's growing capability of mauling the United States, massive retaliation made policy its prisoner as a nuclear response to conventional military or political aggression was no longer credible. Massive retaliation did not make force 'useful' and the Eisenhower budget's trimming of spending on conventional forces put fewer practical tools in the hands of policy-makers. By the late 1950s the arguments had been rehearsed among a new group of defence intellectuals. Then came the Kennedy administration, a new Secretary of Defence, Robert S. MacNamara, and a new policy.

The Age of Mutual Assured Destruction, 1960-70

When the new Kennedy administration took office in January 1961 the United States still enjoyed an unchallenged nuclear superiority over the Soviet Union but the luxurious time of the 'massive retaliation doctrine' and nuclear defence on the cheap was already past. The new government's first budget boosted spending on strategic systems, strategic air and civil defence, and programmes already developed under the Eisenhower administration such as Minuteman and Polaris were accelerated dramatically.

Defence Secretary Robert S. MacNamara expressed the aims of the United States' new doctrine thus: 'We believe in a policy of controlled flexible response where the military force of the United States would become a finely tuned instrument of national policy, versatile enough to meet with appropriate force the full spectrum of possible threats to our national security from guerrilla subversion to all out war.' Although this doctrine of 'flexible response' was applicable first to strategic forces, it was soon expanded to imply that the United States would respond appropriately to any attack, at conventional or tactical nuclear level, and would fight and win at the level at which the attack was made. This meant investment in conventional weapons to revive the utility of force for positive ends, and this path led to the protracted disaster of Vietnam and massive eventual public disillusionment with the sacrifice of the lives of American soldiers in combat abroad.

On the strategic level, the new doctrine meant a switch in targeting policy away from the 'optimum mix' assault, designed to destroy Soviet society and military power in one mighty spasm, to a 'no-cities' counterforce option aimed at destroying remaining Soviet armaments in place. In addition to limiting damage to Soviet cities, active air defence, passive civil defence and the geographic separation of US weapons from populated areas were all part of the same policy. The accuracy and discrimination of manned bombers as compared with missiles was used by the USAF who eagerly embraced counterforce to justify the B-70 bomber programme and senior air force commanders began to speak and write openly about winning a nuclear war as if it was a normal military operation. Just as the new weapons were coming on stream, however, by 1963 MacNamara and his Pentagon advisers were shifting their position to a radically different policy – that of 'assured mutual destruction' (MAD).

The irony was that the new generation of damage-limiting counterforce weapons' accuracy and relative invulnerability in silos or under the ocean made them suitable for use in a first strike. The new doctrine emphasized reduction of damage and trading of military targets like knights jousting at a tournament, all seeming to make nuclear war more 'rational' – even winnable, destabilizing the presumptions on which deterrence depended. The Cuba crisis of October 1962 showed the irrelevance of counterforce strategy. Kennedy threatened the Soviet Union with a 'full retaliatory stroke' unless the missiles were dismantled; meanwhile, SAC's B-47 and B-52 fleets were dispersed to satellite airfields, removing them from Soviet counterforce reach. Further, the Soviet Union was continuing to acquire an ever more punishing capability which could not be passively absorbed in a first strike before choosing an appropriate response. The way out of this conundrum was to switch back to 'city-busting', in effect to threaten another nation with such a terrible level of destruction to its cities and economic assets that it would not dare to attack. Its populations, not its weapons, should be held hostage and the will to turn vengefully on them in their flats, suburbs, schools, hospitals and factories should be undiluted.

Initially their strategic nuclear inferiority forced the Soviets also to rely on city targeting but nuclear war for them never slipped the bounds of policy. Military policy meant stripping an opponent of the means or the will to resist and the technical means of doing just that were coming into the Soviet strategic arsenal in the early 1960s – together with the expanding general-force capabilities of the Soviet Army and Navy – just as the United States was shifting to the policy of 'mutual assured destruction.'

The Soviets always assumed that a war in Europe would be nuclear, although there was a shift in the mid-1960s allowing the possibility of an opening non-nuclear phase. The concentration in the early 1960s was on Europe, for its own sake and because that was where forward American aircraft and missile bases actually were, with IR/MRBMs targeted against western Russia.

The first-generation Soviet ICBMs, the SS-7 and SS-8, were not effective against the new Minuteman silos in continental America but the development imperative for a new generation, the SS-9 and SS-11, had been given even before the Cuba crisis had so shaken Soviet prestige and military confidence. The SS-9 was an enormous rocket once thought capable of cracking silos in the US and the SS-11, built in larger numbers, would be equally effective against soft targets such as airfields. At the same time the decision was taken to mass-produce *Yankee*-class SSBNs armed with the SS-N-6 SLBM. With the Soviet doctrine that class struggle, not deadly weapons, would ensure the triumph of Marxism-Leninism, targeting policy made the primary mission the destruction of as much rival military capability as possible.

By the end of the period the Soviet Strategic Rocket Forces had eliminated the United States' original quantitative advantage in ICBMs and maintained their large advantage in medium-range strategic missiles for use in Europe or against China. The number of SLBM tubes still did not match the US but the gap was closing. This Soviet progress was about to be blunted, however, by the most major advance in delivery system technology since the ICBM itself – the advent of the MIRV.

The doctrine of mutual assured destruction suited the United States through the 1960s, preoccupied as its military machine was with the Vietnam War. The technology of the early 1960s suited the MAD stand-off with ICBMs with single large RVs and SSBNs immune from detection armed with missiles suitable for city attack but not hard target kills. The side which targeted enemy cities could destroy its target list while any attacker who attempted to disarm his opponent with a counterforce strike would not be sure of doing so, given the relative inaccuracy of his weapons. The MAD doctrine was expressed in weapon procurement. US strategic forces were sized according to their ability to destroy the Soviet Union in a retaliatory strike. According to Pentagon sums, 25 per cent of its population and 50 per cent of its economic infrastructure would represent intolerable punishment. This could be achieved by 400 one-megaton-equivalent warheads with delivery systems at a level after which any increase in numbers would produce only marginally 'improved' results in wrecking the Soviet Union as a viable society. US weapons were not engineered to be able to neutralize hard targets nor made responsive enough to be 'time sensitive', that is, to be launched under attack. Congress refused funds to re-engineer Poseidon and Polaris with the new warhead capabilities coming out of the ABRES (Advanced Ballistic Re-entry Systems) programme set up in 1962. As a further corollary to the city-busting logic of MAD, efforts to preserve US cities began to be downgraded on the presumption that the limiting of damage to oneself was irrelevant to the relative numbers of missiles given the assured ability to punish the aggressor.

As strategic parity, not superiority, became the standard of US force structure, so imperatives towards arms control followed. This was first to cap the destabilizing new technologies of MIRVs and anti-ballistic defence which represented investment black holes ready to swallow up defence budgets. Demands for diplomacy and negotiation increased in the period and arms control, which previously had played only a peripheral propaganda role, became an inseparable part of US strategy under direct supervision of the State Department, not the Department of Defence. Five US-inspired disarmament initiatives were concluded in the period between 1963 and 1968 (see Chronology) leading up to the Helsinki summit and the beginning of the Strategic Arms Limitation Talks.

Britain in this period scrapped its own IRBM programme and went shopping in America for a replacement. It got the Polaris SLBM when the Skybolt programme collapsed and, with a British warhead in a British submarine hull, the decision was made in 1962 to go to an all-missile seaborne deterrent, formal responsibility being handed over from the RAF's V-bombers to the Royal Navy in 1969. British targeting policy, while corresponding with the US war plan – the Single Integrated Operational Plan (SIOP) – was largely a retaliatory, city-orientated affair with some command and control targets as the size of the available force gave no real counterforce value and thus none of the flexible options that the Americans were able to debate and adopt. The Nassau agreement stipulated that the British Polaris force would be used for 'the purpose of international defence of the Western Alliance in all circumstances'. However the final decision for use was left with the British, based on their understanding of whether 'supreme national interests were at stake'. Here was the 'second centre of decision' that would deter any Soviet temptation to test the strength of the US nuclear commitment to Europe, but technically the 'independent' deterrent rested on American support. It was left to France to devise the diplomatic and political route to completely self-sufficient forces and to test, build and deploy them. France compressed nuclear weapon and delivery system programmes into the decade with the first atomic weapon exploded in 1960 and strategic bomber, strategic and tactical land-based and seaborne missiles all flying in prototype by 1970 and France pursuing a staunchly independent defence policy outside of NATO.

The Age of Assured Anxiety, 1970-82

The questioning of the enshrined tenets of mutual assured destruction began in the United States in the mid-1960s. Even at the declamatory height of the doctrine the actual US targeting plan assigned four-fifths of available weapons to 'soft' military targets such as ports and factories while the remainder were assigned to key industrial and energy targets plus command and communication centres, usually in the middle of Soviet cities. Even so, the new President of 1968 and his Security Adviser Henry Kissinger found the MAD doctrine sorely wanting. 'Should the President,' Richard Nixon asked in an oft-quoted question, 'in event of a nuclear attack be left with the single option of slaughtering Soviet civilians knowing that millions of Americans would be destroyed in return?'

Two things were happening in parallel to concentrate the minds of US policy-makers on something new. The ever-increasing Soviet quantitative and qualitative ability in strategic offensive and defensive technologies and the choices that these technologies in turn gave to the United States.

The two new aspects of strategic technology were ballistic missile defence and multiple warheads, both born out of fundamental electronic and computer research. US efforts to develop an anti-ballistic missile system began in 1956 with an extension of anti-aircraft technology and the programme developed through the Nike-Zeus and the Nike-X to the Sentinel and Safeguard systems, as the capabilities of the new phased array radars to track attacking RVs and direct defence enlarged all the while. The Soviets reportedly began ABM research in the 1940s in parallel with ballistic missiles themselves. They were able by 1962 to deploy a primitive system round Leningrad and, two years later, to deploy the more advanced *Galosh* missile and phased array radars around Moscow.

An ABM system could be overcome by saturating it with a large number of incoming missiles. The multiple warhead missile or MRV was the answer, in which a single missile carries aloft several RVs which are released in flight to come down separately on one or more target.

In 1964 the Polaris A-3 SLBM became operational with the US Navy with a range of 2500 nautical miles and a warhead consisting of three 200 KT RVs. Although the total yield was less than that of the single RV on the original Polaris, the system was capable of inflicting greater damage to single targets. This was only an interim, however, with the true MIRV (multiple independently targeted re-entry vehicle) following on close behind in which each RV could be programmed to strike an individual target. The first operational US tests of a MIRV system were in 1968 on the Minuteman III and in 1970 the first submarine launches were made of the Poseidon C-3 SLBM with up to fourteen 50 KT MIRVs. The result of MIRVing the US ICBM force increased the available RVs from 1054 and 656 SLBMs to a total of 7274 warheads.

The Soviets, meanwhile, although behind in the basic research, had in their massive SS-9 an ideal system for carrying aloft multiple payloads. Test firings of the SS-9 with an MRV warhead began in August 1968 and Western intelligence was soon crediting the missile with the ability to deliver three 5 KT RVs, each one bigger than any individual US ICBM except the Titan II.

The first-generation anti-ballistic missile research was thus already compromised by MRV technology when the agreement resulting from SALT 1 was concluded between the United States and the Soviet Union in 1972 restricting ABM deployments. Under the ABM treaty each side was allowed to construct and operate one ABM site in defence of the national capital and another in defence of an ICBM site. In June 1974 the allowable ABM sites were further reduced, President Nixon and Party Secretary Brezhnev agreeing to retain only the ABM site guarding the Minuteman field at Grand Forks, N. Dakota, and the *Galosh* system around Moscow. The Minuteman site was in fact probably only operational for one day.

MIRV technology had done more than consign anti-ballistic missiles to the slow lane. The deployment of multiple warhead systems by both sides changed the mutual assured destruction equations on which the assumptions of the 1960s had been built. With MIRV technology the Soviets could at some stage in the 1970s arm 500 large ICBMs with three five-megaton warheads each and count on an 80 per cent reliability rate and quarter-mile accuracy at the target. Thus 1200 RVs could be expected to strike their target and strip the land-based Minuteman core out of the United States nuclear arsenal in a first strike. All that the surviving US seaborne or land-based systems could do would be to make a spasmodic retaliatory strike on Soviet social targets, inviting the launch of the remaining large number of Soviet missiles against US cities.

United States multiple-warhead technology was already mature by the time of the first SALT talks and that of the Soviet Union was in its infancy. Nevertheless for President Nixon and Security Adviser Henry Kissinger opening a dialogue with the Soviet Union on reducing strategic armaments seemed to be the only way to contain the essentially destabilizing new technologies when faced with an adversary who would soon achieve equivalent power. The overwhelming foreign policy issue facing the new Republican presidency was the Vietnam War with over half a million US troops on the ground and turmoil at home. In the same year, 1969, the Sino-Soviet ideological split had turned into armed border clashes and an eastern arms race. Three interlocking policy tasks were isolated and pursued by Kissinger – withdrawal of US ground forces from SE Asia, 'normalization' of relations with China and the establishing of a consistent and far-reaching relationship with the Soviet Union.

Against this background the first session of SALT began in November 1969 and the ensuing negotiations included seven formal sessions over the next two and a half years, the so-called 'back channel communications' and summit interventions at critical points.

SALT 1 included three separate agreements signed by President Nixon and Party Secretary Brezhnev in Moscow in May 1972. These were the Treaty on the Limitation of Anti-ballistic Missile Systems (see above), an interim agreement with a protocol on 'Certain Measures with respect to the Limitation of Strategic Offensive Arms (Interim Agreement)' and a 'Statement on Basic Principles of Mutual Relations' plus complex initialled agreed interpretations and 'noteworthy unilateral statements'.

The interim agreement on Offensive Weapons Limitation provided for a freeze after 1 July 1972 on new construction of fixed-site ICBMs and ballistic missile submarines and launch tubes. This was further split into a distinction between light and heavy ICBM systems and a 'trade-in' agreement on new missiles and submarines for old, all of which in effect substantially favoured the Soviet Union.

It was what SALT left out, however, that was so important. It did not cover strategic aircraft, nor European theatre nuclear weapons. Qualitative improvements in the accuracy of ICBMs and MIRVing were not covered, nor were land-mobile ICBMs, although the US made a unilateral statement that it would view deployment of operational land-mobile ICBMs as 'inconsistent with the objectives of this agreement'. SALT 1 limited only launchers, effectively silos and submarine missile tubes, but did not constrain numbers of delivery vehicles nor the numbers and accuracy of re-entry vehicles. The US was reasonably satisfied that it could verify compliance with the treaty as silos and submarines could be identified with relative ease from satellite reconnaissance whereas technical advances in guidance systems could not.

The Agreement was intended by the US at least to last for five years from October 1972, during which time a permanent comprehensive treaty (SALT 2) would be negotiated. SALT was the core of the wider foreign policy of détente, the means of substituting negotiations for confrontation with its ideal of strategic parity intended to serve broader foreign policy objectives for both the USA and the Soviet Union. With the United States still clinging to policies of mutual assured destruction and minimum deterrence, the quantitative advantages that SALT 1 gave the Soviet Union did not matter. As Henry Kissinger graphically stated it at the time – 'What in God's name do you do with strategic superiority' – even if the Soviet leaders knew what to do with it and planned to acquire it as expeditiously as possible.

It seemed for a while, nevertheless, that armed ideology would give way to the pursuit of mutual self-interest. But a new war came in the Middle East in 1973 to overturn this fragile new balance. The Arab oil embargo and Russian threats to introduce troops to the Middle East (Soviet airborne and US strategic forces were put on alert) displayed the United States' dependence on foreign raw materials and energy and the growing Soviet ability to thwart militarily the global projection of US power. To its domestic opponents détente was just a feeble form of crisis management and a cynical cloak for Russian expansionism. Meanwhile Kissinger (Secretary of State since September 1973 and now in virtual charge of American foreign policy with Richard Nixon's embroilment in the Watergate affair) plunged on. Summits in Washington and Vladivostok in July and November 1974 produced a new arms control agreement establishing a common ceiling on the number of all strategic delivery vehicles and a maximum yield of 150 kilotons for underground nuclear testing.

The policy of détente was coming under attack from all sides of the political spectrum. The liberals in Congress charged that the whole thing was ineffective anyway and wanted 'linkage' to internal liberalization of Soviet domestic policies. The conservatives saw the treaties as simply conceding strategic superiority to the Soviet Union and neither the Vladivostok agreement nor the test ban treaty was presented to Congress for ratification.

Even as the SALT 1 treaties were being formulated, US strategic policy was going through another revision. As always this was as a result of imminently available technical capabilities which in turn caused new ones to be sought after and acquired. In January 1974 Defence Secretary James Schlesinger, finding the MAD doctrine to be wanting, announced a new limited strategic nuclear options doctrine for the US under which 'immediate massive retaliation against Soviet cities was no longer to be the President's only option and possibly not the principal option.' The strategy became known by a variety of names, 'counterforce', the 'Schlesinger doctrine' and 'limited strategic options'. The ability to fight a limited war at a level of destruction which would leave enough surviving assets and individuals to allow bargaining for peace, it was argued, would enhance rather than dilute deterrence.

The Minuteman III force was already fitted with the Command Data Buffer system which enabled targeting orders to be changed rapidly, and funding of the new Mk 12A warhead under development by General Electric was ordered in 1974 to give a greater degree of hypothetical accuracy and (on paper at least) a hard target kill capability – tools for real counterforce options.

A greater revolution in the capabilities of US delivery systems was on the way. Ever since the Triad of strategic forces had emerged in the mid-1950s, development programmes on long lead times had been in hand for over a decade to provide a new generation of replacement weapons systems. The B-52 replacement went to North American Rockwell in 1969 and a $40 million contract to develop a subsonic cruise armed decoy (SCAD) as part of the electronic countermeasures fit for the B-1 bomber went out to tender in 1970/71. SCAD was to emerge five years later as the 'cruise missile'. Research on the Polaris/Poseidon follow-on, the undersea long-range missile system (ULMS), began in 1970 with production orders going to Lockheed for the resulting Trident SLBM in 1974. Work was also well advanced on a Minuteman follow-on with high-yield, high-accuracy RVs developed under the ABRES programme in advanced pre-production stages to arm the new ICBM, which was to be land-mobile.

This new Pandora's box was about to be opened just as the new presidency of Jimmy Carter was declaring that MAD was back in town, that even if a first strike ripped out the core arsenal of the United States a single submarine could inflict enough punishment to keep the deterrent alive. The unbroken evidence that the Soviets were making a reality of their long-published intent to acquire the means to fight and win a nuclear war by creating forces capable of destroying and fending off the US deterrent did not help MAD's brief born-again hour, nor did it help when the administration released a controversial CIA report on Soviet civil defence estimating American dead in a nuclear exchange at 160 million and Soviet dead at 10 million.

Thus began a tragic fall from innocence in which President Carter's attempts at arms control, by cancelling or delaying new weapon systems such as the B-1 bomber and enhanced radiation weapons, by pursuing SALT 2, by pursuing controls on conventional arms sales, by high-mindedly seeking linkage of human rights with strategic concessions, were compromised one by one. The Middle East peace process which reached a pinnacle at Camp David tailed off into anti-climax. The peace imperatives of the Carter presidency collapsed in the face of domestic suspicion and uncertainty, foreign policy disasters in Iran and Afghanistan and the quest for advantage by the Soviet Union at every level. The relative calm that fell over American policy-makers about nuclear parity gave way to doubts that superiority was the Soviet Union's goal, with strategic and general-purpose force modernization proceeding apace accompanied by active opportunist diplomacy and power projection. In the Gulf, in the Horn of Africa, in Angola, in the Caribbean and in Central America the military power and political influence of the Soviet Union was evident and expanding.

It was, however, the deployment by the Soviet Union of strategic systems, the SS-17, -18 and -19 ICBMs and the SS-N-18 SLBM, targeted against the United States, which really rattled the Americans; and it was not the bomber-gap or missile-gap scare all over again. Professor Richard Pipes of Harvard University's famous anti-SALT polemic of 1976, 'Why the Soviet Union Thinks It Could Fight and Win a Nuclear War', found some heavyweight political patronage. 'Window of vulnerability' was a fashionable coining, meaning a period of years in the early 1980s when the Soviet ability to disarm the

United States in a counterforce first strike would be irresistably tempting.*

The first-strike fear was built around this scenario: Soviet ICBMs with their new 'throw-weight' and accuracy attack the Minuteman ICBM force and eliminate it wholesale in a first strike while two-thirds of Soviet missiles still remain in their silos and submarines. With the counterforce option knocked out, the one American response left would be a futile counter-city strike from surviving systems inviting a much greater counter-city strike in return. Surrender would be very attractive. The US would have lost the war with the loss of its counterforce weapons (along with an estimated 10-20 million people). The vulnerability of ICBMs thus became a matter of great importance and the proper response was further judged to be not simply a reduction in vulnerability (such as sea basing) but a matching of the adversary's counterforce ability itself. The Trident missile and the MX mobile ICBM seemed to offer the best possible remedy, able to enhance counterforce capability and ride out or evade the most punishing enemy attacks.

There was a counter-argument that the problem was not so much a factor of Soviet strength of purpose and adventurism but American lack of self-confidence following Vietnam and Watergate. The massive lobbying by all the right-wing think-tanks, arms industry pressure groups and conservative pundits that helped pave the way for the Reagan presidency continually emphasized American weaknesses compared with Soviet strengths. According to them, the United States seemed unable to react to Soviet power projection, either at the strategic level or by conventional confrontation (by such means as the Rapid Deployment Force). The Soviet invasion of Afghanistan and the tragic fiasco of Desert One underlined the same point.

By 1980 Carter's fall from grace was complete. Presidential Directive 59, signed in the summer, was MAD's death

---

* Both the Soviet Union and the United States have been victims of counterforce first strikes. In June 1941 the Germans attacked the Soviet Union without warning and in the opening days destroyed very large numbers of aircraft caught on the ground. In December the same year the US Navy's Pacific Fleet was neutralized, four battleships sunk and 300 aircraft destroyed on the ground at Pearl Harbor by the Imperial Japanese Navy.

certificate, shifting targeting policy once again to Soviet military targets. The prime targets would be 'those the Soviet leadership values most – its military forces and its own ability to maintain control after a war starts'. The plan assessed economic-recovery prospects and the long-term impact of attacks on the economic infrastructure but the really new part was the emphasis on finding the Soviet leaders in their bunkers. Some of its supporters went so far as to say that once the KGB and the Moscow bureaucracy were eliminated, the Soviet Union would disintegrate or its internal nationalities would rebel against Great Russian domination.

PD 59 alarmed so many people because for the first time there was published a US plan for nuclear war which foresaw winners and losers. Ancillary studies showed how 'limited strikes' could be made on government control targets or on a core industry such as oil refining as well as against nuclear weapons themselves. It worked both ways: the Congressional Office of Technology assessment in its 1980 study, *The Effects of Nuclear War*, looked at an attack by ten SS-18 ICBMs carrying eighty-one-megaton MIRVs against the US oil-refining industry concentrated near conurbations such as Philadelphia and Chicago and along the gulf coast of Texas; 60 per cent of the refining industry would be pulverized along with 5 million people. This was not a blueprint for anything which could call itself 'limited war'.

This new bellicosity came too late to steal the clothes of the Republicans. The revelation of the existence of a Soviet ground combat brigade on Cuba caused an uproar and SALT 2, signed in Vienna in June 1979, was now immovably stalled in the Senate. The distortions that the treaty's inspection and verification requirements were imposing on plans to reshape America's strategic forces such as the bizarre M-X 'shell game' were insupportable. Following the invasion of Afghanistan, President Carter asked the Senate to defer ratification.

In the November elections the US electorate turned massively to the presidential candidate who offered security not through arms control but through massive arms procurement and with a plan to spend $1.5 trillion in a five-year build up of American military power and with little or no strategy to go with it.

11 • A Chronology of Nuclear War and Peace

1940

February Peirls and Frisch working at Birmingham University, UK, produce memorandum on a practical military atomic weapon.

August 'Virus House' German atomic weapon research team established in Berlin.

August US Army Air Force issues specification for 'hemisphere defence' long-range intercontinental bomber – to become B-36.

1942

April German heavy-water plant at Rjukan Norway destroyed by Allied saboteurs.

August Manhattan Project, US/UK atomic weapon research programme established with massive funding.

3 October First successful launch of German Army A-4 rocket (V-2), 190 km range.

1943

January Central Committee of USSR directs I. V. Kurchakov to organize a new scientific establishment in Moscow to investigate the 'uranium problem'.

– – Theoretical work begins at Manhattan Project, Los Alamos, on 'super' or fusion bomb.

1944

15 June V-1 cruise-missile offensive against London opens.

September First V-2 ballistic rocket lands on London.

1945

25 March Last V-2 falls on London.

11 April Two task forces of US 3rd Armoured Division capture intact underground V-2 factory at Nordhausen. Operation *Overcast*, evacuation of 100 V-2s to US, commences.

19 April Soviet Army captures wrecked Peenemunde missile research site.

April Soviet Army captures German nerve gas factory at Breslau.

May Soviet Army takes over Nordhausen with remaining V-2s intact.

16 July Trinity – first successful explosion of experimental atomic bomb at Alamogordo, New Mexico.

July 509th Composite Bomb Group, USAAF, begins training for atom bomb mission in Utah desert.

27 July Potsdam Proclamation. Japan warned of utter devastation of the homeland without unconditional surrender.

6 August Hiroshima. Most of the population are caught in the open as the sighting of only three aircraft quickly causes air-raid warning to pass. 78,150 dead, 70,000 injured.

9 August Nagasaki. 40,000 dead, 25,000 injured.

August US Smyth report on atomic energy for military purposes.

September Project *Paperclip* brings German rocket scientists and V-2s from Nordhausen to White Sands Proving Grounds, New Mexico.

1946

January UK Chiefs of Staff report on Britain's atomic bomb requirements.

March First test firings of V-2s at White Sands, Nevada.

21 March US Strategic Air Command (SAC) formed as separate command within USAAF.

May V-VS Dalnaya Aviatsaya (long-range aviation) constituted by USSR as separate military command. First Soviet ballistic missile unit, formed from two Guards *Katyusha* (bombardment rocket) regiments, to use captured V-2s at Kasputin Yar in central Asia.

14 June Baruch Plan. US delegate at UN Atomic Energy Commission, Bernard Baruch, proposes plan for US to give up stockpile of atomic weapons to an international Atomic Energy Development Authority. USSR refuses inspection of atomic energy projects; Baruch Plan vetoed at UN, December.

July Operation *Crossroads*: US conducts atomic bomb tests at Bikini Atoll – air and underwater burst.

8 August Prototype Convair XB-36 first flight, 11,000 km range.

November SAC B-29s arrive in western Germany.

December General Assembly of UN approves resolution for world disarmament. (UN Disarmament Commission meets fitfully 1947-60.)

– – Spaatz report for USAAF emphasizes importance of retaining foreign bases for atomic strike forces.

1947

May Tupolev Tu-4 *Bull* appears at air display, 5000 km range copy of B-29 strategic bomber.

June First meeting of UK atomic bomb staff.

August First UK experimental atomic pile at Harwell goes critical.

18 September US National Security Act creates Department of Defence, United States Air Force, and National Security Council which gives charter to newly established Central Intelligence Agency.

30 October Soviets successfully launch V-2 at Kazakhstan.

17 December XB-47 prototype first flight.

1948

January US DoD requests Atomic Energy Commission to produce nuclear reactor for submarine propulsion.

20 February Boeing B-50 operational with SAC.

17 March Brussels Treaty: military assistance treaty between Britain, France, Netherlands, Belgium, Luxembourg, US and Canada.

March Project *Half Moon*: first US war plan to include nuclear attack on Soviet Union in event of attack on western Europe prepared by Joint Chiefs.
26 June B-36 operational with SAC, 16,000 km range.
June First in-flight refuelling experiments conducted by SAC.
– – US Navy conducts experiments with carrier-delivered atomic weapons using P2V Neptune.
June-July Berlin blockade.
July British Civil Defence Corps reactivated.
December French experimental atomic pile *Zöe* goes critical.
– – British MoS abandons long-range rocket development.

1949

4 April North Atlantic Treaty Organization (NATO) set up.
May Decision to build a British atomic bomb announced.
19 September Detection of first Soviet atomic weapon test announced by President Truman.

1950

January US decision to develop H-bomb announced.
Arrest of Harwell spy, Klaus Fuchs.
14 February Sino-Soviet Treaty of Friendship, Alliance and Mutual Assistance.
March First B-50 Washingtons operational with RAF.
April Aldermaston inaugurated as UK Atomic Weapons Research Establishment.
– – NSC-68 memorandum, prepared by Paul Nitze for National Security Council, emphasizes seriousness of Soviet nuclear threat, inappropriateness of disarmament and necessity of increasing conventional and nuclear arsenals.
25 June Outbreak of Korean war.
July President Truman approves stockpiling of non-nuclear components of nuclear weapons at forward US bases in UK.
September British rearmament announced. UK Chiefs of Staff ask for US bomb-testing facilities and are turned down.
November UK agreement with S. Africa on uranium supplies.
December Wernher von Braun arrives at US Army Redstone Arsenal with orders to develop 500-mile-range guided missile.

– – Non-nuclear components of atomic bombs aboard USS *Franklin Roosevelt* in Mediterranean.

1951

16 January SAC B-36s arrive at RAF Lakenheath.

February US Navy AJ-1 Savages armed with atom bombs operational from carriers in the Mediterranean.

20 March USAF SAC 7th Air Division HQ established at South Ruislip, London.

11 April Vickers Valiant RAF jet bomber prototype flies.

April Specifications for Blue Rapier cruise missile issued by UK government (cancelled 1953).

14 June SAC 5th Air Division established in French Morocco.

22 October Greece and Turkey join NATO.

1952

20 August Avro Vulcan prototype flies.

2 October Boeing XB-52 prototype flies.

3 October Operation *Hurricane*: first British atomic bomb exploded at Monte Bello, Australia.

1 November US explodes H-bomb at Eniwetok.

– – US *Teapot* Committee set up to investigate development of ICBMs with thermonuclear warheads.

– – British Chiefs of Staff prepare global strategy paper.

– – Tactical nuclear weapon research initiated by US Atomic Energy Commission.

1953

January-February First deployment of operational B-47s by SAC.

April SHAPE Chief of Staff affirms that NATO defence plan for Europe called for limited use of ground troops and intensive use of atomic weapons. (In 1953-4 7000 tactical nuclear warheads are deployed in Europe.)

4 June B-47s arrive at RAF Fairford. (One B-47 wing is operational in UK until early 1958.)

12 August USSR successfully tests thermonuclear device or H-bomb.

26 September Spain signs ten-year defence agreement with US.

30 October President Eisenhower announces basic security policy involving use of nuclear weapons at all levels (NSC 162/2).

August-December British civil-defence spending peaks: building of regional 'war rooms' commences, and London tunnels abandoned.

– – CIA opens Moscow station at US Embassy.

1954

22 February First UK civil defence fall-out exercise: 10 KT on Birmingham postulated.

30 September USS *Nautilus* atomic-powered submarine commissioned.

November US and Canada agree to construction of Distant Early Warning (DEW) radar line across Arctic Canada.

– – Honest John unguided battlefield missile operational with US Army in Europe: 40 km range, low-kiloton warhead..

– – Matador US cruise missile operational: equips tactical missile wings forward-based in Germany and Taiwan.

– – China establishes atomic weapons programme.

– – Tupolev Tu-16 *Badger* bomber, 5000 km range, enters service with Soviet air force. Myasischev M-4 *Bison* strategic bomber, 10,000 km range, demonstrated at air display. *PVO-Strany*, Soviet Air Defence, established as a separate command.

1955

12 January US Massive Retaliation concept announced.

February Vickers Valiant B.1 enters service with RAF.

14 May Soviet Union, Poland, Czechoslovakia, Hungary, Romania, Bulgaria, DDR and Albania sign Warsaw Pact.

1 June Royal Observer Corps officially given task in UK of nuclear blast and fall-out reporting.

June First B-52Bs operational with SAC.

15 June US and UK sign bilateral treaty for exchange of information on nuclear defence planning and training.

21 July President Eisenhower outlines 'Open Skies' plan for air reconnaissance inspection of strategic military developments.

July US development contract issued for XB-70 supersonic strategic bomber.

September Russell-Einstein Manifesto calling for world scientists to work for peace.

26 November USAF charged with control of all missiles in US inventory with a range over 200 miles.

– – First launch of ballistic missile from Soviet submarine.

1956

March US Thor IRBM programme announced: SAC to emplace missiles in UK, bring to combat readiness and turn over to RAF.

7/8 April First UK country-wide fall-out exercise, *Cloverleaf.*

May UK Home Office embarks on ROC bunker-building programme and secure communications net.

29 May Regulus II US Navy supersonic cruise missile first flight.

June US begins U-2 reconnaissance flights over USSR.

26 July SAC missile-development programme announced: Titan and Atlas ICBMs, Thor, Navaho and Snark IRBMs.

31 October-6 November Franco-British attack on Suez Canal.

Late 1956 Beginning of UK operational nuclear capability.

– – 'Bomber Gap' hearings in US Senate on supposed Soviet lead in bomber design and deployment.

– – UK drops nerve-gas research and discards chemical-warfare stocks.

– – Israel establishes secret reactor in Negev Desert with French assistance.

– – Lockheed carry out first design studies on Polaris SLBM concept.

– – US Army Nike-Zeus development contracts allocated for nuclear anti-aircraft and anti-missile defence system.

– – Mace, improved Matador cruise missile, operational in West Germany.

1957

– – Tupolev Tu-20 *Bear-A* (14,500 km range) enters service with Soviet Air Force.

– – Twenty-two scientists meet at Pugwash, Nova Scotia, for peace conference.

January SAC B-47s operational in Spain.

4 April UK Defence White Paper delivered by Duncan Sandys: conventional force levels and commitments cut back; manned-aircraft development curtailed; Avro 730 Mach 2+ bomber cancelled; emphasis on deterrence by threat of nuclear retaliation.

April Emergency Committee for Direct Action against Nuclear War formed in UK.

May Avro Vulcan B. 1 enters service with RAF.

15 May Operation *Grapple*: UK explodes first hydrogen bomb.

July Nuclear air-to-air missile, Douglas Genie, test-fired in US.

3 August USSR test-launches SS-6 ICBM.

August US Jupiter missile RV survives re-entry and lands within target area on test.

4 October USSR puts Sputnik 1 into earth orbit.

15 October Sino-Soviet agreement on 'supply of new technology for national defence'.

30 October Bell Rascal US air-launched missile briefly becomes operational.

– – FROG (free rocket over ground) unguided battlefield nuclear missile operational with Soviet Army.

– – SS-3 *Shyster* IRBM operational with Soviet Rocket Troops.

– – USSR deploys diesel submarine able to launch two SS-N-4 *Sark* missiles from surface.

– – Tu-22 *Blinder* first flown, 5600 km range with supersonic dash.

– – Regulus 1 surface-launched cruise missile operational from two US submarines.

1958

1 January 1st Missile Division, SAC, transfers to Vandenberg AFB with Atlas D ICBM (activated April 1).

January Campaign for Nuclear Disarmament (CND) founded in UK.

31 January Explorer 1, first US satellite, put into orbit.

20 February Thor missiles activated at RAF Lakenheath by SAC.

31 March Soviet unilateral test ban. (Tests of atomic weapons renewed 30 September.)

April Handley Page Victor B. 1 enters service with RAF.

12 May NORAD (North American Air Defence Command) established.

June Development begins in US of Subroc nuclear ASW system.

August First flight-trials of Avro Blue Steel UK stand-off bomb at Woomera, Australia.

4 August Anglo-US agreement for 'co-operation on the Uses of Atomic Energy for Mutual Defence Purposes'.

10 October Minuteman ICBM contract awarded to Boeing.

31 October US voluntary one-year test ban; USSR follows in December.

– – Chinese reactor operational.

– – SAC perfects airborne alert procedures and begins training for operations at low altitude in response to improvements in Soviet air defence.

– – US 8-inch howitzer with nuclear shell operational in Europe, 10 km range, low KT.

1959

1 January TSR-2 advanced strike aircraft for RAF contract awarded.

12 June First British nuclear submarine, HMS *Dreadnought*, laid down; reactor and propulsion machinery are American.

20 June Soviets revoke agreement to supply China with nuclear-weapon technology.

8 July France refuses to permit stockpiling of US nuclear weapons unless under French control; 200 USAF tactical nuclear aircraft redeployed to UK and W. Germany.

26 August US extends agreement on unilateral test ban.

– – US-British-Soviet test-ban talks at Geneva.

9 September Atlas D ICBMs operational with SAC.

1 December Antarctic Treaty: area to be used exclusively for peaceful purposes.

3 December Three squadrons of Thor IRBMs operational in UK on 'double-key' system.

December Blue Steel Mk 2, supersonic stand-off bomb for RAF programme, cancelled.

30 December USS *George Washington*, first operational Polaris submarine, commissioned.

– – *1959-63* F-4 and F-104 nuclear-capable tactical strike aircraft become operational in Europe.

– – Mirage IV French supersonic nuclear bomber first flight.

– – SS-1 *Scud* Soviet mobile artillery missile, 130 km range, operational.

– – *Henhouse* Soviet ABM radar system operational.

1960

4 January USS *Halibut* SSN with Regulus 1 cruise missile, 800 km range, operational.

13 February French test atomic bomb in Sahara.

15 March First meeting of Ten Nation Disarmament Committee at Geneva.

13 April UK cancels Blue Streak fixed-site IRBM programme. Warhead development continues.

1 May 'U-2 incident': US reconnaissance aircraft shot down at extreme altitude by SA-2 missile over Sverdlovsk; Paris summit meeting breaks up.

May Soviet Strategic Rocket Troops, *Raketnyye Voyska Strategicheskovo Naznacheniya*, established as separate command.

June UK announces decision to acquire 100 Skybolt air-launched ballistic missiles from US.

August Convair B-58 operational with SAC.

October Pershing I battlefield tactical missile test-fired.

October UK Labour Party adopts resolution for unilateral nuclear disarmament.

1 November US/UK agreement on nuclear submarine base at Holy Loch.

November 'Missile Gap' hearings begin in US Senate.

11 September 'Committee of 100' for civil disobedience against nuclear warfare activist group formed within CND.

15 November First deterrent patrol by US Polaris submarine.

December UK becomes United Kingdom Air Defence region under SACEUR, NATO.

6 December President de Gaulle announces plans for French nuclear striking force, the *Force de Frappe*.

16 December US offers five nuclear submarines to NATO for proposed multi-lateral force (MLF).

– – *Golf*-class submarines with three SS-N-4 *Sark* SLBMs operational with Soviet Navy.

– – British Army of the Rhine (BAOR) receives Honest John and Corporal SRBMs with US warheads under double-key control.

– – Davy Crockett light jeep mounted missile projector with 2 km range and low KT nuclear warhead operational in Europe, remained in service until 1967. The weapon's blast radius exceeded its range.

– – Deployment begins of thirty Jupiter missiles each in Italy and Turkey under joint US/NATO command.

– – US begins development of SAMOS-MIDAS ICBM-site reconnaissance satellite programme.

1961

January Robert S. MacNamara becomes US Secretary of Defence.

February 'Looking Glass' SAC Airborne Command Post becomes operational.

– – First ballistic-missile early-warning system (BMEWS) station operational, Thule, Greenland.

18 March Snark cruise missile operational with SAC (deactivated 25 June 1961).

April USAF B-70 bomber programme cancelled.

15 July First Minuteman I ICBM wing operational.

July Berlin crisis: Berlin wall erected 12/13 August.

1 September USSR resumes atmospheric nuclear testing; US follows, ending two and a half years implied moratorium.

October UK Labour Party conference overturns resolution on unilateral disarmament.

9 December First Skybolt test with RAF Vulcan B.2, Scotland.

9 December Krushchev announces Soviet possession of 100 MT+ superbombs.

– – US civil defence spending peaks.

– – British V-bomber force reaches peak of 180 aircraft.

– – First US satellite reconnaissance of Soviet Union.

– – Soviet Interior Ministry (MVD) transfers responsibility for civil defence to Ministry of Defence.

– – AS-2 *Kipper* stand-off missile operational with Soviet air force.

1962

19 April First Skybolt live launch.

22 October Cuba missile crisis.

November Soviet missile sites in Cuba dismantled and bombers withdrawn.

11 December Skybolt programme cancelled; US proposes submarine-based Polaris and European multilateral nuclear force as alternative.

– – Buccaneer nuclear-capable strike aircraft enters service with Royal Navy, supplementing nuclear-capable Scimitars.

– – Sergeant US battlefield guided missile, 125 km range, operational in Europe.

– – SS-7 Soviet ICBM, with 11,000 km range, operational.

– – *Griffon*, first-generation Soviet ABM, briefly deployed around Leningrad.

– – AS-4 *Kitchen* stand-off missile operational with Soviet air force.

10-12 December Nassau talks and agreement between President

Kennedy and Prime Minister Macmillan: Royal Navy to get Polaris instead of Skybolt.

– – Stanley Kubrick's film *Doctor Strangelove* released.

1963

February UK announcement of intended procurement of four SSBNs.

April SAC ICBM alert force overtakes numbers of SAC bomber alert force.

– – US Navy Polaris submarines enter Mediterranean.

25 July Nuclear Test-Ban Treaty signed prohibiting nuclear testing in atmosphere; effective 10 October.

30 August Inauguration of Moscow-Washington 'hot-line'.

September Titan II operational with SAC.

17 October UN General Assembly passes resolution for the renunciation of nuclear weapons in space.

December Thor missiles in UK deactivated.

December Dyna-Soar USAF sub-orbital manned space programme cancelled.

December UN announces air force space weapons project – 'Manned Orbiting Laboratory' (MOL).

– – US conducts first tests with enhanced radiation (ER) weapons or 'neutron bomb'.

– – US Nike-X programme replaces Nike-Zeus ABM programme.

– – Installation of Atomic Demolition Munitions (nuclear mines) begins in Europe and Turkey.

– – SS-8 Soviet ICBM operational, 11,000 km range.

1964

24 February UK announcement of intended fifth SSBN.

March SAC B-47s withdrawn from UK.

March UK Ministry of Defence established.

April Polaris A-3 SLBM introduced in US Navy, 3000 km range, MRV warhead.

21 July Organization of African Unity announces resolution on denuclearization of Africa.

– – First trials in US of phased array radar at White Sands, applicable as battle-management radar for ABM systems.
1 October United Kingdom Warning and Monitoring Organization becomes separate executive branch within Home Office.
20 October China explodes 20 KT atomic bomb.
5 November US missile levels frozen at 1054 ICBM, 656 SLBMs.
21-22 November New UK Labour government committee decides to continue with Polaris programme.
– – US 155 mm howitzer with nuclear shell operational in Europe, 18 km range, low KT.

1965

1965-73 Vietnam War.
15 February UK fifth SSBN cancelled.
15 March Lance I battlefield tactical nuclear missile test-fired.
6 April TSR-2 cancelled.
– – Atlas E, F and Titan I phased out.
– – SS-1 *Scud-B* Soviet tactical nuclear missile operational, 270 km range.
– – UK V-bombers based briefly in Singapore.

1966

7 January SR-71 strategic reconnaissance aircraft operational with SAC.
9 March France withdraws from NATO.
5 April First Minuteman II squadron activated.
July-October Extensive French nuclear tests at Muroroa Atoll.

1967

8 January USSR tests fractional orbital bombardment system.
27 January Outer Space Treaty bans placing weapons of mass destruction in earth orbit.
14 February Treaty of Tlatelcolo signed in denuclearization of Latin America (Argentina and Brazil do not sign).

29 March Le Redoutable, first French SNLE (*Sousmarins Nucleaires Lance Engins*) launched.

17 June China explodes three-megaton H-bomb.

22 June First UK SSBN, HMS *Resolution*, begins sea trials.

June UK Prime Minister Harold Wilson announces government decision not to procure Poseidon.

– – Aldermaston continues warhead research on Antelope 1, anti-ABM MRV.

September US announces plans for Sentinel anti-ballistic missile system deployed primarily against China and 'accidental' Soviet ICBM launches.

November SS-9 Soviet ICBM with very large throw-weight becomes operational.

– – Rescue and first aid sections of UK Civil Defence Corps disbanded.

– – BBC refuse showing of *The War Game*, post-nuclear-strike film directed by Peter Watkins.

– – Strat-X study in US recommends development of four advanced strategic systems: hardened and mobile land-based ICBMs, submarines and ship-borne missiles.

1968

January UK government announces disbanding of Civil Defence Corps, AFS and TAVR III.

30 March Spartan US ABM test-fired.

30 April Strike Command formed within RAF.

1 July Treaty on non-proliferation of nuclear weapons. Nuclear-potential nations that did not sign are France, China, Argentina, Brazil, India, Israel, Pakistan, South Africa, Spain.

16 August First test-firing of Lockheed Poseidon SLBM and Boeing Minuteman III ICBM with MIRV warheads.

24 August France explodes two-megaton H-bomb at Muroroa.

31 August Soviet invasion of Czechoslovakia.

– – CIA estimate first operational Israeli nuclear weapons.

– – UK abandons plan to base SSBN depot ship in Indian Ocean to support patrols targeted against China.

1969

10 June USAF MOL project cancelled.

1 July Nuclear strike responsibilities formally transferred from RAF to Royal Navy.

6 August US Senate votes narrowly for development and deployment of Safeguard ABM system.

8 October General Dynamics FB-IIIA operational with SAC.

17 November US-Soviet Strategic Arms Limitation Talks (SALT) begin at Helsinki.

25 November US renounces first use of lethal and incapacitating chemical weapons and all biological weapons.

November Advanced Manned Strategic Aircraft Programme announced by US (B-1).

December French Pluton battlefield nuclear missile test-fired by France.

－－ Soviet SS-12 battlefield nuclear missile, 700 km range, test-fired.

－－ US Project *Nemesis* to install ICBMs on the seabed, in wilderness areas and in very deep desert silos abandoned.

－－ Shipment of weapons-grade uranium hi-jacked from ship; Israel is possible recipient.

1970

24 March B-1 bomber contract allocated.

25 May Announcement by US government of deployment of MIRVs.

June First RN Polaris SSBN refit completed.

20 July US intelligence identifies new Soviet bomber – *Backfire*, at Kazan factory.

28 August Successful test of Safeguard US ABM.

－－ CSS-1 MRBM operational in China, 1100 km range, 20 KT.

1971

11 February Treaty to denuclearize the seabed.

24 March Minuteman III US ICBM tested operationally, 13,000 km range, Mk 12 warhead with three 170 KT RVs.

March First Poseidon C-3 patrol with USS *James Madison*, 4600 km range, ten 40 KT RVs.

— — Deployment of eighteen silo-emplaced SSBS missiles begins on Plateau d'Albion in Central France.

— — 'Cornflake saga': Anglo-French talks on joint SSBN operations are so limited they can only agree on submariners' diet.

1972

February ULMS (Trident SLBM) programme accelerated.

4 March Short-range attack missile (SRAM) operational on SAC B-52Gs/Hs.

26 May US-Soviet SALT agreements. At Moscow summit Nixon and Brezhnev signed SALT 1. First is Treaty on Limitation of Anti-ballistic Missiles which allows each nation to establish ABM defences only around national capital and one ICBM site. Second is interim agreement on limitation of strategic offensive weapons providing for a five-year freeze on ICBM deployment at then-existing levels.

27 May Development of Safeguard ABM halted.

November Command data buffer installation programme on Minuteman systems begins: allows rapid electronic retargeting, replacing manual insertion of target tapes.

December *Linebacker II* B-52 raids on Hanoi and Haiphong.

— — Blue Steel stand-off bomb withdrawn from RAF service.

— — Studies for SLCM Tomahawk started in US.

— — Joint RN/USN studies on conversion of RN SSBN fleet to Poseidon are inconclusive.

1973

27 January Vietnam peace treaty signed in Paris.

June USAF *Cobra Mist* over the horizon radar (OTH) station at Orfordness, Suffolk, England, deactivated after being only briefly operational.

July Extensive French nuclear tests at Muroroa.

— — *Delta-1*-class Soviet SSBN operational: twelve SS-N-8 missiles, 9600 km range, 1 MT warhead.

October Middle East War.

1974

April UK Labour government cabinet committee secretly sanctions *Chevaline* Polaris front-end improvement programme. Estimated cost: £250 million.

May Pluton tactical nuclear missiles enter service with French Army.

18 May India explodes 15 KT nuclear device.

3 July Threshold test-ban treaty signed limiting US-Soviet nuclear-weapons tests to maximum 150 KT.

July USA unilaterally destroys stocks of biological weapons.

14 August MRCA Tornado prototype first flight.

November President Ford and Secretary Brezhnev agree at Vladivostok on framework for new SALT treaty: joint ceilings of 2400 strategic nuclear delivery vehicles (SNDVs), 1320 MIRVed missiles.

23 December B-1A prototype first flight.

-- Tu-22M *Backfire* bomber operational.

-- First deployment of Chinese CSS-3 ICBM, 7000 km range, 2 MT.

-- First deployment of SS-18 very large Soviet ICBM, successor to SS-9. Mod 1 has very large single RV. Mod 2 has 8/10 MIRVs, 2 MT each with onboard computer.

1975

March First test of US Mk 500 MARV Manoeuvrable Evader RV.

26 March Convention against Bacteriological and Toxic weapons comes into force.

1 October Safeguard ABM system at N. Dakota Minuteman site declared operational (deactivated next day).

-- Su-19 *Fencer* nuclear-capable tactical strike aircraft becomes operational with Soviet Frontal Aviation.

-- USSR begins development of SS-17 ICBM, 10,000 km range, 4/6 MIRV warhead, 200 KT.

1976

February UK government announces intention of producing tritium in the UK, hitherto imported from US under 1958 agreement.

5 March First launch of ALCM from B-52 at White Sands missile range.

November President Ford authorizes production orders for enhanced radiation ER (neutron) 8-inch howitzer shells and Lance missile warheads.

– – Hound Dog missile retired from SAC.

– – US reconnaissance satellite reports new mobile Soviet IRBM deployed at Alma Ata (SS-20).

– – *Delta-II* SSBN operational with Soviet Navy, sixteen SS-N-8 SLBMs.

1977

March US reveals deployment of Phase III airborne launch control system (ALCS) for Minuteman ICBM force.

30 June B-1 cancelled.

September First *Chevaline* tests at Cape Canaveral.

October NATO Nuclear Planning Group sets up Task Force 10 to report on theatre nuclear force modernization.

October Chancellor Schmidt makes speech at International Institute of Strategic Studies, London, raising urgency of European theatre nuclear imbalance.

– – *Delta-III* SSBN operational with Soviet Navy: sixteen SS-N-18 SLBMs, 9000 km range, 3 KT MIRVs.

– – First reports in West of Soviet charged-particle beam weapons.

– – First flight of prototype Stealth aircraft.

– – USSR begins deployment of SS-20 mobile IRBMs in western Russia and Soviet Far East, 3700 km range, three MIRV warheads.

– – Cobra Dane phased array ICBM-detecting radar operational in US Aleutian Islands.

1978

January Two Polaris replacement committees set up in UK MoD, Foreign and Commonwealth Office.

April President Carter announces decision to postpone production of ER weapons.

May Pershing II advanced development programme completed.

May-1 July United Nations Special Session on Disarmament.

3 August US Army Appeals Board awards service disability pensions to leukemia victims of 1957 *Smoky* nuclear troop exposure tests.

November UK Polaris Replacement Committee reports. Submarine-based system must be sanctioned by the end of 1980.

1979

January At Guadeloupe summit, Callaghan-Carter talks on Polaris replacement.

February Full development contract awarded to Martin Marietta for Pershing II.

– – UK Parliamentary Committee begins examination of Polaris replacement.

– – Update improvements completed at Fylingdales, UK, BMEWs.

9 April Last Nike-Hercules/Hawk SAM systems protecting US cities deactivated.

May New UK Conservative government sets up MISC 7 Cabinet Committee to consider NATO TNF modernization.

June SALT 2 signed in Vienna. Treaty to last until 1985. SNDVs to be limited to 2250, ALCM carriers to 1320, MIRVed IRBMs to 1200, MIRVed ICBMs to 820, heavy MIRVed ICBMs to 308. Mobile missiles, ground- and sea-launched cruise missiles and Tu-22M not resolved.

September US satellite records double flash associated with nuclear weapon test in South Atlantic. South African or Israeli weapon test postulated.

– – President Carter authorizes development contract for MX missile by Martin Marietta.

6 October USSR announces troop withdrawals from East

Germany. Brezhnev offers reductions in SS-20 deployment conditional on non-deployment in Europe of Pershing II and GLCMs.

20 October First operational deployment of Trident I SLBM in converted Poseidon SSBN, USS *Francis Scott Key*.

1 December USAF Aerospace Defence Command (ADCOM) disestablished; space surveillance and missile warning resources absorbed by SAC.

December Deployment begins of Mk 12A advanced RV on Minuteman IIIs.

12 December NATO ministers announce decision on modernization of European theatre nuclear weapons – 'US ground launched systems comprising 108 Pershing II launchers' as substitutes for short-range Pershing IAs, and '464 GLCMs all with single-warheads'. The Pershings are to be based in West Germany, the GLCMs to be emplaced in Great Britain and Italy. Belgium and the Netherlands defer decision to emplace GLCMs.

26 December Soviet invasion of Afghanistan.

– – US suspends military aid to Pakistan in response to continuing atomic-weapons programme.

– – Space Defence Operations Centre (SPADOC) established at NORAD.

1980

January President Carter suspends exports of high technology to USSR, asks for Senate ratification of SALT 2 to be deferred.

January UK government announces intention of producing enriched uranium for SSBN fuel cores by gas-centrifuge process at UK sites.

January UK Minister of Defence announces existence of *Chevaline* Polaris front-end improvement programme costing £1000 million.

March UK government releases Civil Defence pamphlet *Protect and Survive*.

28 April European Campaign for Nuclear Disarmament (END) founded.

April US Congress adds $600 million to USAF development

funding of strategic weapons launcher (SWL) based on B-1. Wide-bodied ALCM-carrier is deleted.

May Flight tests of US ASALM advanced strategic air-launched missiles completed.

May First S-3 SSBS (*Sol-Sol Balistique Stratégique*) French IRBM silos operational, 3000 km range, 1.2 MT warhead, hardened against ABM defences.

29 May US Joint Chiefs testifying before Congress claim President Carter's FY 1981 defence budget insufficient to keep pace with Soviet improvements.

May China tests CSS-X-4 10,000 km ICBM.

June US begins withdrawal of 1000 old tactical nuclear warheads from Europe.

10 June US House/Senate resolution for abrogation of SALT 1 ABM treaty.

19 June UK government announces plans to deploy 110 US GLCMs at Molesworth, Cambridgeshire, and Greenham Common, Wiltshire.

28 June US House Appropriations Committee votes $3.1 million to build binary chemical warfare plant at Pine Bluff, Arkansas.

July French President reveals that France has developed and tested neutron weapons.

July Pave Paws SLBM-detecting radar sites operational on US east and west coasts.

July UK government announces decision to procure Trident I SLBM from US to arm four new Royal Navy SSBNs.

September Test firings of *Chevaline* Polaris SLBM from HMS *Renown* off Florida.

September Soviet *Typhoon*-class, very large SSBN, launched – 30,000 tons displacement, twenty SSN-X-20 8000 km range missiles.

4 September Iran-Iraq war begins.

September E-4B US AABNCP (Advanced Airborne National Command Post) operational.

November First test launch of French M-4 advanced MSBS SLBM from trials submarine *Le Gymnote*.

1981

20 January Inauguration of President Reagan. Caspar Weinberger is Secretary of Defence.

March During attempted assassination of President Reagan, secret war code card is lost. It is revealed that Joint Chiefs of Staff hold duplicates.

May UK Polaris *Chevaline* RV fails to separate in tests at Cape Canaveral.

May Washington radical issues report on 'continuous storage of US nuclear weapons in Japan in 1950s and 1960s'.

June US AEC begins production of tritium for Lance neutron warheads.

June USS *Ohio*, first Trident submarine, completes trials, two and a half years behind schedule.

June Israeli aircraft destroy Iraqi nuclear reactor site at Osirak.

13 July Tomahawk SLCM completes first successful submarine-launched strike against land target.

August US decision to develop and deploy enhanced radiation weapons (neutron bomb) announced.

August BMD terminal defence validation programme successfully tested at Kwajalein Atoll.

1 September M. Hernu, French Minister of Defence, confirms new French Socialist government's intention of continuing to develop ER weapons and completing sixth SNLE (SSBN).

2 October President Reagan announces details of US strategic defence programme:

(i) MX 'race track' scheme to be abandoned; 36 MXs to be based in hardened ex-Titan and Minuteman silos, the first to be operational by 1986. Three alternative basing options to be examined: continuous airborne patrol, BMD protection and superhardening of silos. 100 MXs to be operational by 1990 providing a capacity of 1000 RVs.

(ii) Long-range weapon system (B-1 bomber) under full development.

(iii) Stealth advanced technology radar-penetrating bomber under full development.

(iv) Continued construction of Trident SSBNs, one per year

to be armed with Trident II SLBM; operational in 1989. SLCMs to be deployed from 1984.

(v) Upgrading of strategic C^3 systems and strategic air defence.

Total cost budgeted at $180,300 million (£98,500 million) over six years – 15 per cent of total projected US defence spending.

10 October Very large anti-nuclear demonstration in Bonn.

16 October President Reagan comments on the possibility of a limited nuclear war in Europe not leading to a full US-USSR nuclear exchange.

24 October Simultaneous European anti-nuclear weapons rallies on large scale in London, Paris, Madrid, Oslo, Brussels, Helsinki. UK CND membership passes 300,000.

1 November Exercise *Warmon*, large-scale UK CD exercise.

4 November US Secretary of State, General Alexander Haig, talks of NATO plans to fire a nuclear warning shot in early stages of European war.

5-7 November Public disagreement within US administration on facts of NATO nuclear strategy.

5 November Swedish government announces that Soviet submarine stranded outside Karlskrona naval base probably has nuclear weapons aboard.

15 November Large anti-NATO demonstrations in Madrid and Athens.

19 November M. Hernu announces French government's forward nuclear defence policy:

(i) New tactical missile, the Hades, under development to replace Pluton.

(ii) SX IRBM to replace Mirage IV force in 1993.

(iii) Seventh SNLE (SSBN) to be constructed.

(iv) Sixth SNLE to be operational in 1985 armed with 16 M4 SLBMs.

(v) Five SNLEs in service to be converted to take 16 M4 SLBMs, six 150 KT RVs, 4400 km range.

19 November President Reagan makes 'zero option' offer to cancel deployment of Pershing IIs and GLCMs in Europe in response to Soviet dismantling of SS-20s aimed at Europe.

22-24 November Brezhnev-Schmidt conference in Bonn. USSR offers unilateral reduction of 'certain portion' of IRBM force.

30 November Medium-range-missile-reduction talks begin in closed session at Geneva. Paul Nitze is chief US negotiator, Yuli Kiviisnsky for USSR.

19 December Military takeover in Poland. US imposes sanctions on USSR including suspension of high-technology exports.

1982

January US DoD announces intention of reaching initial operating capability with Minuteman silos for MX by 1986.

– – UK announces re-motoring programme for Polaris missiles and updated guidance systems for submarines.

February US government refuses to agree on date for resumption of Strategic Arms Limitation Talks because of Poland.

– – US government acknowledges intention of expanding production of nuclear warheads. Intention is to scrap 6500 old warheads, and expand arsenal by 10,500 overall to 40,500.

2 March US DoD announces detection by reconnaissance satellite of B-1 type new Soviet bomber.

7 March Test launch of French M4 SLBM.

11 March UK government announces decision to procure Trident D-5.

16 March President Brezhnev announces moratorium on new Soviet missiles targeted on Western Europe. If US went ahead with deploying new systems, Soviet Union would create an analagous situation for the US.

March US Navy announces plan to dispose of old SSBNs and SSNs by sinking in deep ocean trenches.

22 March Operation *Ivy League*: US wargame involving actual National Command Authorities includes US President's death and full retaliatory exchange.

7 April RAF Vulcan force committed to role in Falklands.

2 May HMS *Conqueror* torpedoes and sinks *General Belgrano*, first act of war by a nuclear-powered submarine.

6 June Spain joins NATO.

7 June Second United Nations Special Session on Disarmament opens.

7 June President Reagan affirms intention of seeking dialogue with Soviet Union on strategic weapons. Each side to reduce its long-range arsenal to 5000 warheads, to be followed by discussion on throwweight and number of land-based launchers.

14 June Pentagon document envisages a 'prolonged nuclear war' if necessary.

14 June Very large anti-nuclear demonstrations in New York.

15 June Very large anti-nuclear weapon demonstration greets President Reagan in Bonn and elsewhere in Europe.

23 June UK Defence Estimates shows unbroken commitment to Trident and continued diminution of surface naval forces despite Falklands fighting.

29 June START negotiations open in Geneva.

June First operational RAF Tornado squadron formed.

14 July UN Special Session on Disarmament ends in disarray.

July First Pershing II test flight aborted.

September US DoD reports existence of Blackjack-A, a new Soviet intercontinental bomber.

October UK government announces that RN Trident D-5s will be stocked and maintained at King's Bay, Georgia. Warheads will be stocked at Coulport, Scotland.

October New Soviet solid fuel ICBM fails in test flight.

October China launches first SLBM, 1600 km range.

October Chevaline warhead enters service with RN.

October French aircraft carriers *Foch* and *Clemenceau* complete refit to operate Super Etendard strike aircraft and tactical nuclear weapons.

November US government announces choice of Dense Pack basing mode for 100 MX ICBMs at Warren AFB, Cheyenne, Wyoming.

November Yuri Andropov becomes Chairman of the Soviet Communist Party.

December Boeing ALCM operational on B-52s of 416th Bombardment Wing.

December US Congress approves record peacetime defence budget but MX production money withheld.

December Last RAF Vulcan in strike role retired.

1983

January Rockwell awarded production contract for seven B-1B strategic bombers.

January Japanese government approves transfer of military technology to the USA.

January USS *New Jersey* recommissioned, to be SLCM platform.

January Second group of nine S-3 ICBMs operational on Plateau d'Albion.

February USAF announces ALCM production to stop at 1500, to be followed by AALCM.

February Warsaw Pact summit proposes non-aggression pact with NATO.

February Dense Pack basing mode for MX rejected by US Congress.

February US Army successfully intercepts Minuteman I with experimental ABM (Homing Overlay) outside atmosphere.

February First test flight of Mirage 2000, French nuclear strike aircraft.

March Florennes, Belgium selected as GLCM deployment site.

March CDU victory in German general election.

March President Reagan announces emphasis on high technology space-based defence programme against nuclear attack.

April French defence budget includes two new SSBNs, development of ASMP nuclear stand-off missile for Mirage IV and Mirage 2000, SX mobile ICBM by 1996, Hades MRBM by 1992. Army reduced by 7%.

April MX basing committee reports 100 missiles to be deployed in Minuteman silos, new mobile single warhead missile to be developed.

May US Catholic bishops call for nuclear freeze.

12 • US Strategic Forces

The strategic nuclear forces of the United States are in the process of a huge cycle of replacement and modernization. In the mid-1950s the US Congress approved the so-called 'triad' of nuclear systems: manned penetrating bombers, silo-launched ICBMs and submarine-launched ballistic missiles. Each had relative advantages or disadvantages in terms of accuracy, survivability, range, adaptability and cost but the systems overlapped and were the building blocks from which a flexible range of deterrent strategies could be constructed. This combination was enough until the mid-1970s when the great ICBM vulnerability scare gave the impetus to develop not just replacement systems but ones with new capabilities. They were the Trident SLBM, and MX mobile ICBM, the cruise missile, the B-1 manned bomber and the so-called 'Stealth' aircraft. All these programmes were in an advanced state of research and development when President Reagan came to office and opened the pursestrings.

Capabilities Now: Strategic Air Command

SAC (universally referred to as 'Sack') maintains near to 70 per cent of all US nuclear delivery vehicles, 1053 ICBMs and approximately 400 manned bombers. Virtually 100 per cent of the missiles and 30 per cent of the bombers are on constant alert and SAC operates the USAF tanker fleet, some 600 KC-135s undergoing a long-term re-engining programme and being supplemented by the KC-10A tanker version of the DC-10 wide body airliner. SAC crews also operate the EC-135 Looking Glass Command Posts, the E-4B National Emergency Airborne Command Posts, RC-135 electronic intelligence aircraft and the U-2, TR-1 and SR-71 strategic reconnaissance aircraft.

The Minuteman Force

The total number of US ICBMs has been the same since 1967 in the 'heavy/light' mix of 1000 Minutemen and big Titan IIs (one was lost in a silo fire). The Minuteman force is organized in Flights of ten launchers, each Flight having its own launch control centre. Five Flights make a Squadron and three or more make a Strategic Missile Wing.

Each Wing can be dispersed over a very wide area – the biggest Minuteman field is over 18,000 square miles, while individual missiles are emplaced in silos with a fenced-off surface area of two acres strewn with sensors. The silo is 25 m deep and 4 m in diameter, protected by a six-sided steel and concrete carapace weighing 100 tons. The flight-launch control centre over 5 km from the silo is 15 m underground and contains a blast-resistant, shock-mounted capsule occupied by two SAC officers who control a flight of ten missiles. Inside the launch control centre the first warning of an attack would be an oscillating note on the loudspeaker, at which the crew immediately close the blast doors and go on to emergency air. If it is a real attack the speakers will announce, 'Gentlemen you have received an authorized launch instruction from the National Command Authority,' and simultaneously a printed code of letters and numbers comes through a telex machine. The crew open a strongbox on the wall and check the code inside against the code they have received. If they match, the launch command is valid. They sit in chairs at right-angles to each other, fifteen feet apart, and set their individual codes (unknown to each other) to gain access to the firing circuits, then turn keys within two seconds of each other and hold them in place for two seconds. A second crew in another capsule have to go through the same operations, 'voting' simultaneously for the launch command to be effected. These centres can also control a squadron should other centres be knocked out, and a single centre can override another individual centre's launch command acting independently of the squadron's; but once a missile is fired there is no recall. The Phase III airborne-launch control system now nearing initial operating capability will provide nine EC-135C aircraft able to monitor 200 ICBM's and control and retarget them from the air.

There are 450 Minuteman IIs in the SAC inventory, each tipped with a single RV equipped with advanced penetration aids. The 550 Minuteman IIIs carry a MIRV warhead of three RVs plus chaff and decoys, and installation of the advanced Mk 12A warhead on 300 missiles began in December 1979. The NS-20 guidance system gives the Minuteman III a circular error probable of about 0.12 nautical miles. The 170 KT yield Mk 12 warhead has a 75 per cent chance of crushing a silo hardened to 1000 psi, and each Mk 12A at 335 KT improves that chance to 88 per cent.

Strategic Bombers

SAC currently operates over 300 B-52G/Hs and 60 FB-111 strategic bombers. The venerable B-52s which date back to the 1950s have been extensively re-engineered to keep airframes and avionics up to the mark; they can carry very large yield free-fall bombs or fourteen nuclear short-range attack missiles, designed to destroy terminally defended targets after deep penetration has been effected (using SRAMs to destroy defences along the way if necessary). Improving Soviet defences will go on reducing B-52 probabilities in spite of improved ECM but the force is being reworked as ALCM carriers (see below). FB-111s can carry six B-61 free-fall bombs or six SRAMs and could strike the Soviet Union if forward-based in the UK.

Ballistic Missile Submarines

The nuclear-powered ballistic submarine fleet of the US Navy is in the process of introducing the first of the third-generation strategic systems to become operational, the Trident missile. The Trident I has twice the range of the Poseidon (7000 km), giving the launch submarine more searoom to hide in with no deterioration in accuracy over longer range. It can be fitted with the Mk 500 Evader MARV (manoeuvring re-entry vehicle) capable of pre-selected evasive manoeuvres during atmospheric re-entry to ensure better penetration of any enemy defences, or the Mk 4 with eight 100 KT RVs.

Since its inception the SSBN fleet has provided the assured destruction component of the triad, its original Polaris A-3 and then Poseidon C-3 SLBMs being effective against soft city targets, but neither accurate nor powerful enough to assure 'hard target kills'. The number of SSBNs each with sixteen tubes remained static from 1967 to 1980 – forty-one boats. Now ten of the Polaris boats have been withdrawn and twelve Poseidon boats are being converted to take Trident I by 1983. Eight *Ohio*-class, purpose-built twenty-four-tube Trident submarines are under construction. The current programme called for twelve, however the schedule has fallen into disarray, construction and material faults having seriously shaken confidence.

US Navy SSBNs are based at King's Bay in Georgia, Charleston in South Carolina, Holy Loch in Scotland and Rota in Spain (closed in 1980), and a support base at Bangor, Washington State, is under construction. Four hundred Poseidon warheads are allotted to SACEUR to cover targets in Europe and western Russia outside the implementation of the full US SIOP.

In early 1982 the US government announced its intention of expanding the production of nuclear warheads. The FY 1982 budget had already allotted $1,040 million to warhead manufacture; several hundred million more would be needed. These plans would go far beyond those set in motion in the closing stages of the Carter administration which re-opened the closed plant at Savannah, Georgia. The reactors at Savannah would be redesigned and production boosted at the Hanford plant in Washington State. There would be no revival of the proposal to use fuel from commercial reactors for weapons grade material although it was hinted that Great Britain might provide a source of Plutonium and Tritium. The present stockpile of 30,000 warheads would climb to 40,000, and 6500 non-operational obsolete weapons would be replaced. The effective arsenal would thus expand by 70 per cent and the number of warheads immediately combat-available would climb from 12,000 to 20,000.

Capabilities Now: Strategic Defence

Unlike the Soviet Union, the USA possesses no strategic anti-aircraft missile system. Manned interceptors are up to twenty-five years old although modern equipment is earmarked for their replacement. The strategic air defence of the United States is an early-warning system designed to make deterrent retaliatory forces credible. The joint US/Canadian North American Aerospace Defence Command, NORAD, like the offensive strategic forces, relies on several complimentary and overlapping systems to lessen the likelihood of a successful surprise attack or a false alarm. Two different devices that sense different physical phenomena survey each known relevant launch-site. An early-warning satellite in synchronous orbit over the Indian Ocean uses infra-red sensors to spot ICBM rocket plumes within 90 seconds after launch and relays signals to control stations at Guam and Nurrunger, Australia, which can relay information to NORAD almost instantaneously. Satellites have their limitations: in low orbit they are already compromised by demonstrated Soviet hunter-killer techniques, and, being dependent on reading infra-red, lose track of missiles in mid-course after the boosters burn out but *before* the MIRVs and penaids separate. Ground-based radar systems thus take over where the satellites leave off. The three huge overlapping arcs of the BMEWs (ballistic-missile early warning) system extend outwards from Clear in Alaska, Thule in Greenland and Fylingdales in the UK for 3000 miles, covering anything coming out of the Eurasian land mass. The thirteen tracking radars of BMEWs track ICBMs and IRBMs but not MIRVs or satellites. The Space Detection and Tracking system (SPADATS) station at Shemya, Alaska, called Cobra Dane complements the BMEWs' watch. SPADATS includes the USAF's Spacetrack system composed of large radar-optical and radio-metric sensors located around the world maintaining a catalogue of all objects in space. The US Navy's NAVSPASUR system tracks satellites passing through a fence across the southern USA and, with other test-range radars, including the UK Malvern radar, feeds into the SPADATS net. SPADOC (Space Defence Operations Centre) at NORAD controls commands and communications to all space-associated commands and agencies. One north-facing phased-array radar at Grand Forks, North Dakota, identifies and tracks individual RVs (Perimeter Acquisition Radar Attack Characteristics System – PARCS – a relic of the original ABM defences) and a phased array radar in Florida called FPS-85 looks south, guarding against a Fractional Orbital Bombardment (wrong way round the globe) missile attack. It also watches the Caribbean for SLBM attacks, joining two Pave Paws phased array radars on the Pacific and Atlantic coasts looking out for close-in submarine-launched missile attacks.

Defence against manned aircraft (and the new threat of cruise missiles) has declined from a 1960 peak as the threat of the bomber seemed to recede. The Distant Early Warning (DEW) line crosses northern Canada backed up by twenty-four stations of the Pine Tree line in southern Canada. They can detect aircraft or cruise missiles at 200 miles out and up to 40,000 feet but not at low level, so effort is going into three systems. Over the horizon back scatter (OTH-B) radars in Maine and Washington State and into the thirty-four AWACS aircraft which are entering service with Tactical Air Command, seven of which are allotted to continental air defence. Six Regional Operations Control Centres (ROCCs) will, by 1983, control forty-six radars in the US, Alaska and Canada for the co-ordination and control of military and civil air traffic within the continental United States itself (the Joint Services System – JSS).

In 1979/80 the organization of North American air defences went through a transition. Anti-aircraft missile defence of US cities was scrapped, and ADCOM (Aerospace Defence Command) had its brief reduced. In April 1981, the Aerospace Defence Centre (ADC) was established to support both ADCOM and the joint US/Canadian North American Aerospace Defence Command. Lieutenant General James Hartinger on 1 January 1980 became Commander of ADC as well as NORAD and ADCOM, with the associated SPADOC.

NORAD is based at Colorado Springs on the edge of the Rocky Mountains and has a massive battle headquarters blasted out of the solid granite of Cheyenne Mountain for retreat to on the first hint of an alert. A third of a mile into the mountain are fifteen steel structures shock-mounted on springs, in which the staff of NORAD can operate 'buttoned up' for up to one month with autonomous life-support systems.

Information from satellites and radars is fed into the central command post and displayed on massive screens posting the positions of Soviet SSBNs (detected by sonars, US submarines and by satellites), the movements of aircraft, the tracks of satellites and events deep within the missile fields of the Soviet Union itself. NORAD does not control any retaliatory forces. It passes its information to forty other relevant US agencies and to the National Command Authority.

Civil Defence

The Office of Civil Defence originally came under the Secretary of the Army and has some 10,000 civilian employees with 20,000 part-time volunteers, organized on state and local lines. There are some 3000 protected Emergency Operating Centres (EOCs) for use by key officials and an Emergency Broadcast System which utilizes 600 civil stations hardened by a 'Broadcast Station Protection Programme' with emergency power and secure radio links to the EOCs. Over 1500 warning points are linked to NORAD and there are more than 65,000 radiological monitoring locations. In July 1979 a Presidential Executive Order transferred responsibility for the US Civil Defence Programme from the DoD to the Federal Emergency Management Agency (FEMA) with new funding and new imperatives to 'enhance deterrence and stability in conjunction with our strategic offensive and other strategic defence forces'.

Capabilities to Come

MX

The MX missile is a four-stage ICBM, weighing 86 tonnes and capable of lifting 3600 kg over 11,100 km. The post-boost vehicle (the 'bus') contains the computers, guidance and communications equipment that control the missile and ten independently targetable Mk 12A RVs. The missile's accuracy and the warhead's capabilities give on paper a CEP of 0.05 nm and a kill rate against a 1000 psi hardened silo of 99.9 per cent.

The MX is more than a bigger, more lethal Minuteman. In many ways its counterforce ability is irrelevant in a second-strike context as it would merely crush empty silos. What is much more important is the MX's survivability. MX was designed as a mobile missile, able to be carried and launched from very large transporters and equipped with the AIRS guidance system (Advanced Intertial Reference Sphere) which permits missiles to be shuttled about while the inertial navigation system continuously updates itself, providing a true initial reference.

There were many proposals for using this capability – such as mounting the missiles on railway wagons, in underground closed loops or on linear tracks and by providing 4600 shelters for 200 missiles so that the number of targets would soak up the Soviets' ICBM MIRVed warhead capacity. Friends of the MX said it would cost $34 billion. Its enemies put on it a price-tag three times as much and pointed out that the 'shell game' deceptive basing would consume 40 per cent of US cement production over three years. There had been thirty-six high-powered reviews of the MX basing mode over fifteen years to 1981 and several announced changes of government policy. The Reagan administration has scrapped the 'shell game' and is planning an initial operating capacity by 1986 with MX placed in Minuteman silos. Airborne basing on a wide-bodied aircraft named Big Bird, Deep Under Mountain Basing (DUMB) and Ballistic Missile Defence are also being considered; so is a concept called 'dense-pack' which relies on close spacing so that incoming missiles destroy each other by 'fratricide'.

Trident II

A follow-on Trident SLBM is under development by Lockheed, called the D-5. It will utilize the full volume of the tubes on Trident submarines and have range greater than 7000 km without loss of payload. Further improved accuracy and the Mk 12A or an improved Mk 500 Evader MARV would give the missile a hard-target-kill counterforce ability.

Cruise

The cruise-missile concept – an air-breathing, terrain-hugging, long-range penetration missile that flies to its target with great

accuracy at low level confounding traditional air defences –
embraces a wide range of programmes and diverse means of
basing which are summarized here.

Sea-launched
TASM: tactical anti-ship missile, Tomahawk BGM-109B/E
(non-strategic)
TLAM-C: conventional land-attack missile, Tomahawk BGM-
109C (non-strategic)
TLAM-N: Nuclear land-attack missile, Tomahawk. This
missile combined with the VLS (vertical launch system) will arm
US Navy submarines and surface vessels the size of destroyers,
affording them a nuclear-attack capability over 2500 km range.
900 SLCMs (or 'Slickems', as the Americans call them) are
planned to be operational by 1987 and they will be deployed in
'farms' on de-mothballed battleships.

Air-launched
MRASM: Tomahawk basis for AGM-109H air-to-ground
high-priority target conventional attack missile (non-strategic)
ALCM: the air-launched cruise missile is a key aspect of the US
strategic forces modernization programme. It can fly for 2500
km at 800 km/h and its long, slow approach encourages
accuracies that ballistic missiles cannot achieve. Current plans
call for 170 Boeing B-52Gs to be re-engineered as ALCM
carriers carrying twenty missiles each by 1990.

Ground-launched
The Tomahawk BGM-109G is the 2300 km-range missile that
is coming to the UK and other NATO countries at the end of
1983 to be operated by the USAF.

The combat flight of a GLCM squadron consists of sixteen
Tomahawk missiles based on four transporter-launchers and
two launch-control centres. One flight retains a quick-reaction
alert status at each operating base during normal conditions
while the flights would disperse to 'satellite' stations during full
alert-stations. Eighty per cent will have W-80 nuclear warheads
while the remainder will have conventional warheads including
airfield attack cluster munitions.

The range and capabilities of cruise missiles were not covered in SALT 2 although air launch platforms were, and it was agreed not to deploy SLCMs or GLCMs until 1982 to allow more time to negotiate.

Cruise puts a new chip on the table and all newness is destabilizing. It can be mounted on a very wide range of small launch platforms and the distinction between tactical, tactical-nuclear or strategic nuclear is blurred. However, because it flies at 500 mph and would take three hours to reach the Soviet Union from ground launch in the UK it cannot be a surprise first strike weapon, in spite of its accuracy.

Strategic Aircraft

The cancellation of the B-1 by President Carter in 1977 was regarded by his US domestic opponents not as a sensible realization that the day of the manned, long-range military aircraft was over but as an act of strategic infirmity. When President Reagan announced plans to built 100 B-1Bs in October 1981 (described by its opponents as the most expensive weapons system ever undertaken by the United States) he was fulfilling a long-standing political promise. But many felt the military facts had moved on and that Soviet air defence would compromise any conventional manned penetrator however lavishly equipped with ECM by the end of the 1980s. Nevertheless, at the end of 1981 the House of Representatives and the Senate approved the procurement of the system after intense lobbying by the manufacturers and the USAF who argued that maintaining the B-52 force to the year 2000 would cost nearly as much as the $100 billion bill for a new long-range combat aircraft force. The B-1B can carry twenty-two ALCMs, thirty-eight SRAMs, and up to thirty-eight free-fall nuclear bombs or a range of conventional supermunitions.

Part of the political debate hinged on the allocation of resources between the B-1B and the advanced technology bomber (ATB) – the so-called Stealth aircraft, although according to a statement by the Under Secretary of Defence for Research and Engineering at the end of 1981, Stealth is adequately funded through 1983 and 1984 to reach deployment in the early 1990s.

Stealth

The ATB relies on deception rather than speed to outwit its opponents and is designed to present the lowest possible optical, radar and infra-red 'signatures' to enemy sensors. A product of the famous Lockheed 'Skunk Works' at Burbank, California, which produced the U-2 and SR-71 Blackbird, a twin turbojet prototype is reported to have flown for the first time in 1977. The prototype with the type name X-25 has high-mounted engines, heat-suppression devices and a carefully shaped airframe incorporating much non-metallic composite material, and eliminates as many echo-producing corners as possible. The whole is clad in emission-absorbing tiles. Two prototypes are reported to have crashed in testing.

Command, Control and Communications

A very important component of the strategic force modernization package concerns C^3. The Administration intends spending $18 billion over six years on extending existing and introducing new programmes. The aim is to make US strategic forces less vulnerable to 'decapitation' (eliminating the supreme command machinery) or disruption. Systems will be battlehardened by extensive use of fibre-optics (which is resistant to electro-magnetic pulse) and double-routing. Beyond expanding programmes in progress, the new package includes MILSTAR, a highly survivable satellite-based command and control system using advanced VHF technologies that will provide immune two-way communications between forces in the field and the National Command Authority. MX missiles will further be available to put essential space hardware back into orbit and repair any damage caused by hunter-killer attacks on communications, early-warning or control satellites. The Electronic Systems Division of Air Force Systems Command has set up a 'super SPO', a systems programme office, to manage this very large venture.

Ballistic Missile Defence

Practical ballistic missile defence is under large-scale research and development and is one of the options under review for closing the window of vulnerability on the MX missile. The programme is in two parts, the 'Advanced Technology Programme' and the 'Systems Technology Programme' which turns fundamental research into missiles, computers and radars into practical systems to perform the enormous feats of mathematics and engineering that intercepting a ballistic re-entry vehicle with another missile represents. Concepts developed so far are the Low Altitude Defence system which could be deployed fairly rapidly to defend Minuteman or MX installations. LoAD studies have proved the feasibility of building a BMD system that can intercept ICBM re-entry vehicles, discriminating warheads from decoys and the ICBM's tanks breaking up and have proved by tracking targets of opportunity that the very large radar and data processing loads imposed by a heavy attack can be handled. The second concept is layered defence with LoAD providing the close-in terminal defence and an overlay thinning the attack by non-nuclear means outside the atmosphere. A particular pressure group is pushing a proposal called 'High Frontier' which envisages spending $50 billion over a decade with surface to air 'swarmjet' silo-protecting projectiles becoming operational in 2-3 years, missile armed satellites in 5-6 years and a 'space plane' to tend advanced ABM satellites by 1990. The BMD development programme is seen as an insurance policy against unrestrained, unSALTed growth in the number of Soviet warheads.

13 • Soviet Strategic Forces

The Soviet Union, like the United States, has a triad of strategic nuclear forces: land-based missiles, sea-launched missiles and long-range aircraft with a sophisticated satellite-based command and control system. The force structuring does not, however, represent a mirror image of that of the United States.

Soviet strategic doctrine prizes the frustration of the opponent's nuclear strike and when in the late 1960s MIRV technology aborted the development of anti-ballistic missiles, this doctrine became more important. Regardless of how a war started, the nuclear forces and command systems of the opponent are the first-priority targets and these include silos, launch controls, bomber bases, submarine berths and nuclear storage facilities. Second-priority targets would be those associated with the ability to project power abroad. Third-priority targets would be core industrial and energy targets.

Missiles

The Strategic Rocket Forces, *Raketnyye Voyska Strategicheskovo Naznacheniya (RVSN)*, control all military ICBMs, IRBMs and MRBMs and its carefully selected personnel are the elite of the Soviet armed forces. Missiles with ranges of less than 1000 km are assigned to the rocket and artillery troops of the ground forces. Organization is based on Army, Division, Regiment, Battalion and Battery, a Battery consisting of a single launcher.

Much of the Soviet Union's arsenal of silo-emplaced ICBMs is strung out along the Trans-Siberian Railway, away from population centres. Other fields are in the Arctic and Ukraine. A typical complex consists of a number of launch groups, each launch group being either six or ten silos, plus road, rail-transfer facilities and launch control centres.

Four major design bureaux specialize in strategic missile development, controlling many hundreds of subsidiary development, test and production facilities. Development is concentrating on giving the force ever greater technical capabilities, accuracy, reduction in size of individual RVs and thus more per launcher and 'cold-launch' reload capability. Most Soviet ICBMs can carry warheads with yields of more than 1 MT. The least destructive tips have three times the yield of a MK 12-headed Minuteman III. High accuracy is now joining the equation and if, as US intelligence sources predict, post-boost control will afford SS-18s and SS-19s a CEP of 0.1 nm by the mid-1980s, their capabilities against the hardest silos in the US will be unqualified. The current modernization programme is installing the 10,000 km range SS-17, the very large SS-18 and SS-19 with onboard computer and MIRV warhead. The SS-16 'light' ICBM is a three-stage SS-20 and retains the small system's mobile basing. As such, it was forbidden under the now discarded terms of SALT 2; developments of this programme are being very closely watched by US intelligence.

Among the half-completed German secret weapons captured by the Soviets in 1945 were U-boat-towed containers designed to be able to launch V-2s at the USA. Although never used operationally, the concept was eagerly explored by Soviet scientists and the first experimental launch of a ballistic missile from a Soviet submarine was in 1955, more than four years before the US Navy tested Polaris. In the early 1960s the *Golf*-class diesel and the *Hotel*-class nuclear-powered ballistic-missile submarines began to enter service followed by the successively improved *Delta* and *Yankee* classes (as they are codenamed by NATO). The *Delta III* carries sixteen SS-N-18 missiles, each with a 6500 km range and a seven-MIRV warhead. In September 1980 at Severodvinsk, the largest submarine every built was launched, first of the *Typhoon* class with twenty tubes for the 8300 km range SS-NX-20. Propelled by two reactors, the enormous *Typhoon* is 170 metres long (the length of two and a half Boeing 747s) and displaces 33,000 tons dived.

In the 1970s the number of SLBM tubes climbed from 289

to almost 1000 and target coverage was further increased when SS-N-18s with MIRV warheads first went to sea in 1978. Coverage, however, is still far less than that of the US (1309 to 5210) but the Soviet SSBN fleet can still wage effective counterforce war with US ballistic missile submarine yards, stores and bases as targets. From stations close to US coasts, Strategic Air Command bases could be struck seven minutes after launch although technical difficulties with trajectories impose a minimum range of 300 nautical miles. Flight times to SAC's nearest bomber and tanker bases would triple, however, for missiles fired from the Barents Sea where most patrols are stationed. The Soviet ballistic-missile submarine fleets are based on two major complexes, Polyarny on the Kola peninsula and at Petropavlovsk-Kamschatsky on the Pacific.

Long-range Aviation

The Soviet Union never developed a long-range manned bomber force on anything like the scale of the US although small numbers of the two aircraft originally flown in the early 1950s, the turboprop-powered Tu-95 Bear and M-4 Bison, are still in service with the Long Range Aviation, the *Dal'nya Aviatsaya* (*DA*) and in February 1982 the US Secretary of Defence announced the detection of a new bomber similar to the US B-1 by reconnaissance satellite, the 'Bomber-X'. A major question of the original SALT talks was whether the *DA* was targeted against the continental United States, although the Soviets insisted that it was not exclusively an intercontinental weapons system. The introduction of the very capable Tu-22M *Backfire* in the mid-1970s became a stumbling block of the SALT 2 negotiations and a gift to SALT's US domestic enemies. The unratified treaty's protocol eventually contained an exchange of statements that the *Backfire* was not to be regarded as a heavy bomber unless it was armed with long-range cruise missiles, although American *Backfire*-fanciers pointed out that the aircraft could easily be converted to a strategic system by the addition of an inflight refuelling capacity. More than seventy *Backfires* serve with the *DA*, and the same number with Soviet naval aviation and production continues at an estimated rate of forty-two per year with a target of a strategic/maritime force of 250/400 aircraft. One *Backfire* unit has been based in the Far East since spring 1979.

Strategic Defence

The Soviet Union has put enormous effort and investment into strategic aerospace defence, grouped since 1948 as a separate command, the *Voyska Provivovozdushnoy Oborony Strany – PVO Strany*. By 1955 Moscow was protected by two concentric rings of SAMs and very large numbers of launchers are still deployed despite the decline in numbers of US manned aircraft. Soviet efforts to develop anti-ballistic missile defences and satellite killers have also been strenuous with PKO (anti-space defence) and PRO (anti-rocket) established in the mid-1960s. In 1977 a controversy broke in the United States as to whether or not the Soviets had succeeded in developing high-energy lasers capable of destroying both satellites and missiles (see page 117).

The Soviet Union has two major National Air Defence Districts, Moscow and Baku, grouping most of its assets against NATO and China, and the rest of the country is divided into air defence regions. The PVO forces have three basic components – manned interceptors, radio technical troops and zenith rocket troops – and close ties are maintained between PVO units and civil defence troops.

The *Radiotekhnicheskiye Voyska-RTV* or radio technical troops are responsible for the electronic watch of airspace, operating a dense and overlapping network of more than 6000 radars. Current US electronic countermeasures have difficulty in limiting the performance of the older simpler radars and the most modern Soviet radars are considered to be very good indeed. The *Hen House* ballistic-missile early-warning network informs the ABM defences round Moscow (a total of sixty-four missiles based on four sites), and the BMEW system is being extended with new phased-array radars and two over-the-horizon radars facing the USA. *Moss* AWACS aircraft, which have a limited capability over water and cannot reliably separate targets from ground clutter, will be replaced by an improved system probably based on the 1-76. This network of early-warning and ground control intercept stations feeds information to the Fighter Aviation of Air Defence (*Istrebelbitel'naya Aviatsaya PVO-IA PVO*) which fields some 2700 interceptor aircraft and the *Zenitnyye Raketnyye Voyska* (*ZRV*), controlling 12,400 SAM launchers at over 1000 fixed sites. Capabilities of manned interceptors and surface-to-air missiles are being improved and although *PVO* has not yet deployed a look-down, shoot-down system in the MiG-25 *Foxbat* or any other aircraft, an advanced version of this interceptor called *Foxhound* with snap-down missiles and high-capability radar has been successfully tested.

SAC bomber crews rate Soviet air defence to be a very formidable barrier in its present state, even though half the equipment inventory is obsolete by US standards. Overall effectiveness against low-level penetrations might still be low, however, and US tests indicate that existing Soviet early-warning radars can only detect cruise missile attacks at close range; and current infra-red guided SAMs and air-to-air missiles are ineffective against them for several reasons.

Technical improvements and the introduction of new systems are continuing in all aspects of strategic air defence – new interceptors, new SAMs, and new AWACS and new capabilities against low-level attacks and cruise missiles. There is also continuous ABM research concentrating on more capable battle management radars and rapidity of deployment. The existing ABM defences of Moscow, which are regarded as ineffective against MIRV attacks, are expected to be substantially upgraded. The demonstrated low-altitude orbital anti-satellite interceptor poses a limited threat to some US satellites and it is anticipated that continuing research will eventually produce a system capable of knocking out satellites in high orbit.

The Soviet emphasis on civil defence (CD) is very great and deep within a militarized, ordered society. In 1961 responsibility was transferred from the Interior Ministry of Defence itself, making CD a branch of the Army. The 50,000 regular troops combined with 65,000 reserves are commanded by a Deputy Minister of Defence, General of the Army A.T. Altunin, appointed with a wide-ranging brief and lavish funding in 1972 to reinvigorate the organization after the retreat from anti-ballistic missile defences. Military Civil Defence staffs exist at each echelon of the Soviet government structure with local civilian staffs in towns and factories. The Moscow Higher Command School of Road and Engineer Troops runs a four-year course in civil defence.

The Soviet population, although concentrated in a triangle bounded by Leningrad, Odessa and Kuznetz containing the core areas of Moscow, Donets, Baku and the Urals, is far less compressed than that of the United States. The 1000 largest cities contain less than half the total population, 271 cities have populations of at least 100,000, 18 exceed 1 million and Moscow has 7 million.

Current doctrine reportedly entails clearing these cities in times of crisis while essential services are still manned and functioning with recourse to blast and fall-out shelters in factories. There are deep, very hard urban shelters, a secure communications net and rural dispersal sites for 115,000 key administrators. There is also training and practice to protect the economic assets on which the evacuated populations and any post-war recovery depends. The Boeing Company tested the Soviet civil defence manual's directions on protecting machine tools, covering several kinds with sandbags and exploding 500 tons of TNT close enough to get a pulse of overpressure, simulating a nuclear explosion. At 1300 psi, heavy machinery bedded on Styrofoam and packed with earth and swarf remained operable.

In 1978 there was another 'gap' scare in the US, fulfilling the prophecy of Dr Strangelove's 'mineshaft gap'. It was in response to claims that in a general war Soviet fatalities would be 4-5 per cent and the United States 50 per cent of the population. No matter how crushing or effective offensive strategic forces were on either side, effective civil defence would shield key economic assets, allow a rapid recovery from the war and thus produce a 'winner' and a 'loser'. US strategists and intelligence agencies became very interested in the subject of Soviet civil defence but they produced contradictory conclusions. The US Department of Defence reported that although city evacuation and economic 'hardening' plans looked impressive, they doubted their efficacy in practice. Other experts concluded that 'Soviet preparations substantially undermine the concept of deterrence that forms the cornerstone of US security.'

Nuclear Delivery Vehicles, 1982

NATO/FRANCE

ICBM	52 Titan II 450 Minuteman II 550 Minuteman III	USA
SLBM	320 Poseidon C-3 200 Trident C-4	USA
	64 Polaris A-3 80 MSBS M-20	UK Fr
Bombers	(long/medium range) 151 B-52G 90 B-52H 75 B-52D (phasing out) 60 FB-IIIA (carry 1250 SRAM) 48 Vulcan B2	USA UK (phasing out, Tornado operational 1983)
	33 Mirage IVA	Fr

708 US (inc carrier) nuclear-capable strike aircraft in Europe
704 Other NATO/French nuclear-capable strike aircraft

IRBM	18 SSBS	Fr
SRBM	108 Pershing 1	USA
	36 Lance	

179 Honest John, Pershing and Lance with other NATO
42 Pluton   Fr
300 US nuclear-capable artillery, 1600 nuclear-capable artillery with other NATO

WARSAW PACT

ICBM
520 SS-11
60 SS-13
150 SS-17
308 SS-18
300 SS-19 Mods 1/2

SLBM
18 SS-N-5
165 SS-N-6 Mods 1/2
288 SS-N-6 Mod 3
291 SS-N-8
12 SS-NX-17
256 SS-N-18

Bombers
105 Tu-95
45 Mya-4
580 Tu-16
165 Tu-22
135 Tu-22M
2785 strike aircraft, some nuclear-
capable

IRBM
300 SS-4
40 SS-5
280 SS-20 (deployment continuing)

SRBM
650 SS-12, SS-21, SS-22, SS-23, Scud,
FROG 350 SRBMs with other WP

SLCM
650 SS-N-3, SS-N-7, SS-N-9, SS-N-12,
SS-N-19

ALCM
350 AS-2, AS-3, AS-4, AS-6

300 nuclear-capable artillery

14 • Other Nuclear Powers

France

France is a true nuclear superpower in miniature with a triad of systems almost entirely developed within its own competence. The French *Force Nucleaire Strategique* at present consists of five subsystems: the *Gendarmerie FNS* and *Developments et Experimentations* which provide its security and technical backup; the land-based missile force, the *Soutien Terre FNS*; the long-range manned bomber force, the *Force Aeriennes Stratègique*; and the submarine missile fleet, the *Force Oceanique Stratégique (FOST)*.

The *Soutien Terre FNS* deploys two squadrons of S3 IRBMs, each carrying a 1.2 MT warhead over 3000 km in groups of nine launch areas on the Plateau d'Albion. Each group is controlled by a heavily protected underground launch centre.

The *Force Océanique Stratégique* is based on the Ile Longue naval base in Brest Bay and consists of five SSBNs (or *SNLE – Sousmarin nucleaire lance engins*), each able to launch sixteen M-20 missiles with a one-megaton warhead and a 3000 km range. *Le Redoutable* was launched in 1967 followed by *Le Terrible, Le Foudroyant, L'Indomptable* and *Le Tonnant*, this last completed in May 1980. The *FAS* deploys thirty-seven Mirage IV strategic bombers each capable of carrying a single AN22 free-fall 60 KT nuclear weapon backed up by eleven KC-135 tanker aircraft. In July 1976 the Fourth Programme Law for Military Expenditure and Equipment for the Armed Forces began the process of developing replacement systems and the Socialist government of President Mitterrand, installed in summer 1981, showed no slackening of the nuclear commitment. It announced plans in November for their implementation as operational weapon systems (see page 203).

France also has the *Arme Nucleaire Tactique*, five regiments equipped with six Pluton 120 km range battlefield support missiles, Mirage III and Jaguar aircraft capable of delivering 25 KT AN-52 free-fall bombs and the capability of developing enhanced radiation weapons. Air-launched cruise missiles and new stand-off nuclear weapons are also under development.

China

Chinese defence policy has tried to square the ideological circle of 'People's War' with the acquisition and development of nuclear weapons and delivery systems. The People's Liberation Army (PLA) numbers over 4½ million with air and naval forces accounting for a fifth of total manpower, but the PLA is a mass defensive force lacking the facilities for protracted large-scale interventions outside China.

China exploded its first nuclear device in 1964 and acquired an operational capability with 1000 km+ range missiles, the CSS-1, in about 1966. The 'Second Artillery' of the PLA, the strategic rocket forces, are now believed to deploy up to six CSS-3 7000 km range ICBMs with a two-megaton warhead; and deployment may have started after a successful test in May 1980 of a new ICBM with a 13,000 km range with a five-megaton warhead known as the CSS-X-4. The Chinese Navy has a single *Golf*-class diesel missile submarine but no missiles. The air force deploys 90 B-6 bombers (based on the 1955-vintage Soviet Tu-16). 85 SAM sites with six missiles per site, 4000 fighter aircraft and over 15,000 anti-aircraft guns provide air defence for key civil and military targets while shelter and city-evacuation-based civil defence is rigorously rehearsed.

15 • Nuclear Accidents

US Accidents

This list is based on the US Department of Defence report released in 1981 in response to the accident involving a Titan II ICBM which exploded in its Arkansas silo in September 1980. There has never been an accidental full or even partial nuclear explosion as part of an accident involving the USAF, US Navy or US Atomic Energy Commission, even given the severe detonation stresses encountered in some accidents, and the US Army apparently has never experienced a reported accident. With some early nuclear weapons it was standard operating procedure to keep the 'capsule' of nuclear material separate from the weapon itself containing the high explosive (HE) and a small quantity of unenriched uranium as a trigger. This technique was superseded in the early 1960s, by building extensive safety devices into the weapons themselves, a process hastened by the Goldsboro accident (see below).

Only two accidents, at Palomares, Spain, and at Thule, Greenland, resulted in widespread dispersal of nuclear material. Most of the accidents occurred during ferry missions or during the period to 1968 when the US Strategic Air Command employed the continuous airborne alert procedure. This is one of the basing modes under review for the new MX ICBM force and is favoured by the Secretary of Defence although not by the USAF.

In the early 1970s a reconnaissance satellite saw a missile test launch deep in the Soviet Union and a computer predicted it would land in California. SAC went on high alert. In October 1975 a satellite saw a flare which was interpreted as an ICBM launch. It was a fire in a natural gas pipeline.

In November 1979 a computer at NORAD HQ in Cheyenne Mountain was loaded with simulated data indicating that a nuclear attack on the US was in progress and NORAD briefly took it for real. Bomber and missile alert procedures went into effect before the fault was corrected. In June 1980 a faulty microchip repeated the alarm and three days later there was a deliberate false alarm to locate the faulty microprocessor. In each case the alert lasted less than two minutes. As NORAD's Commanding General, James V. Hartinger, said at the time, 'We can contact every one of our sensors in less than sixty seconds. Each time they showed nothing was coming our way. So I say no, no, no. There is no way a flock of geese could start a nuclear war.'

US Department of Defence Nuclear Accident Codes

NUCFLASH
Accidental or unauthorized incident involving detonation of a nuclear warhead by US forces which could create risk of war with USSR.

BROKEN ARROW
(a) Unauthorized or accidental nuclear detonation, no war risk.
(b) Non-nuclear detonation of a nuclear weapon.
(c) Radioactive contamination.
(d) Seizure, theft or loss of nuclear weapon including emergency jettisoning.
(e) Public hazard, actual or implied.

BENT SPEAR
Any nuclear weapon incidents other than nuclear weapon accidents or war risk detonation actual or possible.

DULL SWORD
Any nuclear weapon incident other than significant incidents.

FADED GIANT
Accident involving nuclear reactors.

13 February 1950 B-36 bomber shut down three engines at altitude and was forced down by severe icing while en route from Alaska to Texas on simulated mission. Bomb dropped into Pacific off coast of British Columbia and high-explosive content detonated. Sixteen crew parachuted to safety and aircraft crashed in Arctic Canada. Nuclear weapon not recovered.

11 April 1950 B-29 crashed into Manzano Mountain, New Mexico, used as dead storage for outmoded weapons. Partial high-explosive detonation. Nuclear capsule not inserted.

13 July 1950 B-50 (improved B-29) crashed at Lebanon, Ohio, sixteen crew killed, high explosive detonated on impact.

5 August 1950 B-29 crashed near trailer camp at Fairfield AFB, California. Sixty hurt, nineteen crew and rescue personnel killed including USAF General. High explosive detonated, nuclear capsule not inserted.

10 November 1950 B-50 jettisoned nuclear weapon over water somewhere outside United States. Not recovered.

10 March 1956 B-47 with two capsules of nuclear weapons material disappeared over Mediterranean. Never found.

27 July 1956 B-47 making a training landing crashed into storage igloo at Lakenheath RAF station, twenty miles NE of Cambridge. Inside igloo were three Mk 6 nuclear bombs each with 8000 lb of TNT as part of trigger mechanism. Rescue services played hoses on the igloo and the crew were burned but TNT did not explode. 'It is possible that a part of Eastern England would have become a desert had the TNT exploded and showered radioactive materials over a wide area,' said a retired USAF General.

22 May 1957 B-36 dropped nuclear weapon at Kirtland AFB, New Mexico, while release mechanism locking pin was being inserted. High explosive detonated but capsule not inserted. Recovery and clean-up operations effected by Field Command Armed Forces Special Weapons Project.

28 July 1957 C-124 Globemaster transport aircraft carrying three nuclear weapons and one nuclear capsule jettisoned two nuclear weapons off Delaware coast after engine failure en route to Europe. C-124 force-landed and weapons were never found.

11 October 1957 B-47 crashed at Homestead, Florida,, with weapon in ferry configuration in bomb bay and nuclear capsule in crew compartment. Crew killed and aircraft burned for four hours. Partial high-explosive explosion.

4 January 1958 Five railroad cars carrying Atomic Energy Commission classified material derailed at Hamburg, New York.

31 January 1958 B-47 crashed at Sidi Slimane AFB, French Morocco. Fire crew fought blaze for allotted ten minutes and then evacuated. Aircraft blazed for seven hours but HE did not explode. Some contamination to fire crew. B-47 alert exercises suspended.

5 February 1958 B-47 collided in mid-air with F-86 but was still flyable. Attempted to land at Hunter AFB, Georgia, but could not decrease to safe landing speed. Weapon jettisoned into Savannah River. After extensive search, weapon was not found.

11 March 1958 B-47 accidentally jettisoned unarmed nuclear weapon over Mars Bluff, South Carolina. Detonated in garden of Mr Walter Gregg who was awarded $54,000 compensation by USAF for injuries to himself and family. Extensive clean-up effected and bomb fragments carried off by souvenir hunters were recovered. Air Force crews order to lock in nuclear bombs, increasing hazards if plane crashed, but diminishing risk of inadvertent jettisoning.

4 November 1958 B-47 caught fire on take-off from Dyass AFB, Abilene, Texas. HE exploded but nuclear materials were recovered.

26 November 1958 Eighth and last B-47 incident at Lake

Charles, Louisiana. Aircraft caught fire on ground, destroying onboard weapon. Local contamination.

6 July 1959 C-124 on ferry mission crashed on take-off at Barksdale AFB, Louisiana, with nuclear weapons aboard. Safety devices functioned and no HE or nuclear explosion occurred.

25 September 1959 US Navy P-5M ditched in Puget Sound. Nuclear ASW weapon containing no nuclear material was lost and not recovered.

15 October 1959 B-52 on airborne alert collided with KC-135 tanker during refuelling over Hardingsberg, Kentucky. Two unarmed nuclear weapons recovered intact, one partially burnt.

18 January 1960 F-100 Super Sabre at Okinawa inadvertently jettisoned fuel tanks while still on ground. Fire engulfed nuclear weapon but capsule not inserted.

7 June 1960 Bomarc SAM missile helium tank exploded and the missile melted and burned for forty-five minutes. Nuclear warhead destroyed but did not explode. Local radioactive contamination and in fire-fighting water drain-off.

8 June 1960 New York Times report of nuclear weapons accident at US base near Tripoli, Libya.

24 January 1961 Four days after President J. F. Kennedy's inauguration, a potentially very disastrous incident occurred over Goldsboro, North Carolina, when a B-52 broke up in mid-air. Two 24 MT bombs were released, one came down by parachute and the other impacted without exploding. A portion of this weapon was not recovered despite excavation to a depth of fifty feet, and the land was taken over by the USAF. Upon recovering the intact bomb, it was found that five of the six safety devices had failed and as a result many more safety devices were incorporated into existing weapons. Kennedy was reportedly told of sixty nuclear accidents since 1945.

14 March 1961 B-52 experienced pressurization failure over Yuba City, California, and all crew except commander bailed out. Nuclear weapons were torn away on ground impact but did not explode.

3 December 1962 Train derailed at Marietta, Georgia, carrying nuclear components.

13 November 1963 HE component of nuclear bomb began to burn spontaneously while being dismantled at AEC storage igloo, San Antonio, Texas. Fire spread to other weapons and 123,000 lb of HE explosion results.

13 January 1964 B-52 broke up in turbulence over Cumberland, Maryland. Two weapons in tactical ferry configuration on board when aircraft crashed were recovered relatively intact from deep snow.

5 December 1964 Minuteman I missile was on strategic alert in its silo at Ellsworth AFB, South Dakota, when retrorocket on RV fired during maintenance and RV crashed to bottom of silo. Did not detonate when safety devices did not receive proper arming sequence.

8 December 1964 B-58 lost control on runway at Grissom AFB, Indiana. Portions of five nuclear weapons on board were burned, causing contamination to area of crash. Two crewmen escaped with minor injuries; navigator used ejector capsule and was killed.

9 August 1965 Fire in Titan II silo at Searcy, Arkansas, killed fifty-three.

11 October 1965 C-124 transport on nuclear ferry mission caught fire on ground during refuelling. Fuselage containing weapon components destroyed releasing local contamination.

5 December 1965 US Navy A-4 Skyhawk with nuclear weapon aboard fell off US aircraft carrier in mid-Pacific. Weapon, pilot and aircraft lost.

17 January 1966 B-52 collided with KC-135 during in-flight refuelling and both aircraft crashed near Palomares, Spain, strewing wreckage over 100 square miles. Tanker boom ripped through the B-52 along its spine and it began to break up, while flames ignited the KC-135's 40,000 gallons of jet fuel, killing the crew immediately. Four out of seven B-52 crew got out by parachute. Four H-bombs (20-25 MT each) were aboard. One fell to earth relatively intact, two scattered plutonium when their HE exploded, and one fell into the sea. Up to 1750 tons of contaminated soil were taken from Palomares area to nuclear dumping site at Aiken, South Carolina. Ships of the US Sixth Fleet sealed off the area of the bomb lost underwater while a midget submersible searched two weeks for the bomb, finding it entangled in its parachute at 2500 feet. It was finally recovered on 7 April, dented but intact.

21 January 1966 B-52 on airborne alert was flying Arctic Circle route over Greenland when fire broke out on board. The pilot headed towards Thule Air Base, 700 miles above Arctic Circle, while crew ejected four miles south of the runway. Aircraft crashed on to ice of North Star Bay, skidded in flames and exploded into fragments. HE on four 1.1 MT weapons exploded, scattering plutonium but no nuclear explosion occurred. Contaminated ice and crash debris was removed to United States and soon afterwards the SAC airborne alert procedure was suspended.

21 May 1968 US Navy SSN, USS *Scorpion*, lost 450 miles SW of the Azores with ninety-nine men. Subroc nuclear depth bombs aboard.

24 August 1978 Two killed, thirty injured by gas leak at Rock, Kansas, Titan II ICBM site.

September 1980 Department of Energy vehicle crashed on icy roads near Fort Collins, Colorado, carrying nuclear material to Los Alamos, New Mexico.

19 September 1980 During maintenance at a Titan II silo at Damascus, Arkansas, a repairman dropped a wrench which hit the missile's pressurized fuel tank. The missile complex was evacuated and a team of specialists called in from the support base at Little Rock AFB. Fuel vapours building up in the silo exploded $8\frac{1}{2}$ hours after the initial puncture, killing one and injuring twenty-one other USAF personnel. The 740-ton steel silo door was blown off and the warhead blown 600 feet. It did not explode.

The Titan II is one of the biggest and oldest missiles in the US inventory, operational since 1963. The Air Force disclosed that between 1975 and 1979 there were 125 accidents at Titan sites in Arkansas, Arizona and Kansas, and ten in 1979/80 in Arkansas Titan silos. In spite of a patchy safety record, a USAF review of the weapon's safety and supportability concluded that the weapon was satisfactory but recommended additional safety precautions. In January 1982 it was announced that the first phase basing of thirty-six MX missiles would not be in Titan silos as originally planned but in Minuteman fields.

Soviet Accidents

No details are available of accidents involving nuclear materials in the Soviet Union, but there have been several accidents to Soviet nuclear-powered or armed submarines.

10 January 1970 The Italian cruise liner *Angelina Lauro* reported hitting an unidentified object in the Bay of Naples. A few days later, a diesel-powered *Foxtrot*-class submarine was seen with 25 feet of her bows missing. It can be assumed that if nuclear torpedoes were aboard at the time of the accident, some of them may have sunk inside the bow section.

January/February 1970 A very large explosion occurred in the Gorki submarine yards. The Volga River and its Black Sea estuary were afterwards contaminated with radioactive material.

12/13 April 1970 Nuclear-powered *November*-class attack submarine sank 150 nm south-west of Land's End in Cornwall. For some years a *Don*-class submarine-support vessel remained on station over the *November*'s wreck.

27/28 February 1972 Hotel-class (three SS-N-5 SLBM) was seen in difficulties 600 nm north-east of Newfoundland. There was no radiation leak and the submarine was towed back to its Murmansk base by Soviet units. It is thought that the reactor was damaged.

12 March 1972 Yankee-class (sixteen SS-N-6) remained surfaced in the north-east Atlantic for some time. It is thought she had reactor trouble which was repaired.

September 1973 Echo II was seen in the Caribbean with an 'immense' gash in her hull.

August 1980 Echo II was disabled on the surface off Okinawa. Meanwhile men in radiation suits appeared on deck – to 'keep off the sun', according to Soviet sources.

November 1981 Whiskey-class diesel-powered submarine stranded on rocks outside Swedish Karlskrona naval base. Nuclear torpedoes probably aboard.

Part Three
The Battle for the
Third World

16 • Power Projection

The fundamental stability in the confrontation of East and West with its organized structure of deterrence has meant there has been very little war and a fossilization of political alignment in the countries of the North. All the firepower of the West can do nothing for Poland – even if it should wish to. This surly stability has been mirrored by war and turbulence in the countries of the South. The old European empires have been dismantled (nearly always accompanied by some form of war of liberation) while the ideological superpower rivals have striven to fill the vacuum. The client successor states have grafted modern politics and modern weapons (or at least as modern as their patrons will let them have) on to much older divisions of race or religion and, without the ritualized deterrent processes of the Northern Hemisphere or the threat of total destruction that war represents, their search for security often ends in conflicts with their neighbours or within.

These wars are usually on a small scale, fought with obsolete weapons, and are often brief, spasmodic or represent guerrilla insurgencies. The wars of the Middle East, between India and Pakistan and China and Vietnam, with their large consumption of first-division conventional weapons and head-on, all-out engagements, have been dangerous exceptions.

Not only have these conflicts of the Third World represented proxy ideological battlefields, but genuine carve-ups to secure materials and markets as much as in the old imperial days. Energy is the key – the oil of the Middle East and the protection of its terribly vulnerable gathering infrastructures and tenuous supply routes (the US in 1981 imported 44 per cent of its total petroleum requirements, half its total energy need), and the oil embargo that followed the 1973 Middle East war underlined the extent of the West's dependence on imported oil. And it is not simply energy. The United States relies on foreign sources for a great deal of critical materials: all of its industrial diamonds for machine tools are imported, as are 90 per cent of defence-related strategic metals such as manganese, cobalt (from Zaire), bauxite and chrome (from Zimbabwe and South Africa).

The British Empire was founded on seapower with a first class battle fleet bottling up European challengers while gunboats, frigates and cruisers projected power around the world, shelled recalcitrant harbours, landed punitive expeditions and brought back the goods. Strategic nuclear weapons perform the first fixing function for the superpowers while, in Kissinger's phrase, 'beneath the nuclear umbrella the temptation to probe with regional forces and proxy wars increases'. Britain's nuclear weapons did not ensure a 'hands-off' when it went to war with Argentina. They could not be used to get the junta to withdraw its forces on the Falklands and their expense had truncated general-purpose forces able to apply an 'appropriate level of violence'.

Nuclear weapons cannot guarantee that very powerful instruments of power projection can operate with impunity – in fact, the opposite. It's relatively simple for the US Navy to mount a blockade of El Salvador, but what could it do if Soviet adventurism brought a direct military threat to the supply of Gulf oil – would it trigger a nuclear conflict? Or what could it do militarily to prop up a regime threatened from within?

Before looking at power projection in action, it is useful to look at the above-the-line (as opposed to economic or covert) means available and how these military tools match long- or short-term policy demands.

The United States

The USA has always been in the business of power projection overseas (at least since Pershing's 1916 Mexican expedition against Pancho Villa) because it has to cross oceans to get to its enemies and aid its friends. Between 1946 and 1977 the US made 215 'shows of force' in support of diplomatic ends. The US Navy deploys 30 per cent of its power away from the continental United States in peacetime and the Mediterranean Sixth and Pacific Seventh Fleets have become permanent features. The

US forces in Europe, maintained since 1945, represent the greatest investment in projected power, with the security of Israel as the second great constant from the late 1950s. Throughout the period of the Vietnam War the US sought to field enough conventional forces to cope simultaneously with conflicts in Europe and Asia with a contingency in reserve ('half a war'). This shrank to '1½ wars' in 1970 with an emphasis on burden-sharing by America's allies including NATO. This pattern of decline continued through the 1970s until the perceived threat to the nation's oil supplies caused an urgent reappraisal.

A deep-grained policy debate is going on within the Reagan administration which hinges on two traditionally divergent trends within American politics. The traditionalists (exemplified by ex-SACEUR Alexander Haig) hang US power projection on Europe, Israel and Korea. The new guard (exemplified by Secretary of the Navy John Lehman, backed by an influential triumvirate in the Reagan White House of Deaver, Meese and Baker) seeks a global imperative based on seapower as a pragmatic instrument of power projection in areas of US interest abroad. Ironically, this embraces the old 'America first' themes of isolationism and also includes the concept of 'horizontal escalation' – responding to one crisis by initiating another one elsewhere.

The shift began in the previous administration. The Carter State of the Union message delivered in January 1980 following the invasion of Afghanistan declared that 'The Soviet Union is now attempting to consolidate a strategic position that poses a grave threat to the free movement of Middle East oil.' This is the background to the formation of the Rapid Joint Deployment Task Force (RJDTF).

The concept is not new. A joint services task force was set up to expel the Soviets from Cuba in 1962 if necessary and was actually used in the Dominican Republic in 1965, but these rapid-response specialists were suborned into the Vietnam War and the concept all but disappeared until dusted off in Presidential Decision 18 (PD-18) of August 1977. The early studies were hastened along by events in Iran and Afghanistan and a staff was therefore set up, commanded by a Marine Lieutenant-General to draft plans to combine Army, Navy and

Marine Corps units into an operational fleet-footed long-range force of up to 200,000 men. Strategic Air Command also provides a component – a 'Strategic Projection Force' of B-52H bombers.

By mid-summer 1981 the RDF was still only an administrative cadre, 242 officers now commanded by an Army Major-General operating out of an old air force base at Tampa, Florida. They have two problems to reconcile – actual availability of forces in terms of manpower and equipment, and the means to move them by land and sea – before the policy-makers can dream up schemes for their use.

Two of the sixteen active US Army divisions are transported by air, the 82nd Airborne Division (which reaches the battlefield by parachute and fights as light infantry) and the 101st (which is air-mobile, fighting from helicopters, and thus is not a long-range, quick-reaction force). The 82nd has over 16,000 men organized into three brigades, supposedly ready to go into action with no warning time anywhere in the world. 850 men of the 82nd Airborne dropped into the Egyptian desert in November 1981 a week after President Sadat was assassinated, going straight into mock action as part of exercise *Bright Star* having flown direct from Fort Bragg, North Carolina, in Lockheed C-141s. They might equally be earmarked for jungle fighting or for war in NATO's Central Sector so the airborne has to maintain a flexible mix of tactics and equipment hoping to defeat tanks with fluid attacks and heavy anti-tank missile armament. Product-improved, reworked Sheridan light tanks, Huey Cobra helicopters, Hawk missiles and Vulcan 20-mm anti-aircraft weapons support its corps, battalions and brigades. Large-scale contracts are out with US industry to provide new-generation light tanks and high-mobility vehicles ('Humvees') for such forces (the British Alvis company picked up contracts for two light tanks).

The US Marine Corp's role remains the securing of hostile coastlines by amphibious assault. Its three active divisions are equipped with their own armoured fighting vehicles and air wings, with fighter ground attack, helicopter and support squadrons. The USMC has three squadrons of the McDonnell

Douglas AV-8A, variant of the British VTOL Harrier close-support aircraft with the advanced AV-8B on order. Two Marine Divisions are based in the USA and one on Okinawa.

Counting US commitment to NATO as a constant, the pressures begin to crowd in on available forces. Seven active US Army divisions support NATO. Four divisions with elements of two others are actually forward-deployed in Europe while the rest remain in the US as ready reserves. One division is in Korea and another in Hawaii. Seven US-based divisions constitute a strategic reserve but at least six out of sixteen active Army divisions must remain in the US to act as a rotational and training base. Only one of six active separate brigades is available for contingencies, the rest being tied to training commitments in Alaska, Panama and Europe.

In optimum circumstances the US could put four Army and two Marine divisions along with an independent brigade and an armoured cavalry regiment (light tanks) into a contingency force. If NATO and Korea called on its full commitment of earmarked forces, one army division would be all there was. Reserve mobilization was an important part of the NATO Long-term Defence Programme and since 1980 US diplomats have been urging European NATO allies to expand reserve capabilities to free uncommitted US forces for the Persian Gulf.

USAF Military Aircraft Command (MAC) operates thirteen bases in the United States, has a mid-Atlantic stage at Lajes in the Azores and its European 'terminal' is at Rhein-Main air base outside Frankfurt. According to the USAF Almanac, 'While training for ultimate use in conflict, MAC supports readiness forces and projects the American spirit at home and abroad through its many humanitarian air-lift operations.'

The Command, however, is the flexible backbone of US power projection and in 1980 shifted 439,000 tons of cargo and more than 2 million people. Its long-range lift is provided by 77 giant C-5s and 270 C-141 StarLifters. The C-141 fleet is being modified to C-141B standard by the addition of extra fuselage stretch and in-flight refuelling capability. Two hundred and sixty-six C-130 Hercules provide tactical mobility.

MAC C-5 Galaxys and C-141 StarLifters delivered 22,395 tons of war supplies to Israel (staging in the Azores) in thirty-three days during the October 1973 war. The first ship to arrive contained more tonnage but by then the war was over. The US Civil Reserve Air Fleet has 123 specially strengthened long-range cargo and 250 passenger aircraft available to MAC in time of crisis.

There are problems. US strategic airlift is expected not only to get its high-priority charges to the centres of decision in the opening stages of any conflict but keep them maintained until sealift can take over. A move from Fort Bragg, North Carolina, to the Gulf with the combat elements of an airborne division (11,000 men) with enough ammunition and fuel for a week's operations would take twelve days and 700 equivalent sorties by C-141s. The C-5 fleet consumes enormous amounts of maintenance and is being reworked with new wings (at present they can lift only one M-1 tank and require very long runways). The KC-10 tanker-transport programme was cut back in a defence pruning but the advanced McDonnell Douglas C-17 transport (the 'C-X'), which combines the C-5s' ability to handle outsize loads with the C-130 Hercules' battlefield mobility, was given a production engineering contract in 1982.

Sealift

At the end of the Vietnam War the US Navy retired a generation of Second World War vintage cargo ships, and Military Sealift Command (MSC) shrank from several hundred to twenty-eight dry cargo ships (most of them chartered) and thirty tankers by 1980. With the move of a carrier group into the Indian Ocean to cover Iran, the US Navy was forced to charter a Royal Navy replenishment ship (RFA *Lyness*) and open negotiations to buy another. Bound up with the progress of the RJDTF are plans by the Reagan administration to build a new fleet of logistic support ships. The shift from general cargo to container ships which do not suit the transport of military equipment in the US Merchant Marine has not helped the US Department of Defence's sealift readiness programme, but about 250 merchant transports are contracted to meet defence requirements along the lines of the Civil Reserve Air Fleet and captains of some US merchant ships have packets of sealed orders to be opened in an emergency. All merchant ships provide US Navy controllers with a daily reference to maintain continuous plots of position.

There is also the National Defence Reserve Fleet – 161 mothballed dry cargo ships. But the time required for reactivation of these ships (many of Second World War vintage) is estimated in months. The British experience in the Falklands, however, in which power was successfully and rapidly projected across 7000 miles to the South Atlantic, showed the efficacy of expedient and flexible use of available merchant sealift.

Europe: the Replenishment Imperative

NATO has contingency plans for the rapid projection of American power into Europe during a time of crisis. The US rapid reinforcement programme is designed to double US land combat strength and triple tactical airpower within fourteen days. Practical application depends, however, on more pre-positioning of stocks of ammunition and storage sites for heavy equipment, the airlift itself being composed of lightly armed manpower. In a shooting war MAC is realistic about losses which its packed transport fleets might suffer. If a European war lasted long enough for sealift to enter the equation, then the Soviet attack submarines fleet is there to tilt the balance in its favour. Two convoy strategies are under consideration: 'pulsing' which sends infrequent surges of large numbers of ships (300–500) with heavy ASW escort across the Atlantic, and smaller convoys running fast in expanded formation (35–50) which would not pose the same kind of logistic burdens on port facilities even if these were left intact.

Reforger 80 was a very large-scale Europe reinforcement exercise conducted by the US Army at the end of 1980 to test the system. MAC moved 1700 fighting vehicles from bases within the United States to ocean ports where they were loaded on to Military Sealift Command vessels. These roll-on, roll-off ships ran straight for Antwerp where they unloaded their cargoes virtually straight into battle. 1700 men were flown meanwhile to Belgium and Germany. The 2nd Armoured Division flew from Fort Hood in one hop aboard C-141s which were refuelled in flight and drew their stockpiled equipment as they left the airfield. The 82nd Airborne went straight into action having flown from North Carolina. Ten C-141s dropped 650 very tired soldiers with their weapons and vehicles after a nine-hour non-stop flight and put them on the ground in well under four minutes.

Amphibious Assault

The US has enough amphibious craft to enable a marine assault echelon to storm a defended coastline and bring up its tactical airpower but not enough to land heavy equipment and sustain an advanced force inland without the assistance of the MSC or Merchant Marine. The Reagan administration plans to increase 'trooplift' capability from 1.15 Marine Amphibious Forces (one MAF = 3 x mechanized Marine amphibious brigades totalling 52,000 men) to 1.5 in the near future and two MAFs by the end of the decade. To do this will require the construction of at least five new amphibious ships per year.

The Middle East

Assuring the continued supply of Middle East oil has joined the defence of Western Europe as a priority US military commitment. Four problems stand in its way – distance, the conflict of Arab and Israeli, dependence on Arab oil and rival Soviet power projection.

The Gulf is a long way from centres of US power. The Subic Bay base in the Philippines is 6000 miles away and Norfolk, Virginia, is 11,000 miles via the Cape. The Indian Ocean base of Diego Garcia, taken over from the British in 1972, has a 12,000 foot runway than can take a C-5 or a B-52 and enough fuel storage to keep a carrier task group going for thirty days. Its natural coral reef harbour can shelter a single carrier plus support ships but is 2300 miles from the head of the Gulf.

This is not enough to sustain a major expeditionary force, so when events speeded up in the autumn of 1979 the search was hastened for allies willing to make a jumping-off base available with pre-positioned stocks. The RDF could not fight its way ashore. Present plans for its deployment depend on being invited in by a 'friendly' government such as Saudi Arabia to help in resisting attacks from outside or subversion from within.

But as long as the US is seen to take a pro-Israeli line over the Palestinians no Arab country can openly act as broker of US power projection without the risk of disaster. Djibouti is out and the Soviet-built complex at Berbera in Somalia was largely dismantled by the Russians when they left. Mombasa in Kenya is farther away than Diego Garcia and Oman, after an initial flirtation, backed away in the summer of 1980. When Margaret Thatcher declared blandly in the United Arab Emirates that Great Britain would participate in US intervention initiatives, the local reaction was intensely hostile.

Thus by the end of 1981 the Reagan administration had formed a strategy which overcame the logistical problems of bringing a large military force to bear to engage an enemy on equal terms in the Middle East. It is a restaging of the 'tripwire' policies of the 1950s in Europe in modern dress. The new tripwire plan envisages, if Russian land forces were to move into northern Iran, for example, rushing a token force of 500 men to form an arc north of the oilfields (how the Iranians would react is not recorded). If Soviet shoots American, the whole ladder of retaliation is now open – as in Europe linking rifle bullets up a chain to ICBMs.

As well as Iran the line runs through Turkey, Pakistan, the Gulf, Egypt, Sudan, Somalia and Kenya – and a $1000 million package is going into extending facilities at Diego Garcia, sustaining a marine brigade in the Arabian Sea, equipping the Pakistani port of Gadawar to take US warships and the Omani island of Masirah to take transport and combat aircraft. The Gulf, however, is beyond the reach of most Soviet fighter and ground-attack aircraft based in the south of the country or even in Afghanistan. Parachute assaults and ground forces attempting to make link-ups would lack air cover unless strips were used within Arab or Iranian territory. Warships in the Black Sea or Indian Ocean would be compromised without composite land-based air cover.

Whether the RJDTF could do anything militarily to secure intact oilfields is highly problematic. The oil-gathering infrastructure is highly vulnerable and one bomb in a remote pumping station (outside the tripwire arc) could shut down a refinery for many months. Direct intervention by a first-class military power would make an airborne mission virtually impossible. Electronics take away the surprise, and fighters controlled by an AWACS could devastate troop transports in mid-air. The tripwire policy and the RJDTF therefore are designed not just to check regional enemies and reassure friends but to deter Soviet adventurism. In doing so the nuclear switchboard is connected to one of the world's most volatile areas.

The Far East

The pullback from Vietnam accelerated the withdrawal of US military power from the rest of southeast Asia. The US is bound by mutual defence treaties to Australia and New Zealand (ANZUS), the Philippines, Japan and Korea. One US infantry division and four fighter squadrons remain in Korea as a 'tripwire'. The Republic of Korea army itself is the second largest in non-communist Asia with half a million men in forty-one divisions under arms.

The US recognized the People's Republic of China on 1 January 1979 and withdrew military support from Taiwan. In spite of the efforts of some Western politicians eager to court China with the promise of high technology weapons, according to a US Congressional report, 'The People's Republic of China remains far apart from the United States and Japan in terms of political values and ideology. The question of its long term aims in Asia, although apparently dormant today, is a potentially troublesome element in the relationship. Recent Chinese instability raises the issue of Chinese reliability. In short China is probably the most uncertain factor in the East Asian power balance.'

Soviet Power Projection

Until the 1970s the Soviet Union lacked the capability to project its conventional military power far beyond its own land frontiers. From the mid-1950s onwards, other than police actions in East Berlin and Hungary, projection was below the line, expressed in alliances (Sino-Soviet in 1950, Warsaw Pact in 1956), economic assistance, arms sales or grants and military missions. In the 1970s such support for Marxist-Leninist movements brought results with the installation of pro-Soviet governments in Vietnam, Laos, Angola, Ethiopia, South Yemen and Cambodia where the pro-Chinese Khmer Rouge were defeated. Meanwhile Egypt, Somalia and Equatorial Guinea fell out of the pack and Afghanistan needed a full-scale invasion to be kept in line. Cuba has provided highly motivated manpower, training and equipment for bold ventures in Africa. US intelligence estimates have put at 20,000 (including the elite MININT special forces) the number of Cuban troops in Angola and 17,000 in Ethiopia and South Yemen.

Seapower

The Soviet Union has now acquired the means of above-the-line military action at long range. The Soviet Navy has grown both in size and in its global coverage, concentrating on cycles of visits and exercises in the Mediterranean, West Africa and the Indian Ocean, building up a contingent chain of port facilities and bases for maritime reconnaissance aircraft.

The Soviet Merchant Marine disposes 350 tankers and over 1300 modern ships and, like the state airline Aeroflot, is able rapidly to integrate with military needs. Amphibious sealift is still modest although investment is going into a large hovercraft fleet and a new class of amphibious warfare vessels named after the first of the class, the 13,000 tonne *Ivan Rogov* capable of embarking over 500 naval infantrymen and first deployed to the Indian Ocean in 1980. Soviet naval infantry composes six regiments of 2000 men each, a fraction of the USMC's 190,000 total. As currently constituted, they are really only suitable for commando operations in the Baltic.

Airborne Forces

Soviet Transport Aviation (*Voyenno Transportnaya Aviatsaya – VTA*) controls a very large number of strategic and tactical transport aircraft, 1400 medium/long range transports backed up by the resources of Aeroflot. 575 An-12 *Cubs* provide basic tactical transport and although generally inferior to the US C-130 Hercules can handle all the equipment assigned to airborne divisions. The huge An-22 has been a failure in service but the new four-jet I-76 *Candid*, the equivalent of the US C-141, has been slowly entering service since 1974. Soviet heavy-lift helicopters proved very effective in the 1978 Ogaden war and Soviet industry still turns out more than 750 Mil MI-8 *Hip* battlefield assault helicopters a year. The very large *Halo* heavy-lift helicopter with an eight-bladed rotor was unveiled to the West in 1980 and is said to be very advanced.

Soviet airborne troops (*Vozdushno-Desantnyye Voyska-VDV*) are a service assigned as a reserve of the High Command under the direct command of the Ministry of Defence. They comprise eight divisions distinguished in dress by a blue beret and naval collar, although the Soviet Air Force can transport only two divisions with supplies for three days without recourse to pre-positioning.

Seven divisions (8500 men each) are kept at Category I readiness in peacetime, emphasizing their value as a rapid-reaction, long-range force. The 103rd Guards Airborne seized Prague airport in 1968 and was reportedly flown to Romania ready to intervene in the October 1973 war if ordered. The 105th Airborne Division was the vanguard of Soviet forces into Kabul in 1979. Soviet special forces include naval infantry commandos trained in para, frogman and clandestine landing techniques, airborne commando Special Operations Brigades called *Raydoviki*, the equivalent of the US Rangers, and the *Vysotniki* which correspond with the US Special Forces or SAS and who specialize in deep penetrations in squad strength. GRU Military Intelligence troops in addition have several diversionary battalions available and trained for special missions.

Part Four
Coming Soon to This Planet

17 • Future Weapon Systems

200 major weapon systems under development or entering service for the 1980s, 1990s and beyond.

Note: this selective inventory does not include radar systems, reconnaissance and electronic surveillance, electronic counter-measures, laser weapons, C^3 systems, electro-optical guidance systems, air defence, fire control or simulators, all of which are commanding large-scale funding and research and development programmes.

Strategic Systems

ACM: Extended range ALCM under development by Boeing. Parallel with DARPA directed research programme into new cruise missile technology for 1990s.

ALCM: US Air Launched Cruise Missile. In production by Boeing. 3418 by 1990.

ASALM: Advanced Strategic Air-Launched Missile under development by Martin Marietta. Main element of USAF Strategic Bomber Penetration programme to cover postulated improvements in Soviet defensive capability in late 1980s. Version also being developed to disable Soviet AWACS system (SUAWACS).

AS-X-? Reported Soviet ALCM under development with range of 1200 km.

AS-X-? Soviet air-launched stand-off missile under development.

Chevaline: UK Polaris front-end improvement programme begun 1974. Summer 1980 test explosions in Nevada, HMS

Renown made test-launch off Florida, autumn 1980. Six 40 KT RVs with advanced penaids. Final development stage, in service until early 1990s.

CSS-4: Chinese ICBM under development.

CSS-N-X: Chinese SLBM under development.

MSBS M4: New-generation French SLBM under development by Aerospatiale operational from mid-1980s. First test launch made March 1980.

MX: US ICBM under development by Martin Marietta. Three basing modes under review. First flight 1983, operational 1989.

SRAM-L: Advanced Short-range Attack Missile proposal by Boeing.

SS-18: Large Soviet ICBM. Mod 4 carries fourteen warheads, with high accuracy and advanced penaids.

SS-19: Soviet's most effective ICBM. 300 deployed by 1980.

SS-20: Soviet mobile IRBM with three MIRVs.

SS-X-?: New Soviet solid propellant ICBM under test. To be deployed in super-hardened silos.

S-X-?: New Soviet mobile ICBM similar in size to US MX.

SS-X-?: Large liquid propellant ICBM follow-on to SS-18 under development.

SS-N-8: SLBM with impressive range and accuracy. Mod 3 with three MIRVs under test.

SS-N-17: Solid propellant SLBM under development.

SS-N-18: Liquid propellant SLBM under development, range up to 16,000 km.

SS-N-20: Large SLBM under development to arm *Typhoon*-class SSBNs.

SX: French mobile IRBM under development by Aerospatiale. In service 1985.

Tomahawk: US Navy ship/submarine-based cruise missile, operational 1982. Tomahawk is also weapon element of GLCM (ground-launched cruise missile). 160 in UK, 112 in Italy, 96 in Germany, 32 each in Belgium and Netherlands by December 1983. Total cost: $2000 million.

Trident I (C4): US SLBM under development since late 1960s by Lockheed. First Trident SSBN *Ohio* operational 1982, follow-on vessels *Michigan* and *Florida* late 1982, 1983 (see below: *Ohio*). UK decision to acquire Trident I announced

1980, to be fitted with US post-boost MIRV system and British warheads.

Trident II (D5): Follow-on to Trident I under development by Lockheed. Projected range of 11,000 km and CEP of 120 m using Mk 12A RV makes system effective against hard counterforce targets. UK decision to acquire Trident II announced March 1982.

Tactical Nuclear Weapons

ASMP: French air-launched attack missile with 150 KT nuclear warhead. Mach 3 top speed with terrain-following capability. Firing trials 1982.

Pershing II: Advanced US battlefield missile under full-scale development. Operational in Germany by 1984.

Lance: US Army to procure W70-4 warhead in 1981-3 offering enhanced radiation capability for Lance missile stocks.

Hades: French ramjet-powered tactical missile with twice the range of Pluton which it will replace in mid-1980s.

Israeli Battlefield Missile: Reported long-range tactical missile with nuclear warhead.

SS-X-23: New Soviet battlefield nuclear missile.

XM753: US ER rocket-assisted nuclear artillery round.

Aircraft Weapons

AA-7 *Apex*: New Soviet AAM becoming operational.

AA-XP-1/AA-XP-2: New-generation Soviet AAM with look-down/shoot-down performance. In service mid-1980s.

ACSM: Advanced conventional stand-off missile development, part of USAF's Advanced Attack Weapons programme.

AIAAM: US Navy advanced intercept AAM designed for long-range fleet defence. Proposal request stage.

AMRAAM: US/UK/German advanced medium-range AAM under development.

ASAT: Air-launched anti-satellite weapon under development since 1975. Compatible with F-15.

AS-15 TT: Aerospatiale air-launched anti-ship missile. In service 1984.

ASRAAM: UK/German short-range AAM under development.

AS-X-10: Soviet laser-guided ASM to arm tactical aircraft in mid-1980s.

AS-8: Soviet fire-and-forget air-launched A/T missile.

AS-X-9: Soviet anti-ship missile under development.

AS-X-?: Soviet advanced tactical ASM under development.

Axe: Lockheed project for ballistic missile airfield destruction weapon.

Exocet AM: 39 Air launched anti-ship missile. Launched from Argentine Super Etendard and sank HMS *Sheffield* in May 1982.

HARM: US high-speed anti-radiation (radar) missile, operational 1983.

Harpoon: US all-weather air-launched anti-ship missile. In production, 3000 by 1987.

Hellfire: US helicopter-launched A/T missile. Operational 1984.

LAD: Low-Altitude Dispenser for sub-munitions under test by USAF.

Laser Bombs: Laser-guided aircraft munitions under development by Soviet Union.

Laser Maverick: US precision-guided tactical missile for laser-designated targets. Navy Maverick operational 1984.

MICA: *Missile Intermédiat de Combat Aerien.* Advanced French fire and forget AAM for 1990s.

MRASM: US attack missile based on Tomahawk cruise missile technology for air launch against high-value targets. Under test.

MW-1 Mehrzweckwaffe: German submunition area weapon under development for Tornado.

Paveway III: US family of laser-guided bombs. Production 1983.

Penguin Mk 3: Norwegian ASM, operational 1987.

Phoenix: Improved version of long-range, high performance AAM under development for US Navy. Anticipated total of 1400 by 1990.

Python: Israeli AAM under development.

Sea Eagle: UK sea-skimming, air-launched, anti-ship missile under development.

Sea Skua: UK helicopter-launched anti-ship missile. Entered service 1981.

Sidewinder AIM-9L: Third-generation development of widely used AAM. 3000 planned procurement for USN and USAF. Licence production for RAF and RN.

Sky Flash: UK AAM becoming operational, licence production in Sweden.

Sparrow III AIM/RIM 7M: Advanced version of US Sparrow AAM under full development.

WAAM: USAF wide-area anti-armour munitions multiple-kill air-launched anti-tank system under development. Complements US Army's Assault Breaker project. Part of USAF's advanced attack weapons programme.

McDonnell-Douglas/BAe/MBB: US/UK/German joint project for long-range fire-and-forget stand-off missile. Under development.

AST1228: UK Air Staff Target for defence-suppression weapon to arm manned penetrators such as Tornado. Could be harassment drone.

Surface-to-air Weapons

Strategic Systems
US Army continues development of BMD (ballistic missile defence) system. US DoD funding Low-altitude Defence system (LoAD) using existing technologies. BMD research is in two parts – advanced technology programme (ATP) and systems technology programme (STP). ATP is investigating alternative solutions including directed energy (beam) weapons. STP uses layered concept – first layer of long-range missiles with long-wavelength infra-red optics intercepting attacking RVs outside the atmosphere by non-nuclear means; second layer uses conventional radars and missiles to kill RVs leaking through overlay. Homing Overlay Experiment test-launch planned in 1982.

SH-4: Soviet ABM able to loiter at very high altitude.

SH-8: Soviet hypersonic ABM which could form last-ditch defence underlay below SH-4 net.

Land-based Surface-to-air Weapons

FMS Eurosam: UK/France/Germany joint development of medium-range SAM for 1990s.

Ford Gunfighter: Tracked US Army Division Air Defence system (DIVADS). 50 operational by 1982.

Patriot: US Army's air defence system. Operational 1982, full deployment by 1990.

Rapier: UK low-level SAM. Ordered in 1981 to protect USAF air and GLCM bases in UK. Tracked Rapier operation with British Army 1984.

SA-X-12/SA-X-13: New-generation Soviet SAMs under development.

Storads: French air defence system under development. Shanine missile component sold to Saudi Arabia.

Improved Hawk: Product improvement programme for SAM missile widely deployed by US and allies.

Naval Air Defence

Aegis: US advanced SAM anti-anti-ship missile system. First Aegis cruiser operational 1983.

Goalkeeper: Dutch rotary cannon close in weapons system.

Outer Perimeter Defence Missile: Long-range air defence missile under development by Martin Marietta.

Phalanx: US close-in ship defence system. 450 systems by 1986. Deployed on HMS *Illustrious*.

RAM: US anti-anti-ship missile under development by General Dynamics. Production 1983.

SA-NX-6: New Soviet vertically launched SAM. To arm new class of missile cruiser.

Seawolf: UK missile component of GWS 25 weapon system. Lightweight Seawolf with Dutch VM 40 radar tracker under development for corvette-size vessels.

SIAM: Self-initiating anti-aircraft missile under development by Ford Aerospace for US Navy.

Naval Weapons

ALWS: Advanced lightweight torpedo under development for US Navy.

ASW-SOW: US long-range ASW stand-off weapon with over-the-horizon and deep-diving capability. Under development for service in late 1980s.

Captor: US Navy anti-submarine torpedo launched from mine.

EX 41 VLS: Vertical launch system under development for US Navy for range of weapons including Tomahawk SLCM. USS *New Jersey*, WW2-vintage battleship, will undergo two-year refit to take VLS magazines for 400 cruise missiles in late 1980s.

MM40 Exocet: Advanced surface to surface Exocet under development.

NSR 7525: UK naval staff requirement for new heavyweight torpedo to deal with deep-diving submarines, under development.

OSCAR: US Navy project to communicate with submerged submarines by satellite-borne lasers.

Quick Strike: US Navy mine warfare programme. Production 1983.

Sting Ray: UK acoustic homing lightweight torpedo. Total development and production cost, 1969-89, could amount to £800 million.

SS-NX-12: New Soviet anti-ship missile.

SS-NX-19: New VLS Soviet anti-ship missile arming *Kirov*-class battlecruisers.

SS-N-?: New anti-ship missile arming *Oscar*-class submarine.

Sub-Harpoon: US anti-ship cruise missile system ordered for RN fleet submarines. Operational 1983.

US Navy ASW programmes: IUSS, integrated undersea surveillance system; SOSUS, sound surveillance system; SURTASS, surveillance towed array sensor system; RDSS, rapidly deployable surveillance system; TACTAS, tactical towed array sonar.

Anti-tank Weapons

ADATS: US/Swiss anti-tank/air defence system, production 1985.

Assault Breaker: US project name for extensive research programme under direction of US Defence Advanced Research Projects agency (DARPA) to counter large enemy armoured formations. US Army project uses missiles releasing 'smartlet' submunitions.

AT-4/5/6: New-generation Soviet anti-tank missiles in early operational deployment stage. NATO names, *Spigot, Spandrel, Spiral*.

Copperhead: Laser-guided anti-tank weapon for US Army. Production end 1984. Naval version cancelled.

European Third-generation weapon: UK/France/Germany collaborating on advanced A/T missile.

LAW-80: UK light anti-armour weapon under development by Hunting for mid-1980s.

Multiple launch rocket system: US mobile rocket bombardment system, production 1982.

SADARM: US Army artillery-delivered anti-armour multiple-target system, under development.

Tank Breaker: Development contracts issued for US Army man-portable anti-tank missile.

TOW-2: Improved US heavy anti-tank missile. Full system operational mid-1980s.

Armoured Fighting Vehicles

MPlus: USMC requirement for mobile protected weapons system. Light tank for US Rapid Deployment Force through year 2000.

LAV: USMC/US Army requirement for light armoured vehicle for RDF. In service by 1983.

T-72: Soviet MBT, 125 mm gun-firing fin-stabilized projectiles able to penetrate current or future NATO counterparts. Laser range-finder and automated fire control. In production, in service. 22,000 by mid-1980s.

AMX-32: New French MBT, prototype stage.

Leopard II: Advanced German MBT, high velocity 120-mm gun.

M-1 Abrams: US MBT, incorporates high technology but has technical shortcomings in reliability. In service in Europe by 1984. MIEI to be armed with 120-mm smoothbore to defeat advanced Soviet armour, standardized as M1A1.

T-80: New Soviet MBT under development with composite armour.

BTR-70: New Soviet eight-wheel APC under development.

OF-40: New Italian export tank based on Leopard I.

SP-70: UK/Italy/Germany 155 mm SP howitzer under development.

Merkava Mk 2: Improved Israeli MBT under development.

Challenger: Phase 3 development of Chieftain originally undertaken for Iran as Shir 2. MBT-80 cancelled for British Army mid-1980 and replaced by order for 240 Challenger MBTs. Operational 1985.

Valiant: Vickers private venture MBT under development.

M2: US infantry fighting vehicle, entering service.

Aircraft

USA

Bell Model 209 AH-1S: Advanced TOW-capable Huey Cobra assault helicopter for US Army. 1000 by 1983. Supply authorized to Israel and Japan.

Boeing E-3A Sentry: Airborne warning and control system (AWACS) delivery commenced 1977. 34 to be operational by 1984, NATO to operate additional 18 under dual funding from 1983.

Chinook H C Mk 1: Boeing-Vertol heavy-lift helicopter for RAF. 33 to be delivered by 1982.

General Dynamics F-16 Fighting Falcon: USAF's multi-role fighter operational with US, NATO and Israel. MSIP (multinational staged improvement programme) to F-16 C/D standard operational in 1984. F-16 programme derivatives include FX export fighter and F-16E advanced technology development, first flight scheduled summer 1982.

Grumman F-14: US Navy fleet fighter. F-14C development flying by 1984 and studies continuing for Super Tomcat.

Grumman EF-IIIA: ECM tactical jamming derivative of F-111 designed to counter Soviet air defence lead in conjunction with AWACS. Operational in 1982.

Hughes AH-64: US Army advanced attack helicopter with Hellfire missiles and Chain gun. 536 ordered, operational 1984.

Lockheed Project Stealth: Single-seat strike/reconnaissance aircraft X-25 with low radar, infra-red and optical signatures. High development priority since first flight in 1977.

Lockheed TR-1: Tactical reconnaissance aircraft derivative of U-2. 33 operational by 1984.

Lockheed C-5: New wing retrofit programme to 77 heavy lift transports between 1982 and 1987.

McDonnell-Douglas F-15 Eagle: Air superiority fighter, 749 for USAF by 1983, 40 for Israel, 60 for Saudi Arabia delivered from January 1982, and 88 for Japan. ECM and Strike Eagle variants under development.

McDonnell-Douglas AV-8B: VTOL strike-fighter development of British Harrier. 336 for USMC and 60 for RAF by 1986.

McDonnell-Douglas F/A-18 Hornet: US Navy air combat fighter. 1337 for USN and USMC by 1990. 137 for Canada by 1988, 75 for RAAF by 1990. RF-18 reconnaissance version under development.

McDonnell-Douglas KC-10A Extender: Advanced tanker/-cargo aircraft for USAF. 36 by mid 1980s.

McDonnell-Douglas C-17: Short-field heavy-lift long-range military transport, winner of USAF's CX request for proposals. Operational 1990.

Northrop F-5G Tigershark: Advanced lightweight tactical aircraft designed for export.

Rockwell International B-1B: Strategic ALCM launcher (SAL) derivative of original ASMA concept of late 1960s. 100 B-1Bs able to carry 30 ALCMs and with some stealth qualities operational by 1987.

Rockwell International XFV-12A: US Navy VTOL fighter technology programme continues on low funding.

Sikorsky UH-60A Black Hawk: Combat assault helicopter for

US Army. 337 operational by 1983. Armed and battlefield
radar versions under development.
Sikorsky Seahawk S-70: Light airborne multi-purpose system
(LAMPS) helicopter for US Navy.

United Kingdom
BAe VC-10 K Mk 2: Flight refuelling tanker for RAF, 9 by
1983-4.
BAe Hawk: Trainer/ground attack. 150 in service with RAF,
orders from Finland, Abu Dhabi, Kenya, Indonesia and US
Navy.
BAe Sea Harrier: VTOL naval strike fighter. 34 on order for
Royal Navy, 6 for Indian Navy by 1983.
BAe Nimrod AEW Mk 3: AWACS aircraft for RAF, oper-
ational 1982.

China
Shenyang J-8: Variable geometry combat aircraft comparable
with MiG-23, under development.
Shenyang J-12: Mach 2.4 fighter, under development.

France
Dassault-Breguet F-1: All-weather interceptor, will remain in
production until 1984.
Dassault-Breguet Mirage 2000: Strike fighter, deliveries to
begin in 1983 with single basic type making up French Air
Force's planned first line strength by second half of 1980s.
Dassault-Breguet Super Mirage 4000: Private venture MRCA.
Twin-engined scale-up of Mirage 2000 backed by Middle
East development moncy.
Dassault-Breguet Atlantic NG: New-generation maritime pa-
trol aircraft, in production 1986.

International
Aeritalia/Aermacchi/Embraer AM-X: Italian/Brazilian light-
weight combat aircraft project. Operational 1987.
MBB/Aérospatiale HAC: Franco-German anti-tank helicopter,
planned operational late 1980s.
Panavia Tornado: UK/Italy/Germany MRCA. First flight 1974.

385 total for RAF first becoming operational in 1982, 212 for Luftwaffe, 100 for Italy.

Sepecat Jaguar: Anglo/French strike aircraft. Advanced versions under development.

Israel

IAI Lavi: Lightweight strike fighter under development, planned operational 1986.

Italy

Agusta A129: A/T helicopter. First flight planned September 1983.

Sweden

SAAB 2105: Advanced MRCA under development. To enter service 1990.

Soviet Union

Ilyushin Il-76: Large Soviet jet transport. Flight refuelling tanker for *Backfire* force under development. AWACS version reportedly operational by mid-1980s.

Foxhound: Reported two-seat development of Foxbat interceptor with AA-X-9 missiles and high-capability radar. Tested in 1978 and shot down target drones at 200 ft from 20,000 ft.

Ram L: US reporting name of new Mikoyan fighter comparable with F-18. Has look-down/shoot-down radar.

Mil Mi-26 *Halo*: Soviet heavy-lift helicopter, production imminent.

Mil Mi-28 *Helix*: New naval helicopter under development.

Ram J: US reporting name for Sukhoi-designed close-support aircraft similar in concept to US A-10.

Sukhoi Su-24 *Fencer*: Advanced variable geometry strike fighter. Has UK range from forward Warsaw Pact bases.

Tu-22M *Backfire B*: First flown in 1970, more than 150 of these large long-range advanced bombers are in service with production rate boosted after collapse of SALT 2. It represents a very effective strategic and tactical weapon aimed at NATO in Europe and at US Atlantic and Pacific replenishment routes.

Bomber-X: New Tupolev B-1 like design reported early in 1982 (Ram-P).

Ram-H: High-altitude recce type similar to U-2 with twin tail.

Fighting Ships

France

L'Inflexible: Sixth nuclear ballistic missile submarine with M4 SLBM, operational 1985. 5 French SSBNs in service will be converted to M4 by 1990.

Rubis-class: 5 nuclear patrol submarines under construction.

Bretagne, Provence: 2 nuclear aircraft carriers planned for 1990, 1995.

Georges Leygues: ASW destroyer class. 6 by 1990 with 2 more advanced destroyers planned.

USA (under construction or planned)

2 *Nimitz*-class nuclear aircraft carriers.

Ohio-class Trident nuclear ballistic missile submarines.

4 modified *Virginia*-class guided-missile cruisers, 1987-91.

21 *Ticonderoga*-class guided-missile cruisers.

New-design DDGX guided-missile destroyers.

Spruance-class destroyers.

7 *Oliver Hazard Perry*-class guided-missile frigates.

6 *Los Angleles*-class nuclear patrol submarines.

Large auxiliary force-building programme including cargo and replenishment ships for the Rapid Deployment Force.

4 *Iowa*-class battleships (Reactivations).

UK

Trident: 4 Trident-armed nuclear ballistic missile submarines announced 1980. In service early 1990s.

Trafalgar-class: 3 nuclear patrol submarines ordered 1977-9, fourth cancelled. First to be launched 1982.

Invincible-class: HMS *Invincible* light aircraft carrier commissioned June 1980. Follow-on *Illustrious* 1982, *Ark Royal* 1985.

Broadsword-class: ASW destroyers, 6 in service by 1985.

USSR

Typhoon-class: Very large nuclear ballistic missile submarine armed with new SS-NX-20 SLBM, first of class launched 1980.

Oscar-class: Very large fast nuclear cruise-missile submarine, first of class running trials 1981.

Possible nuclear aircraft carrier under construction.

Kirov-class: Nuclear battle cruiser commissioned 1981, second in 1984.

Kiev-class: Third and fourth light aircraft carriers in this class to be completed 1982, 1984.

Udaloy: ASW cruiser, completed 1982, 4 to be commissioned 1982-4.

Sovremenny: ASW cruiser, 4 to be commissioned by 1983.

3 large cruisers also under construction. Ambitious air-cushion vehicle and light forces construction programme.

Glossary

ABM: anti-ballistic missile

ABRES: advanced ballistic re-entry system

ABRV: advanced ballistic re-entry vehicle

ACDA: US Arms Control and Disarmament Agency

ACTIVE DEFENCE: the employment of weapons systems to deter, deflect, or otherwise defeat enemy offensive forces.

ACTIVE PENETRATION AID: a weapon such as a decoy missile that helps a nuclear delivery system breach enemy defences.

ACTIVE SONAR: sound navigation and ranging equipment that transmits pulses and records reflections to detect and locate submarines.

AEROSPACE DEFENCE: measures to intercept and destroy hostile aircraft, missiles and space vehicles.

AFV: armoured fighting vehicle

AIRBORNE ALERT: state of bomber readiness to reduce reaction time and increase survivability by maintaining combat-equipped aircraft aloft on a continuing basis. Dropped by SAC in 1968 but would be used again in a crisis.

AIRBORNE WARNING AND CONTROL SYSTEM (AWACS): aircraft-mounted radar system designed to detect and track attacking enemy aircraft and cruise missiles and direct defensive actions. Able to scan large area with look-down capability not available to ground radars.

AIR DEFENCE: all measures to intercept and destroy hostile aircraft and cruise missiles, or otherwise neutralize them. Equipment includes interceptor aircraft, surface-to-air missiles, surveillance devices, and ancillary installations.

AIR-LAUNCHED BALLISTIC MISSILE (ALBM): ballistic missile transported by and launched from aircraft. Skybolt of 1961 an example, MX basing mode under review.

AIR SUPERIORITY: control of airspace to a degree that permits friendly forces to operate at specific times and places without prohibitive interference by enemy air forces.

ALCM: see CRUISE MISSILE

ANTI-BALLISTIC MISSILE (ABM): missile capable of destroying hostile ballistic missiles or their payloads in flight at short, medium or long range inside or outside the atmosphere.

ANTI-SUBMARINE WARFARE (ASW): active and passive measures to reduce or nullify the effectiveness of hostile submarines.

APC: armoured personnel carrier

AREA DEFENCE: measures to protect key targets such as cities by engaging enemy forces at a considerable distance. See also POINT DEFENCE.

ARMS CONTROL: international agreements governing the numbers,types, deployment, and use of armed forces and armaments. See also ARMS LIMITATION; DISARMAMENT.

ARMS LIMITATION: an agreement to restrict numbers or capabilities of weapons. See also ARMS CONTROL; DISARMAMENT.

ASALM: advanced strategic air-launched missile

ASAT: anti-satellite weapon

ASCM: anti-ship cruise missile

ASM: air-to-surface missile

ASSURED DESTRUCTION: the ability to inflict unacceptable damage on an aggressor, even after absorbing a surprise nuclear first strike.

ASW: anti-submarine warfare

A/T: anti-tank

ATOMIC EFFECTS: blast and shock, heat, initial nuclear radiation, and residual radiation (fallout) generated by the detonation of fission or fusion weapons.

ATTACK AIRCRAFT: tactical aircraft used primarily for interdiction, denial of enemy use of an area, and close air support purposes. A – prefix in US military aircraft designation system.

ATTACK CARRIER: an aircraft carrier designed to accommodate high-performance fighter/attack aircraft whose primary purpose is to project offensive striking power against targets ashore and afloat.

ATTACK SUBMARINE: a submarine intended primarily to destroy enemy shipping and naval vessels, including other submarines.

AWACS: airborne warning and control system (*qv*)

BALLISTIC MISSILE: a pilotless projectile propelled into space by one or more rocket boosters. Thrust is terminated at some early stage, after which re-entry vehicles follow trajectories that are governed mainly by gravity and aerodynamic drag. Mid-course corrections and terminal guidance permit only minor modifications to the flight path. See also RE-ENTRY VEHICLE.

BALLISTIC MISSILE DEFENCE (BMD): all measures to intercept and destroy hostile ballistic missiles, or otherwise neutralize them. Equipment includes weapons; target acquisition, tracking, and guidance radars; and ancillary installations.

BALLISTIC MISSILE EARLY-WARNING SYSTEM (BMEWS): electronic surveillance screen designed to detect attacks by ballistic missiles. The three US BMEWS stations, tied to NORAD's Operations Centre, also have tracking capabilities.

BINARY WEAPON: a shell or bomb filled with two harmless chemicals which react on impact to produce a supertoxic weapon.

BIOLOGICAL WARFARE: the use of micro-organisms such as bacteria and viruses, toxic agents derived from micro-organisms, and herbicides to produce casualties among humans, animals and/or plants. See also CHEMICAL WARFARE.

BMD: ballistic missile defence.

BMEWS: ballistic missile early-warning system

BUS: RV carrier vehicle of MIRV systems

BW: biological warfare

C^3: Command, Control and Communications

CD: civil defence

CEP: circular error probability

CHEMICAL WARFARE: the use of or defence against asphyxiating, poisonous and corrosive gases, sprays, and smoke to produce casualties among humans and animals and/or damage to plants and material.

CIRCULAR ERROR PROBABLE: the radius of a circle within which half of all missiles delivered by any given weapons system are expected to land. The lower the figure, the more accurate the system.

CIVIL DEFENCE: measures designed to protect the population and production base.

CLOSE AIR SUPPORT: air strikes against targets near enough to ground combat units that co-ordination between air and ground elements is needed.

COLD LAUNCH: a 'pop-up' technique that ejects ballistic missiles from silos or submarines using propellants that are separate from the delivery vehicles. Primary ignition is delayed until projectiles are safely clear of the launcher, and technique offers reload capability.

COLLATERAL DAMAGE: physical harm done to persons or property near to targets such as missile silos.

COMBAT RADIUS: the distance an aircraft with military load can fly from base to target and return.

COMMAND, CONTROL AND COMMUNICATIONS: facilities, equipment and personnel used to acquire, process and disseminate data needed by decision makers to plan, direct, and control operations. Expressed as C^3.

CONFLICT SPECTRUM: span of levels of hostilities ranging from sub-crisis manoeuvring to the most violent form of general war.

CONTROLLED COUNTERFORCE WAR: war in which concentration is on reducing enemy strategic retaliatory forces with action to minimize collateral casualties and damage to civilians.

CONUS: Continental United States

CONVENTIONAL (FORCES, WAR, WEAPONS): military organizations, hostilities and hardware that are not nuclear, chemical or biological having mass destruction effects.

COUNTER-CITY: targeting policy aimed at enemy population centres; or 'city-busting'.

COUNTERFORCE: the use of strategic forces to destroy the military capabilities of an enemy force. Bombers and their bases, ballistic-missile submarines and their shore facilities, ICBM silos, ABM and air defence installations, command and control centres and nuclear stockpiles are typical counterforce targets.

COUNTERVALUE: strategic concept which involves the destruction of selected enemy cities and resources which constitute the social fabric of a State.

CRUISE MISSILE: a pilotless aircraft, propelled continuously by an air-breathing engine operating aerodynamically within the earth's atmosphere. In-flight guidance and control offering terrain-following capability can be accomplished remotely, by satellite or by onboard computer.

ALCM: air-launched cruise missile

GLCM: ground-launched cruise missile

SLCM: sea-launched cruise missile

CW: chemical warfare

DARPA: US Defence Advanced Research Projects Agency

DETERRENCE: steps taken to prevent opponents from initiating aggressive actions and to inhibit escalation if such actions occur. Promises of punishment or reward both may contribute.

DEW LINE: distant early-warning line

DIA: US Defence Intelligence Agency

DIRECTION TECHNIQUE DES ENGINS: French missile agency.

DISARMAMENT: the reduction of armed forces and/or armaments as a result of unilateral initiatives or international agreement. See also ARMS CONTROL; ARMS LIMITATION.

DISTANT EARLY-WARNING LINE (DEW): the northernmost stations in NORAD's air defence surveillance system. The line, which stretches across the arctic from Alaska through Canada to the Atlantic, comprises isolated radar stations.

DSARC: US Defence Systems Acquisitions Review Council

ECCM: electronic counter-countermeasures

ECM: electronic countermeasures

ELECTRONIC COUNTER-COUNTERMEASURES: electronic warfare carried out to ensure effective use of the electromagnetic spectrum despite enemy ECM efforts.

ELECTRONIC COUNTERMEASURES: electronic warfare techniques that prevent or degrade enemy uses of the electromagnetic spectrum such as jamming.

ELINT: electronic intelligence

EMP: electromagnetic pulse

ER: enhanced radiation (neutron bomb)

EXCLUSION ZONE: area of blockade within which intention of using military force has been announced.

FALLOUT: the precipitation of radioactive particles from clouds of debris produced by nuclear blasts. Surface bursts send up huge amounts of material in mushroom stems which can be dispersed over very wide areas by wind.

FEBA: forward edge of the battle area

FIGHTER AIRCRAFT: tactical aircraft used primarily to gain and maintain air superiority. It lacks internal bomb capacity. F – prefix in US system.

FIRST STRIKE: the first offensive move of a war. Applied to

general nuclear war, success implies the ability to eliminate retaliation by the opposition by counterforce targeting.

FIRST USE: the initial employment of specific military measures, such as nuclear weapons, during the conduct of a war. A belligerent could execute a second strike in response to aggression, yet be the first to employ nuclear weapons.

FISSION: splitting of heavy nucleus (uranium or plutonium) accompanied by release of large amounts of energy.

FLEXIBLE RESPONSE: a strategy based on meeting aggression at an appropriate level or place with the capability of escalating the level of conflict if required or desired.

FOBS: fractional orbit bombardment system

FORWARD DEFENCE: a strategic concept which calls for containing or repulsing military aggression as close to the original line of contact as possible to protect important areas.

FRACTIONAL ORBIT BOMBARDMENT SYSTEM: a method of launching ballistic missiles into low orbit (about 100 miles). Retro-rockets fired after less than one earth orbit permit a rapid descent to targets, reducing defensive radar reaction times.

FRATRICIDE: the destruction or neutralization of one nuclear weapon by another under same control.

FREE ROCKET: a missile that is not controlled in flight.

FROG: free rocket over ground; Soviet tactical rockets of 1950s/60s.

FUSION: thermonuclear process in which nuclei of light elements (Deuterium or Tritium hydrogen isotopes) combine to form nuclei of heavier element releasing large amounts of energy.

GCHQ: UK Government Communications Headquarters

GENERAL PURPOSE FORCES: all combat forces not designed to accomplish strategic offensive/defensive or mobility missions.

GENERAL WAR: armed conflict between major powers in which the national survival of one or more belligerents is contested.

GKO: Soviet State Committee for Defence

GLCM: ground-launched cruise missile

GROUND ALERT: readiness-state designed to reduce reaction time and increase survivability by maintaining aircraft fuelled and armed with crews ready to take off quickly.

GUIDED MISSILE: missile whose trajectory can be altered by internal or external mechanisms.

GUIDED MUNITIONS: bomb or missile warhead that can be steered to its target by internal or external mechanisms.

HARD TARGET: point protected against the blast, heat and radiation effects of nuclear explosions.

HEAVY ICBM: SALT definition of US Titan II; Soviet SS-7, SS-8, SS-9, SS-18, SS-19.

ICBM: intercontinental ballistic missile

INERTIAL GUIDANCE: an onboard guidance system that measures acceleration and altitude and relates it to distances travelled in certain directions and steers ballistic missiles over pre-determined courses.

INFRA-RED SIGNATURE: the image produced by sensing electromagnetic radiations emitted or reflected from a target in the infra-red spectrum.

INTERCEPTOR: an air defence aircraft designed to identify and/or destroy hostile aircraft or missiles.

INTERCONTINENTAL BALLISTIC MISSILE (ICBM): a ballistic missile with a range of 3000 to 8000 nautical miles.

INTERDICTION: operations to prevent or impede enemy use of an area or route.

INTERMEDIATE-RANGE BALLISTIC MISSILE (IRBM): a ballistic missile with a range of 1500 to 3000 nautical miles.

IRBM: intermediate-range ballistic missile

KILOTON (KT): the yield of a nuclear weapon equivalent to 1000 metric tons of TNT (trinitrotoluene).

LASER (light amplification by stimulated emission of radiation):

amplified light beams which can be focused. Has military applications in range finding and target illumination. Developed as a weapon itself.

LAUNCH-ON-WARNING: retaliation launched in time to prevent any losses to strike forces by discerned approaching enemy nuclear attacks.

LIMITED WAR: armed encounters, exclusive of incidents, in which one or more major powers or their proxies voluntarily exercise various types and degrees of restraint to prevent unmanageable escalation. Objectives, forces, weapons, targets and geographic areas all can be limited.

LOGISTICS: plans and operations associated with the design, development, acquisition, storage, movement, distribution, maintenance, evacuation and hospitalization of personnel; the acquisition or construction, maintenance, operation and disposition of facilities; and the acquisition or furnishing of services.

LOITER TIME: the length of time an aircraft can remain airborne in any given location, pending receipt of further orders. Depends primarily on fuel capacity, consumption rates, refuelling capabilities and pilot fatigue. Loiter capabilities for missiles are under development.

LOOK-DOWN, SHOOT-DOWN CAPABILITY: airborne radars that discriminate aerial targets from ground clutter below, combined with air-to-air weapon systems that can destroy supersonic targets.

MAC: US Military Airlift Command

MAD: magnetic anomaly detection; mutual assured destruction

MAGNETIC ANOMALY DETECTION: ASW equipment designed to locate enemy submarines by detecting disturbances in normal magnetic fields of force.

MANOEUVRABLE RE-ENTRY VEHICLE (MARV): a missile warhead that can be steered to its target by internal or external mechanisms. See also PENETRATION AID; WARHEAD.

MAP: US Military Assistance Programme

MARV: manoeuvrable re-entry vehicle

MASSIVE RETALIATION: countering aggression of any type with tremendous destructive power; particularly a crushing nuclear response to any provocation deemed serious enough to warrant military action.

MBFR: mutual and balanced force reductions

MEDIUM-RANGE BALLISTIC MISSILE (MRBM): a ballistic missile with a range of 600 to 1500 nautical miles.

MEGATON: the yield of a nuclear weapon equivalent to 1,000,000 tons of TNT (trinitrotoluene).

MIRV: multiple independently targetable re-entry vehicle

MOBILE MISSILE: a ballistic or cruise missile mounted on and/or fired from a moving platform.

MRBM: medium-range ballistic missile

MRV: multiple re-entry vehicle

MSBS: *mer-sol balistique stratégique*, French SLBM.

MT: megaton

MULTIPLE INDEPENDENTLY TARGETABLE RE-ENTRY VEHICLE (MIRV): a single-missile payload comprising two or more warheads that can engage separate targets.

MULTIPLE RE-ENTRY VEHICLE (MRV): a missile payload comprising two or more warheads that engage the same target.

MUTUAL ASSURED DESTRUCTION: reciprocal capabilities of two or more rivals to inflict unacceptable damage on each other at any time during the course of a nuclear war, even after absorbing a surprise first strike.

NATIONAL COMMAND AUTHORITIES: the top national security decision-makers of a country. In the United States, they are limited to the President, the Secretary of Defence, and their duly deputized alternates or successors.

NATIONAL MILITARY COMMAND SYSTEM: the priority component of the United States' World-wide Military Command and Control System, designed to support the National Command Authorities and the Joint Chiefs of Staff.

NAVAL SUPERIORITY: dominance on the high seas to a degree that permits friendly land, aerospace and naval forces to operate without prohibitive interference by the enemy.

NCA: National Command Authorities

NDAC: NATO Nuclear Defence Affairs Committee

NEACP: US National Emergency Airborne Command Post

NFCS: nuclear forces communications satellite

NMCS: National Military Command System

NORAD: North American Air Defence Command

NORTH AMERICAN AIR DEFENCE COMMAND: combined US and Canadian HQ responsible for global aerospace surveillance and the defence of North America against air and ICBM attack.

NUCLEAR DELIVERY SYSTEM: a nuclear weapon, together with its means of propulsion and associated installations.

NUCLEAR FREE ZONE: area in which manufacture and deployment of nuclear weapons is forbidden.

NUCLEAR FUEL CYCLE: Uranium ore mining, refining, fuel element fabrication, reprocessing, waste disposal.

NUCLEAR WEAPON: a bomb, missile warhead or other deliverable ordnance item (as opposed to an experimental device) that explodes as a result of energy released by atomic nuclei through fission, fusion or both. See also NUCLEAR DELIVERY SYSTEM.

NUCLEAR YIELD: the explosive power of a nuclear bomb or warhead expressed in kilotons or megatons.

OTH-B RADAR: over-the-horizon backscatter radar

OTH RADAR: over-the-horizon radar

OVER-THE-HORIZON BACKSCATTER RADAR: an OTH radar that transmits signals that extend beyond line-of-sight along the ground. Effective range is about 1800 miles. If signals detect an airborne target, return waves reflect back along the same path to a receiver near the transmitter. See also OVER-THE-HORIZON RADAR.

OVER-THE-HORIZON RADAR: a surveillance radar whose signals hug the earth's surface for distances well beyond line-of-sight, bounce off the ionosphere and return to earth several times in waves, finally activating a receiver.

OVERKILL: destructive capabilities in excess of those which logically should be adequate to destroy specified targets or attain specific objectives. Overkill can be diminished by defence measures such as silo-hardening.

OVERPRESSURE: blast effect of nuclear weapons which give ability to destroy missile silos.

PASSIVE DEFENCE: all measures, other than the application of armed force, taken to deter or minimize the effects of enemy actions. These include the use of cover, concealment, dispersion, protective construction, mobility and subterfuge. See also ACTIVE DEFENCE.

PASSIVE PENETRATION AID: a non-destructive device that aids a nuclear delivery system breach enemy defences, such as electronic countermeasures.

PASSIVE SONAR: sound navigation and ranging equipment that listens for sounds radiated by hostile submarines. See also ACTIVE SONAR.

PAVE PAWS: US phased-array radar

PB: particle beam weapon

PENAID: penetration aid

PERIMETER ACQUISITION RADAR: part of the US Sentinel and Safeguard ABM systems which was designed to track ballistic missiles beginning at a maximum range of about 1000 miles and predict probable impact points.

PLUTONIUM SEPARATION: reprocessing of spent reactor fuel to separate plutonium. Research continuing on laser enrichment to produce weapon-grade material linking civil and military nuclear technology.

POINT DEFENCE: measures to protect key targets of any kind by engaging during terminal stages of the attack. See also AREA DEFENCE.

POINT TARGET: a target whose dimensions are small enough to be identified by a single co-ordinate on operational maps. Missile silos are typical.

PONAST: post-nuclear attack study

POSITIVE CONTROL: standard procedures prohibit the accidental launch of ballistic missiles. Aircraft launched on warning return to base unless they receive coded voice instructions that can be authenticated.

POST-LAUNCH SURVIVABILITY: the ability of any given delivery system to breach enemy defences and attack designated targets. See also PRE-LAUNCH SURVIVABILITY.

POST-STRIKE ASSESSMENT: the acquisition and evaluation of data that indicates the success of a nuclear attack and thereby assists subsequent decision-making.

POSTURE: the combined strategic intentions, capabilities and vulnerabilities of a country or coalition of countries, including the strength, disposition and readiness of its armed forces.

PRE-EMPTIVE WAR: conflict initiated on the basis of incontrovertible evidence that an enemy attack is imminent. See also PREVENTIVE WAR.

PRE-LAUNCH SURVIVABILITY: the ability of any given delivery system to ride out surprise first strike successfully and retaliate. See also POST-LAUNCH SURVIVABILITY.

PREVENTIVE WAR: conflict initiated in the belief that armed combat, while not imminent, is inevitable, and that delay would involve greater risk.

PVO: Soviet Air Defence

RADAR CROSS-SECTION: the picture produced by recording radar waves reflected from a given target surface. The size of the image is not determined entirely by the size of objects. Structural shape, the refractory characteristics of materials, and locations with regard to receivers all are important.

RAPID RELOAD CAPABILITY: the ability of a delivery system to conduct multiple strikes. Land-mobile missiles and hard-site ICBMs have the potential.

RDF: US Rapid Deployment Force. Also Rapid Deployment Joint Task Force (RDJTF).

RECALL CAPABILITY: the ability to retrieve weapons and their carriers after launch on warning. Recall may be directed by communications or occur spontaneously in the absence of authenticated orders to continue attack.

RE-ENTRY VEHICLE (RV): that part of a ballistic missile designed to re-enter the earth's atmosphere during terminal stages of its trajectory.

SAGE: semi-automatic ground environment

SALT: Strategic Arms Limitation Talks (*qv*)

SAM: surface-to-air missiles

SATURATION ATTACK: the multiple use of weapons to overload enemy defences and/or to blanket areas that contain known or suspected targets.

SEA CONTROL: the employment of naval forces, supplemented by land and air forces as appropriate, to destroy enemy naval forces, suppress enemy commerce, protect shipping lanes, and establish local superiority in areas of naval operations.

SECOND STRIKE: a strategic concept which excludes pre-emptive and preventive actions before the onset of war. After an aggressor initiates hostilities, the defender retaliates. In general nuclear war, this implies the ability to survive a surprise first strike and respond effectively. See also FIRST STRIKE.

SEMI-AUTOMATIC GROUND ENVIRONMENT (SAGE): network of US air defence facilities designed to receive early warning of unidentified and/or hostile aircraft, then direct intercept operations.

SILO: underground facilities for ballistic missiles and/or crew, designed to provide pre-launch protection against atomic effects. High-yield, precision weapons are needed to destroy the most durable construction.

SINGLE INTEGRATED OPERATIONAL PLAN: the US contingency plan for strategic retaliatory strikes in event of a nuclear war. Targets, timing, tactics and force requirements are considered for a variety of responses. Prepared by the Joint Strategic Target Planning Staff, which is located with SAC Headquarters at Offutt AFB outside Omaha, Nebraska. UK targeting integrated with US SIOP.

SIOP: single integrated operational plan

SLBM: submarine/sea-launched ballistic missile

SLCM: submarine/sea-launched cruise missile

SNLE: *sousmarin nucléaire lance engins*, French SSBN.

SOFT TARGET: a target not protected against the blast, heat and radiation produced by nuclear explosions.

SSBS: *sol-sol balistique stratégique*. French term for IRBM.

STANDOFF WEAPON (SOW): an air-to-surface missile for air defence suppression purposes or to strike primary target, permitting aircraft to attack multiple targets without physically penetrating to any of them.

STEALTH: US technology programme for aircraft with low radar, infra-red and optical signature.

STRATEGIC AIR WAR: aerospace operations directed against the enemy's war-making capacity. Typical targets include industry, stockpiles of raw materials and finished products, power systems, transportation and communications centres, strategic weapon systems and cities.

STRATEGIC AIRLIFT: transport aircraft, both military and civilian, used to move armed forces, equipment and supplies expeditiously over long distances, especially intercontinentally. See also TACTICAL AIRLIFT.

STRATEGIC ARMS LIMITATION TALKS (SALT): negotiations between the United States and the Soviet Union to curtail the expansion of, and if possible reduce, strategic offensive and defensive weapon systems of both countries in an equitable fashion.

STRATEGIC BALANCE: the comparative national power of two competing countries or coalitions.

STRATEGIC DEFENCE: the strategy and forces designed primarily to protect a nation and/or allies from the effects of general war.

STRATEGIC MOBILITY: the ability to shift personnel, equipment and supplies effectively and expeditiously between theatres of operation.

STRATEGIC OFFENCE: the strategy and forces designed primarily to destroy the enemy's war-making capacity during general war or to so degrade it that the opposition collapses.

STRATEGIC RESERVE: uncommitted forces of a country or a coalition of countries which are intended to support national security interests and objectives, as required.

STRATEGIC SEALIFT: naval and merchant ships, together with crews, used to move armed forces, equipment and supplies over long distances, especially intercontinentally.

STRATEGIC STABILITY: a state of equilibrium which encourages prudence by opponents facing the possibility of general war. Tendencies towards an arms race are restrained, since neither side has undue advantage.

STRATEGIC WARNING: notification that enemy offensive operations of any kind may be imminent. The alert may be received minutes, hours, days or longer before hostilities commence.

SUBMARINE/SEA-LAUNCHED BALLISTIC MISSILE (SLBM): ballistic missile transported by and launched from a ship. May be short-, medium-, intermediate- or long-range.

SUBMARINE/SEA-LAUNCHED CRUISE MISSILE (SLCM): air-breathing missile transported by and launched from a ship. May be short-, medium-, intermediate- or long-range.

SURVIVABILITY: the ability of armed forces and civilian social structures to withstand attack and still function effectively. It is derived mainly from active and passive defences.

TACTICAL AIRCRAFT: land- and carrier-based aircraft designed primarily as general purpose forces.

TACTICAL AIRLIFT: transport aircraft used to move armed forces, equipment and supplies within theatres of operation.

TACTICAL/MOBILITY FORCES: general purpose elements designed for theatre nuclear, conventional and/or chemical/biological warfare; airlift, sealift and land transportation elements that move those forces between or within theatres of operation.

TACTICAL NUCLEAR FORCES: see THEATRE NUCLEAR FORCES

TERCOM: terrain contour matching

TERMINAL GUIDANCE: in-flight corrections to the trajectory of a ballistic or cruise missile during its final approach to the target.

TERRAIN CONTOUR MATCHING (TERCOM): correlates contour map data with terrain being overflown by ballistic or cruise missiles.

THEATRE NUCLEAR FORCES (TNF): nuclear combat power designed for deterrent, offensive and defensive purposes that contribute to the accomplishment of regional military ends.

THERMONUCLEAR WEAPON: device in which fission (A-bomb) provides high temperatures for fusion of nuclei of hydrogen isotopes (H-bomb).

THROW WEIGHT: the payload capacity of a ballistic missile expressed in total weight for re-entry vehicles of all types (warheads, decoys).

TIME-SENSITIVE TARGET: any counterforce target which is vulnerable only if it can be struck before it is launched.

TRIAD: tripartite strategic retaliatory force, which comprises manned bombers, intercontinental ballistic missiles and ballistic-missile submarines.

TRIPWIRE: a largely symbolic force positioned on an ally's soil to advertise the owner's commitment to a particular country or coalition of countries. Attacks against the token contingent would trigger a larger response.

TUBE ARTILLERY: howitzers and guns, as opposed to rockets and guided missiles. May be towed or self-propelled.

URANIUM ENRICHMENT: process of increasing content of Uranium 235 above that found in natural conditions for use in reactors or nuclear weapons.

VERIFICATION: inspection and/or surveillance measures to determine compliance with arms control agreements.

VULNERABILITY: the susceptibility of any country, military force or weapon system to any action by any means through which its effectiveness may be diminished.

VVS: Soviet Air Force

WARHEAD: that part of a weapon system which contains explosives.

WORLD-WIDE MILITARY COMMAND AND CONTROL SYSTEM: provides the means for operational direction and administrative support of US Armed Forces deployed globally. Components include the Advanced Airborne National Command Post (AABNCP), satellite communications, the National Emergency Airborne Command Post (NEACP), the Post-Attack Command and Control System (PACCS), communications systems for ballistic missile submarines, the WWMCCS Information System, and Commander-in-Chief (CINC) programmes.

YIELD: released energy in a nuclear explosion expressed as equivalent in metric tons of TNT high explosive.

Major Electronics Projects

This is an inventory of major electronics projects currently being undertaken by the United States Air Force and serves to emphasize the fundamental importance of electronics (see Chapter 5) in every aspect of modern conventional and nuclear warfare, ranging from programmes to reduce the vulnerability of tactical radios to very large-scale projects such as GEODSS to track objects in deep space for military purposes.

Name and Mission	*Status*	*Contractor*

COMMUNICATIONS AND INFORMATION SYSTEMS

Air Force Satellite Communications System (AFSATCOM)

A programme for acquisition of UHF airborne, ground terminals, airborne/ ground command post terminals, ancillary equipment for operational control and communications transponders on selected Air Force satellites.	Development Acquisition/ Deployment	Rockwell Linkabit Corp

Air Force Single Channel Ground and Airborne Radio System (AFSINCGARS)

Air Force portion of the Army Single Channel Ground and Airborne Radio System for VHF/FM communications. Purpose of the Air Force programme is to provide jam-resistant, secure VHF/FM communications between Air Force elements and US Army ground forces.	Development	Not yet named

Combat Theatre Communications

A programme for acquisition of new hybrid analog/digital communications equipment for both Air Force-unique tactical requirements and for the DoD Joint Tactical Communications (TRI-TAC) programme.	Definition, Research and Development and Acquisition	Martin Marietta, ECI, Raytheon

Name and Mission	Status	Contractor
Digital European Backbone (DEB)		
Incremental upgrade of portions of the European Defence Communications System (DSC) from a frequency division multiplex (FDM) analog system to a time division multiplex (TDM) digital system with higher reliability components. This will provide a modern wide-band, digital, bulk-encrypted capability with increased capacity between Defence Satellite Communications System Earth Terminals and major commands.	Acquisition and Deployment	Many
Joint Tactical Information Distribution System (JTIDS)		
A programme to develop a high capacity, reliable, jam-protected, secure digital information distribution system which will provide a high degree of interoperability between data collection elements, combat elements, and command and control centres within a military theatre of operations.	Engineering Development	Hughes, ITT, IBM, Singer-Kearfott, McDonnell Douglas
Operational Application of Special Intelligence Systems (OASIS)		
Improvement of tactical command control and communications capabilities through the application and interfacing of appropriate surveillance and special intelligence systems. Initially, improvements to the USAFE Tactical Fusion Centre (TFC) in its role in support of Allied Air Forces Central Europe are being addressed. Although the OASIS programme will concentrate initially on needs of the TFC, the programme will, as required, develop operational acquisition of special intelligence systems for other commands.	Development and Acquisition	Martin Marietta
Strategic Air Command Digital Network (SACDIN)		
A programme for a secure record data communications system to support the command and control requirements of the Strategic Air Command. It will replace parts of the SAC Automated Command and Control System (SACCS).	Development	ITT, IBM, ECI

Name and Mission	Status	Contractor
HAVE QUICK A programme to reduce the vulnerability of UHF radios to enemy jamming, HAVE QUICK provides the Air Force an improved near-term air-to-air and air-to-ground-air jam-resistant UHF voice communications capability that will allow mission accomplishment in an enemy jamming environment through 1985.	Development and Production	Magnavox
SEEK TALK A long-term solution to reducing the vulnerability of UHF radios to enemy jamming. SEEK TALK will develop and acquire equipment for a Class V Modifications programme which will provide the Air Force the capability to conduct air-to-air and ground-air-ground UHF voice communications in a jamming environment. This will be achieved by modifying existing UHF voice radios and adding a spread-spectrum modern and null steering antenna array.	Development	General Electric, Hazeltine
Tactical Air Control System Improvement (TACSI) This programme will increase Tactical Air Control System capabilities for combat command and control of tactical aerospace operations. Improvements consist of mobile communications and electronic systems, capable of nuclear worldwide deployment, that are interoperable with Army, Navy and Marine Corps tactical data systems. Projects include ECCM improvements to the AN/TPS-43E Tactical Radar, the AN/TPN-28 Dual Band Radar Bombing Beacon, a weapons controller training system, and the improved Forward Air Control Post.	Definition, Engineering Development, Production	Goodyear, Applied Devices Corp., GTE Sylvania, Westinghouse

Name and Mission	Status	Contractor

Tactical Information Processing and Interpretation System (TIPI)

The USAF TIPI/USMC MAGIS (Marine Air General Intelligence System)/ USA MAGIIC (Mobile Army Ground Imagery Interpretation Centre) will provide more timely and accurate intelligence to tactical commanders at various echelons. Air transportable and housed in mobile shelters, separately deployable segments of the system use automated aids for rapid processing, interpretation, and reporting of intelligence from airborne electronic reconnaissance infra-red, photographic and radar sensors.	Development Acquisition and Deployment	Many

SURVEILLANCE AND CONTROL SYSTEMS

Air Force SAFE Programme

Acquisition and deployment of commercially available and DoD BISS Programme-developed physical security equipment to approximately sixty USAF bases and 130 sites worldwide. These systems will protect mission-critical/high-value resources such as weapons storage sites, strategic/tactical alert aircraft areas, special mission aircraft parking ramps and specified command posts.	Acquisition/ Deployment	Many

ARIA Phased-Array Telemetry System (APATS)

A phased-array telemetry system for installation on the ARIA aircraft in support of the MX and Trident test programmes.	Development	Not yet named

Traffic Control and Landing System (TRACALS)

TRACALS encompasses fixed and mobile ground facilities, with associated avionics to support the USAF Air Traffic Control function. Major systems being acquired include navigation aids, radar approach control equipment, landing systems and simulators.	Continuing Development and Acquisition	Many

Name and Mission	Status	Contractor

TECHNICAL OPERATIONS

Command Management Information System/Graphics (CMIS/Graphics)

Design, implementation and test of an automated graphics and telebriefing for each of the product division elements of AFSC. Includes local graphic stations within system programme offices and selected functional elements, centralized photocomposition, typesetting and graphics processing and large-screen display with interbase voice and graphics connections.	Prototype Acquisition	Booz, Allen, and Hamilton

Competitive Acquisition for the Scientific Environment (CASE)

Acquisition of computer replacement for all AFSC data-processing installations. The programme includes systems engineering to address inter- and intra-AFSC data-processing installations requirements and a fifteen-year programme of replacement and upgrade of existing equipments.	Acquisition	Booz, Allen, and Hamilton

Improved Administrative Capabilty Test (IMPACT)

Design, implementation, test and evaluation of a prototype automated office system for AFSC. Objective is to ensure the introduction of modern office technology to management and support functions for the purpose of increasing office efficiency while reducing manpower requirements and operating costs.	Prototype Demonstration	Booz, Allen, and Hamilton

Name and Mission	*Status*	*Contractor*

AIRBORNE COMMAND POST SYSTEMS

E-4 Airborne Command Post

This programme is to provide the National Command Authorities and the Commander in Chief of Strategic Air Command with a survivable airborne command and control system that will operate during the pre-, trans- and post-attack phases of a nuclear war. As a survivable emergency extension of NMCS and SAC ground command and control centres, the E-4 Airborne Command Post provides high confidence in US ability to execute and control SIOP forces in a nuclear environment.	Development Production/ Deployment	Boeing E-Systems

Air Force Support to MEECN

This programme upgrades the Air Force and Army Survivable Low Frequency Communications Systems (SLFCS) as part of the Minimum Essential Emergency Communications Network (MEECN). Major developments include airborne LF/VLF transmitters, new receive antennas for transverse electric mode reception, incorporation of the Navy MEECN Message Processing Mode (MMPM), and mini-LF/VLF receive terminals for bomber aircraft. This programme is designed to meet the requirements of the Joint Chiefs of Staff, CINCSAC, and theatre CINCs.	Definition, Development, Production/ Deployment	Westinghouse, Sonicraft Inc.

Name and Mission	*Status*	*Contractor*

AIRBORNE WARNING AND CONTROL SYSTEMS

E-3A Airborne Warning and Control System (AWACS)

This system provides airborne air surveillance capability and command control and communication functions. Its distinguishing technical feature is the capability to detect and track aircraft operating at high and low altitudes over both land and water. Used by Tactical Air Command with Tinker AFB, Okla., as the main operating base, aircraft may deploy throughout the US and overseas to provide surveillance, warning and control in a variety of peacetime and wartime situations.	Acquisition and Operational	Boeing, Westinghouse for radar

NATO E-3A

Acquisition of E-3A Sentry aircraft for NATO, with special modifications to meet NATO requirements.	Acquisition	Boeing, Dornier and others

DEVELOPMENT PLANS

Air Force World-Wide Military Command and Control System (AFWWMCCS)

Involves systems planning and engineering for Air Force elements of the Worldwide Military Command and Control System. Activities will focus on intersystem engineering of selected AFWWMCCS existing and planned assets.	Conceptual/ Validation/ Development	Not yet named

Command and Control Countermeasures

A programme designed to degrade an adversary's capability to engage effectively in combat. This would be accomplished by electromagnetic means (jamming, deception or exploitation) or force, i.e., physical destruction, to inhibit use of his command control and communications for managing his combat.	Development	Not yet named

Name and Mission	*Status*	*Contractor*
C³I Interoperability		
This effort involves a process that emphasizes user/developer interaction in defining interoperability requirements for systems being developed by ESD. Includes a study of trade-offs between technical, operational, and procedural requirements and options so that C³I systems will interoperate where required.	Continuing	Not yet named
Ground Target Attack Control System (GTACS) Assault Breaker		
GTACS is a programme to design and develop a near-real-time capability to detect and destroy hostile second-echelon ground forces. Assault Breaker is a series of technology demonstrations designed to illustrate the technical feasibility of accomplishing real-time detection and attack of forces. ESD's responsibility includes coordinating and conducting the Air Force portion of Assault Breaker demonstrations and preparing for full-scale engineering development.	Concept Development Demonstration or Validation	Not yet named
Space Communications Architecture		
To develop and update annually a time-phased programme for satisfying a critical subset of Air Force command and control information flow requirements via satellite relays. Provides basis for formulating portions of the Air Force Budget Submission and Five-Year Development Plan. Analyses current capabilities and deficiencies, projected requirements, and enemy threat, structures needed development and acquisition programmes.	Continuing	Not yet named

Name and Mission	*Status*	*Contractor*
Vanguard		
A comprehensive planning process that measures capabilities against mission responsibilities, identifies deficiencies and proposes solution with each Air Force mission area. ESD is responsible for the strategic, tactical and support C^3 plans, the ballistic missile and atmosphere surveillance and warning plans, electronic counter-countermeasures, C^3 and correlation/fusion plans.	Continuing	Not yet named
Automated Weather Distribution System (AWDS)		
AWDS will enhance Air Weather Service's meterological support for the Army and Air Force. The system will reduce labour-intensive tasks using advanced computer technology, colour graphic displays, and sophisticated meteorological and graphic presentation software. Automation of 163 base weather stations worldwide, and twenty tactical versions will interface with two communication networks for distribution of global alphanumeric and graphic meteorological data.	Development	Not yet named
BMEWS Modernization Programme		
The purpose of the BMEWS Modernization Programme is to upgrade the three operational sites (Greenland, Alaska, England) operated by SAC and the Royal Air Force. The eight Tactical Operations Room consoles at each site are being replaced by four modern consoles to improve operating efficiency and reduce personnel requirements. The Missile Impact Predictor is being upgraded by replacing the aging computers now in use with off-the-shelf computers and translating software assembly language into a higher-order language. Radar improvements are planned that will meet the threat expected in the 1980s, and give the system an attack assessment capability to meet the need of the National Command Authorities.	Acquisition	RCA

Name and Mission	Status	Contractor

DoD Base and Installation Security Systems (BISS)

An evolutionary RDT&E programme to provide DoD standard electronic security system for exterior physical security of DoD resources worldwide. This system's components include sensor imaging entry control, and command and control equipments. The system concept emphasizes maximum commonality of major items and a variety of supporting subsystems. It offers a flexible choice of equipment to assemble a system tailored to the physical characteristics of the location and to the threat.

Advanced Development Engineering Development

Many

CONSUS Over-the-Horizon Backscatter Radar (OTH-B)

This programme provides long-range detection of aircraft approaching North America as part of the NORAD air surveillance and warning capability. Distinguishing technical feature of the OTH-B is its ability to detect targets at all altitudes at extended ranges. The present programme is to build and test an experimental radar system.

Development/ Validation

General Electric

COBRA JUDY

COBRA JUDY is a USAF shipborne phased-array radar system. It will serve as a national technical means for collecting data on foreign strategic ballistic missile tests. Air Force and Air Force contractor personnel will manage, operate and maintain the technical systems on board the ship. The Navy's Military Sealift Command will own and operate the ship.

Acquisition

Raytheon

Enhanced Perimetre Acquisition Radar Characterization System (EPARCS)

The EPARCS programme consists of hardware and software modification to the present PARCS system. It will include range extension of the radars, and increasing the accuracy and improvement of the traffic-handling capability in support of the launch-under-attack mission.

Acquisition

Bell Telephone

Name and Mission	Status	Contractor

Ground Electro-Optical Deep Space Surveillance System (GEODSS)

The GEODSS system will extend the Strategic Air Command's and North American Air Defence Command's spacetrack capabilities for detecting and cataloguing space objects out to the 3000–20,000 nautical mile range. This will be a global network of five sites to detect, optically track and identify satellites in earth orbit.	Acquisition	TRW

Joint Surveillance System (JSS)

The JSS programme is to acquire and deploy a peacetime air surveillance and control system to replace the Semi-Automatic Ground Environment (SAGE) System for the US and Canada. For Canada the mission is expanded to include support of wartime air defence functions, and in Alaska the mission includes the performance of tactical air control functions.	Implementation	Hughes Aircraft

NORAD Cheyenne Mountain Complex Improvements

Acquisition of data-processing equipment, software, displays and communications for the NORAD Cheyenne Mountain Complex. The Core Processing Segment, Modular Display Segment and Communications System Segment will provide NORAD with an integrated responsive capability and a growth potential over a projected ten-year life span without major changes to equipment of software.	Operational	Ford Aerospace & Communications

Pacific Radar Barrier (PACBAR)

The PACBAR system will provide space surveillance coverage and early detection of new space launchers in the Central and Western Pacific areas by placing improved radars at three sites.	Development/Acquisition	GTE Sylvania (Armtract)

Name and Mission	*Status*	*Contractor*
PAVE PAWS		
Two dual-faced phased-array radars, one on the East Coast and one on the West Coast. This system will be operated by the Strategic Air Command and will provide warning to the National Command Authorities of a sea-launched ballistic missile attack against CONUS.	Operational	Raytheon
SEEK IGLOO		
Upgrading or replacement of all thirteen Air Force long-range radar sites in Alaska on a Minimally Attended Radar concept with maintenance by not more than three medium-skill radar technicians and no on-site radar operators. A major objective is a large-scale reduction in the life-cycle cost of Alaskan radar surveillance systems.	Development	General Electric
SEEK SCORE		
This programme is to develop and produce a radar bomb scoring system for SAC for training and evaluation of aircrews in a realistic operational environment.	Development	Not yet named
Space Defence Operations Centre (SPADOC)		
SPADOC, to be located in the NORAD Cheyenne Mountain Complex, is the central command control communications and intelligence (C^3) element of the Space Defence Command and Control System (SPADCCS). It will consist of a new ADPE, displays, interface equipment and communications upgrades. It will act as the focal point for higher echelon command and control and disseminate space-related information to other US commands. SPADOC will collect and disseminate real-time information on system status, warning and operational direction.	Acquisition	RFP (request for proposals) issued

Index